LEXICON OF MUSICAL INVECTIVE

NICOLAS SLONIMSKY

Lexicon of Musical Invective

Critical Assaults on Composers Since Beethoven's Time

W. W. Norton & Company
New York • London

First published as a Norton paperback 2000

Library of Congress catalog card number 65-26270
Printed in the United States of America

ISBN 0-393-32009-X

W. W. Norton & Company, Inc.
500 Fifth Avenue, New York, NY 10110
www.wwnorton.com

W. W. Norton & Company Ltd.
10 Coptic Street, London WC1A 1PU

1 2 3 4 5 6 7 8 9 0

CONTENTS

FOREWORD: IF YOU CAN'T THINK OF SOMETHING NICE TO SAY, COME SIT NEXT TO ME

by Peter Schickele

THE *Lexicon of Musical Invective* is probably the most entertaining reference work ever assembled. That he even came up with the idea is a testament to the liveliness of Slonimsky's mind and the mischievousness of his soul; that he actually went ahead and realized it shows the same kind of impish industry that produced a book-length thesaurus of scales and melodic patterns; and that the finished product is both funny and instructive befits the personality of a man who once reviewed his own autobiography. What we have here is the supermarket tabloid of classical music criticism, but, thanks to Slonimsky's impeccable credentials, you don't have to pretend that you're buying it for someone else.

It is a widely known fact—or, at least, a widely held belief—that negative criticism is more entertaining to read than enthusiastic endorsement. There is certainly no doubt that many critics write pans with an unbridled gusto that seems to be lacking in their (usually rarer) raves, and these critics often become more famous, or infamous, than their less caustic colleagues.

Commentators who have no respect for the object of their comments feel no compunction about showing off their incendiary wit at the expense of their hapless and more-or-less defenseless victims; they know that responding in print to a negative review (except to correct factual errors) is almost always a no-win proposition. (Some victims, it's true, are not completely defenseless. The big Hollywood studios have been known to throw lavish parties for selected critics—on movie sets, in fancy restaurants, even on cruise ships—and it requires an extraordinary amount of innocence not to suspect that this practice encourages certain reviewers to sound like my son at the age of eight: "I've never seen a movie I didn't like.")

Most of us feel constrained, in person, to say politely pleasant things to creative artists no matter what we think of their work; perhaps this penchant of ours endows blisteringly bad reviews with a cathartic strength that makes us read them aloud to our friends even when we don't agree with the reviewers' opinions. I can't believe he said that! (Or she, as when Dorothy Parker, under the pen name "Constant Reader," reviewed the latest A. A. Milne book for *The New Yorker*, ending, "And it is that word 'hummy,' my darlings, that marks the first place in *The House at Pooh Corner* at which Tonstant Weader fwowed up.")

So there's a lot of delectable venom in this book. It's strong medicine, and, since it is such a powerful dose of invective, the responsible druggist might do well to list a couple of cautions on the label: (1) do not swallow whole, and (2) take with a grain of salt. It seems worthwhile to distinguish between the cheap thrills and the surprising insights to be gleaned from this festival of dyspepsia.

The cheapest thrill—sweet, perhaps, but definitely cheap—is mean-spirited exultation over bad prophecy: What a jerk that guy was, not to realize that *The Rite of Spring* is a masterpiece! What kind of a dunderhead could think that *Rigoletto* has "hardly any chance" of being kept in the repertoire? One of the most egregious (and therefore most satisfying) examples of the colossally bad judgment call occurred in the non-classical realm, when an executive at a British record label turned down a new act called The Beatles because, as he told them, "Groups are out."

These little bits of myopia, embedded in the amber of history, may allow us to feel superior as we indulge ourselves in a few unearned chuckles, but there are some things that should be pointed out to the too-easily-amused reader, beyond Slonimsky's observation that many people find it hard to accept the non-familiar.

First, as the title of the work makes clear and as its compiler correctly but fleetingly points out in the introduction, the entries are culled only from the admittedly vast trove of fiercely negative reviews. It is taken for granted—it literally goes without saying—that most of these composers received plenty of favorable comments as well, and indeed part of the value of the *Lexicon* is as an antidote to knee-jerk dead-composer idolatry, the belief that the masterpieces of the mainstream classical canon were brought down from Mount Sinai one day by Moses and immediately embraced as the law of the land. Nevertheless, the nature of this book inherently deprives it of any sense of proportion, and it seems entirely possible that a lay reader might peruse it without, for instance, realizing that Beethoven, in spite of being one of the most iconoclastic composers of all time, was so highly regarded that when he made noises about leaving Vienna, members of the aristocracy initiated a subscription to create an annual stipend for the composer, just to keep him in town. Or that twenty thousand people attended his funeral. Or that Stravinsky's *Rite of Spring*, a decade before Slonimsky decrees that it had finally established itself as a masterpiece, was the only work by a living composer—indeed, the only work written in the twentieth century—to be included in *Fantasia,* created by that most populist and savvy producer of musical entertainment, Walt Disney. (The fact that *Fantasia* was not an immediate financial success is surely not attributable to the presence of Stravinsky's music; the dinosaur section was one of the most memorable and most highly thought of—except, of course, by the composer.)

Second, it is not the job of music critics (despite what they and some of their readers might say) to predict with accuracy which of today's premieres will become tomorrow's acknowledged masterpieces. To be sure, one of the most frequently encountered sentiments in these pages is, "If this is the music of the future, . . ."—to be completed, in essence, either by "I'll eat my hat!" or "I hope I'm not around!" But the market in music futures is, or ought to be, irrelevant. What we want from music is to be moved by it, and there is some music, it's true, that is capable of moving us only after we overcome our lack of familiarity with it. But who cares what pieces will move our great-grandchildren? Depending on your point of view, music is either blessed or hindered by the fact that it is not very investor-friendly, compared with the graphic arts. Since reading a score, even for the few who can do it, is hardly the most satisfying way of experiencing a musical work (there are, to be sure, some ultra-Platonic super-aesthetes who might take exception to that statement), even the most honored composer's manuscript will never fetch as much on the market as a top painting or sculpture. What a pity: we are forced to listen to music for its own sake, not because buying it now might make us rich later on down the line.

Also, a lack of familiarity with a piece is not the only reason to dislike it. How often have you had some repetitive, predictable tune stuck in your mind, playing over and over again? (*Strangers in the Night* is one of my bêtes noires in this regard.) It's the very familiarity that drives you up the wall. When a sophisticated and cosmopolitan composer-critic like Virgil Thomson dismisses Sibelius's Second Symphony, when a sensitive and highly educated violinist-composer like Louis Spohr confesses that he cannot get any enjoyment out of Beethoven's Ninth Symphony, and when my friend Bill Walters says that the Bruckner Expressway (which traverses the South Bronx in New York City) is called that because it's long and boring and doesn't go anywhere, we are talking about a lack of appreciation that has survived familiarity.

And that's as it should be. Once we've given a piece a chance (to paraphrase John and Yoko), we shouldn't worry about what others think or will think. A senior music critic at the *New York Times* recently wrote that he still found Beethoven's *Grosse Fuge* indigestible, and you can be sure that a lack of exposure is not the problem. Beethoven wrote the piece as the finale for his String Quartet Op. 130, but because it was so long and far-out, his publisher talked him into releasing it separately and writing a new last movement for the quartet. Recently, leaving the auditorium after a performance of Op. 130 in its original version (i.e., with the *Grosse Fuge* as the finale), a musicologist friend of mine muttered, "His publisher was right."

When I was a teenager, I told my father that I didn't like Beethoven's Ninth Symphony, and he, with the linguistic felicity that is often given to those not speaking their native tongue, said to me, "Peter, you're a mouse barking at an elephant." Well, more than four decades have passed, and I still haven't come around to the last movement. (The first three, though, I have come to believe, are terrific.)

The *Lexicon* covers a century and a half, from about 1800 to 1950. So why start with Beethoven? First, as Slonimsky suggests, it was the beginning of a golden era of popular music criticism that resulted from the changing demographics of musical presentation. But there's another reason Beethoven makes a good starting point: in spite of his success, he was the first embodiment of two nineteenth-century Romantic ideals, the mad genius and the artist against society. H. C. Robbins Landon, describing the premiere of Haydn's "Military" Symphony in the London of 1793–94, has written: "It was the example par excellence of a composition being totally integrated in the society that first heard it; perhaps it was the last time in music history when the public completely understood and appreciated great music at its first performance." I'm not sure how true that is, but it's a provocative statement.

The cut-off date of the *Lexicon* simply has to do with when Slonimsky completed it, but in retrospect the date seems entirely appropriate: some time after the middle of the twentieth century, the era of the great and widely known classical composers ended.

Perhaps the most fascinating insight to be gained from these pages is not that some intelligent people miscalculated posterity's judgments, or that they didn't like music that most of us now love, but rather that their ears were, in some cases, tuned *so* differently from ours. It's not hard to empathize, for instance, with the statement written in 1911 about Schoenberg's *Three Piano Pieces:* "I see in them a complete dissolution of all that was heretofore regarded as musical art." Even if you love them, the Op. 11 pieces represent, in fact, a more-or-less complete dissolution of all that was theretofore regarded as musical art. But to find little or no melody in *Carmen,* or Brahms's Second Symphony, or the early operas of Verdi—that takes your breath away, and makes you realize what a boundless variety of wiring exists between different pairs of ears.

It's curious that Schubert is not represented here—why is that? Is it because nobody doesn't like Schubert? (Can't be: *everybody* is disliked by *somebody.*) Is it because most of Schubert's major works, outside of the songs, took such an inordinately long time to become widely performed? Or is it simply that the critics in Boston and New York (Slonimsky's principal hunting grounds) had few qualms about the composer whose friends had nicknamed him "Little Mushroom"?

One more thing: it is difficult after reading this book to believe that there are critics who fault pieces for not being modern *enough*, and yet, of course, there are, especially in late-twentieth-century New York City. The reservation implicit in the following comment by a *New York Times* reviewer, presented in its entirety, is evident: "Paul Schoenfield's Sonatina for Flute, Clarinet and Piano, with its clattering Charleston, rag and jig movements, is a zesty piece, though hardly more daring than what Darius Milhaud was doing in the 1930's." You can't win for losing.

As a serious composer and also as the sole discoverer of the putative music of P. D. Q. Bach, I have been on the receiving end of both pans and raves, and, everything else being equal, I prefer raves. Any highly flattering review I get is, of course, humbly accepted and appreciated, but one stands out, head and shoulders above the rest. It appeared in a respected magazine, and it can only be described as an artist's wet dream: "Having banished Mr. Schickele some time ago from my conscious mental life as being a fellow whose spoofs of Baroque music, both on records and television, struck me as labored, clumsy, and utterly sophomoric, it was not with alacrity that I reached for the latest sample of his wares. Mr. Schickele, I recant! I grovel before your genius, an abject idolater. Obtuse and inattentive, I have grossly misunderstood your methods and your motives. You are the most."

Now that's what I call music criticism.

NON-ACCEPTANCE OF THE UNFAMILIAR

The only things we really hate are unfamiliar things.

SAMUEL BUTLER: *Life and Habit*

NON-ACCEPTANCE OF THE UNFAMILIAR

Prelude to a Lexicon

THIS is an anthology of critical assaults upon composers since the time of Beethoven. The criterion of selection here is the exact opposite to that of a press agent. Instead of picking a quotably flattering phrase out of context from an otherwise tepid review, the LEXICON OF MUSICAL INVECTIVE cites biased, unfair, ill-tempered, and singularly unprophetic judgments.

The present collection is, then, not a chrestomathy but a Schimpf-lexicon. Its animating purpose is to demonstrate that music is an art in progress, and that objections leveled at every musical innovator are all derived from the same psychological inhibition, which may be described as Non-Acceptance of the Unfamiliar.

The music critics whose extraordinary outpourings are detailed here are not necessarily opinionated detractors, grouching and grumbling at anything new just because it is new. Many of them are men of great culture, writers of brilliant prose, who, when the spirit moves them, excel in the art of imaginative vituperation. They are adept at effective figures of speech, and they apply metaphorical language with considerable inventiveness to demolish the musical transgressors. Their only failing is that they confuse their ingrained listening habits with the unalterable ideal of beauty and perfection.

The Phenomenon of Non-Acceptance of the Unfamiliar is revealed in every instance when custom clashes with an alien mode of living or a heterodoxal mode of thinking. The Polish language is unpronounceable to non-Slavs; words in Czech and Bulgarian, containing nothing but written consonants, are monsters to the eye.

Unfamiliar customs offend. Gestures have widely divergent social connotations in different lands. A Tibetan sticks out his tongue and hisses when he greets a friend, but such salutation is an insult to an Occidental. Lusty whistling after a theatrical number is an expression of delight among American audiences; but in Europe it is equivalent to booing, as American soldiers found out to their dismay in 1945, when they wished to show their appreciation of a Paris ballet performance. The ballerinas were in tears at what they thought was an ill-mannered expression of displeasure.

To listeners steeped in traditional music, modern works are meaningless, as alien languages are to a poor linguist. No wonder that music critics often borrow linguistic similes to express their recoiling horror of the modernists. The Chinese language, as the ultimate of incomprehensibility, serves the critics particularly well for such comparisons.

The *Musical World* of June 30, 1855 gives this account of the music of *Lohengrin*: 'It has no more real pretension to be called music than the jangling and clashing of gongs and other uneuphonious instruments with which the Chinamen, on the brow of a hill, fondly thought to scare away our English blue-jackets.'

Ninety-five years later, by an ironic turn of history, the Chinese actually played *Lohengrin* music to British and American soldiers in Korea, to scare them away! An International News Service dispatch from the northwest Korean front, dated December 5, 1950, quotes Henry Roose, twenty-year-old private from Lima, Ohio, as saying: 'I was one of five hundred men who fought their way out of a Chinese Communist trap. . . . Around 9 P. M., an eerie sound sent shivers along my spine. A lone bugler on a ridge one hundred yards away was playing Lohengrin's Funeral March.* A Chinese

* There is no funeral march in *Lohengrin*—presumably it was the introduction to the third act of the opera, the melody of which can be played by a single bugler.

voice speaking English floated across the valley, saying: "That's for you, boys—you won't ever hear it again."'

H. T. Finck wrote in 1910: 'Strauss lets loose an orchestral riot that suggests a murder scene in a Chinese theater.' A Philadelphia critic said about Schoenberg's Violin Concerto that it was as comprehensible as 'a lecture on the fourth dimension delivered in Chinese.'

If to Western traditionalists modern music sounds Chinese, to some unoriented Orientals all Western music is unintelligible. One Jihei Hashigushi spoke his mind on the subject after attending the New York première of *Madama Butterfly* in February 1907. He wrote to a New York daily: 'I can say nothing for the music of *Madama Butterfly*. Western music is too complicated for a Japanese. Even Caruso's celebrated singing does not appeal very much more than the barking of a dog in faraway woods.'

When Russian music made its incursion into Europe and America during the last quarter of the nineteenth century, the critics were fascinated and shocked at the same time. The very sound of Russian names seemed forbidding. 'Rimsky-Korsakov—what a name!' exclaims the writer in the *Musical Courier* in 1897. 'It suggests fierce whiskers stained with vodka!'

The Boston *Transcript* wrote of Tchaikovsky's B♭ minor Piano Concerto in 1875: 'This elaborate work is as difficult for popular apprehension as the name of the composer.' One wishes that the critic might have lived to see the day when the opening theme of Tchaikovsky's Concerto became a popular song under the inviting title, *Tonight We Love*!

Stravinsky and Prokofiev were greeted by a horrified chorus of music critics whose ears were still attuned to the aural comforts of nineteenth-century harmonies. *Le Ménestrel* of June 6, 1914 suggested that *Le Sacre du Printemps* should be called 'Massacre du Printemps.' As late as December 1918 a writer in *Musical America* was profoundly shaken when he heard Prokofiev conduct and play his works: 'Those who do not believe that genius is evident in superabundance of noise, looked in vain for a new musical message in Mr. Prokofiev's work. Nor in the *Classical Symphony*, which the composer conducted, was there any cessation from the orgy of discordant sounds. As an exposition of the unhappy state of chaos from which Russia suffers, Mr. Prokofiev's music is interesting, but one hopes fervently that the future may hold better things both for Russia and listeners to Russian music.'

Incredible? Then read this by Henry Fothergill Chorley, reviewing a Chopin recital in London in 1843: 'M. Chopin increasingly affects the crudest modulations. Cunning must be the connoisseur indeed, who, while listening to his music, can form the slightest idea when wrong notes are played.'

The same Chorley wrote that Schumann's harmonies were 'so obtrusively crude that no number of wrong notes would be detected by the subtlest listener.' This species of *argumentum ad notam falsam* is stock-in-trade with reactionary music critics.

After the American première of *Salome,* an American critic echoed Chorley's argumentation: 'Thanks to the prevailing dissonance, nobody knows—or cares—whether the singers sing the right notes, that is, the notes assigned to them, or not.' When Alban Berg's opera *Wozzeck* was produced, there was more of the same: 'Whether one sings or plays wrong notes in such an insalubrious style is utterly immaterial,' wrote one newspaper reviewer.

The Russian critic Hermann Laroche wrote in the St. Petersburg *Golos* of February 11, 1874: 'The overabundance of dissonances and the incompetence in handling vocal parts in *Boris Godunov* reach the point where the listener is unable to distinguish intentional wrong notes from the wrong notes of the performers.'

Another Russian critic, Nicolas Soloviev, described *Boris Godunov* as 'Cacophony in Five Acts and Seven Scenes.'

Professional music critics rarely possess any aptitude for mathematics. Hence, they like to compare musical processes unintelligible to them with the equally darksome methods of mathematical thinking. Here is an assortment of such expressions of helplessness before a modern enigma: 'The science of Monsieur Berlioz is a sterile algebra' (P. Scudo, *Critique et Littérature Musicales,* Paris, 1852); 'The music of Wagner imposes mental tortures that only algebra has a right to inflict' (Paul de Saint-Victor, *La Presse,* Paris, March 1861); 'The Brahms C minor Symphony is mathematical music evolved with difficulty from an unimaginative brain' (Boston *Gazette,* January 22, 1878); 'Herr Bruckner realized and extended the acoustician Euler's belief that it is possible to figure out a sonata'

(New York *Tribune,* November 13, 1886); 'The Russian composer Rimsky-Korsakov has evidently evolved a musical enigma which is too complex of solution now' (Boston *Globe,* March 13, 1898); 'Mathematics . . . are not music, and to non-dodecaphonists the effect of Schoenberg's works on the ear is one of unintelligible ugliness' (*Musical Opinion,* London, July 1952).

The art of musical invective flourished in the nineteenth century and the first decade of the twentieth, when music critics indulged in personal attacks on non-conformist composers. Nowadays, a critic will say that the music he doesn't like is ugly, but he will not say that the composer himself is ugly. And he will not defame the composer by comparing him with a member of an 'inferior' race. James Gibbons Huneker did both in his extraordinary description of the physical appearance of Debussy. He wrote in the New York *Sun* of July 19, 1903: 'I met Debussy at the Café Riche the other night and was struck by the unique ugliness of the man. His face is flat, the top of his head is flat, his eyes are prominent—the expression veiled and sombre—and altogether, with his long hair, unkempt beard, uncouth clothing and soft hat, he looked more like a Bohemian, a Croat, a Hun, than a Gaul. His high prominent cheek bones lend a Mongolian aspect to his face. The head is brachycephalic, the hair black. . . . The man is a wraith from the East; his music was heard long ago in the hill temples of Borneo; was made as a symphony to welcome the head-hunters with their ghastly spoils of war!'

Paul Rosenfeld, the subtle chronicler of the arts, forsakes the customary elegance of his prose to inveigh against the music and the physical features of Max Reger. In his *Musical Portraits,* Rosenfeld describes Reger as 'an ogre of composition . . . a swollen, myopic beetle with thick lips and sullen expression.'

A century ago, music critics freely mixed esthetic invective with scandal-mongering. The *Musical World* of October 28, 1841, having first dismissed Chopin's music as 'ranting hyperbole and excruciating cacophony,' plunged headlong into Chopin's liaison with George Sand: 'There is an excuse at present for Chopin's delinquencies; he is entrammelled in the enthralling bonds of that arch-enchantress, George Sand, celebrated equally for the number and excellence of her romances and her lovers; not less we wonder how she who once swayed the heart of the sublime and terrible religious democrat Lamennais, can be content to wanton away her dreamlike existence with an artistical nonentity like Chopin.'

No newspaper today would publish a piece of music criticism in which the composer is called an idiot or a madman. Yet, on April 19, 1899 the *Musical Courier* suggested that Richard Strauss is 'either a lunatic, or is rapidly approaching idiocy.' The same journal declared some years later: 'Arnold Schoenberg may be either crazy as a loon or he may be a very clever trickster.'

The *Musical World* of June 30, 1855 castigated Wagner as a 'communist,' purveying 'demagogic cacophony, the symbol of profligate libertinage.'

The German-American *Newyorker Staatszeitung,* in its issue of May 23, 1888, suggested that the proper title for *Götterdämmerung* should be 'Goddamnerung.'

There is no more scornful epithet in the vocabulary of partisan critics than impotence and its paronyms. Hugo Wolf, out of Wagnerophilic factionalism, described the music of Brahms as 'die Sprache der intensivsten musikalischen Impotenz.' Nietzsche spoke of Brahms as having 'die Melancholie des Unvermögens.' A French critic wrote of *Pelléas et Mélisande*: 'Les amoureux de M. Debussy semblent fatigués de naissance, des amants anémiés, qui ne peuvent se hausser jusqu'à la volupté et prennent leurs petits spasmes d'une seconde pour des transports d'amour et de passion.'

Music critics of the uninhibited era liked to embellish their invective with gastro-intestinal figures of speech. 'Wagner takes himself for a Dalai Lama,' wrote Heinrich Dorn, 'and his excrement for the emanation of his godlike spirit.'

In an article entitled 'On the Cult of Wrong Notes,' published in the *Musical Quarterly* of July 1915, the English writer Frederick Corder describes the music of Béla Bartók as 'mere ordure.'

After listening to a performance of *Sun-Treader* by Carl Ruggles, a Berlin critic suggested that the title should be changed to 'Latrine-Treader.' He said he had a sensation of 'bowel constrictions in an atonal Tristanesque ecstasy.'

The composers under attack have not been remiss in answering the critics in scatological language. When Gottfried Weber published an article accusing Beethoven of desecrating the high purpose of his art in writing the score of *Wellington's Victory*, Beethoven scrawled on the margin of his copy of the magazine *Cæcilia*, in which the article appeared: 'O du elender Schuft! Was ich *scheisse*, ist besser als du je gedacht!'

The most outspoken letter in its specific imagery was the one that Max Reger dispatched to the Munich critic Rudolf Louis: 'Ich sitze in dem kleinsten Zimmer in meinem Hause. Ich habe Ihre Kritik vor mir. Im nächsten Augenblick wird sie *hinter* mir sein.'*

Animal noises, particularly the meowing of amorous cats, furnish the critics with a vivid vocabulary of invective. Oscar Comettant, writing in *Le Siècle* of May 27, 1872, found cat music in Bizet as well as in Wagner. 'M. Bizet et son patron Wagner ne changeront pas la nature humaine. Ils ne feront pas que les miaulements chromatiques d'un chat amoureux ou effrayé . . . remplacent jamais, chez un auditeur sain d'esprit et d'oreille, une mélodie tonale.' The Boston *Gazette*, in its issue of February 28, 1886, described Liszt's music as 'a choice selection of the various shades of expression of which the voice of the nocturnal cat is capable.'

The atonal music of Wallingford Riegger's *Dichotomy* inspired the Berlin critic of the *Signale* to draw this surrealist animal landscape: 'It sounded as though a pack of rats were being slowly tortured to death, while, from time to time, a dying cow moaned.'

The Mozart-loving Oulibicheff heard 'odious meowing' and 'discords acute enough to split the hardiest ear' in Beethoven's Fifth Symphony! He referred specifically to the transition from the *Scherzo* to the *Finale*.

Lawrence Gilman described the music of one of the *Five Orchestral Pieces* by Anton von Webern by the striking phrase: 'The amoeba weeps.'

New musical instruments, too, have been likened to animal sounds. The London *Times* wrote of the Theremin after a demonstration of the instrument in London in April 1950: 'In the Theremin we have a machine which in the baritone register suggests a cow in dyspeptic distress.'

An anonymous cartoon printed by G. Schirmer in New York in 1869 under the title, 'The Music of the Future,' displays eight cats

* 'I am sitting in the smallest room of my house. I have your review before me. In a moment it will be behind me.'

(labeled A, B, C, D, E, F, G, A), several donkeys, and a group of goats, as participants in a Wagnerian orchestra. The score on the conductor's stand reads: 'Liszt's Symphonic Poem.' Another score, at the conductor's feet, is marked: 'Wagner, not to be played much until 1995.'

Anti-modernists like to use the *argumentum ad tempora futura* to shoo away the immediate assault on their fossilized senses. 'If the future can relish such a chaotic piece of music,' wrote Max Kalbeck about Bruckner, 'we wish this future to be far from us.'

Fiorentino, the French anti-Wagnerian, gallantly declined the blandishments of the musicians of the future: 'J'honore infiniment la musique de l'avenir,' he wrote, 'mais souffrez que je m'en tienne à la musique du passé.'

The New York *Musical Review* of December 23, 1880 published the following aphorism about Liszt's *Faust* Symphony: 'It may be the Music of the Future, but it sounds remarkably like the Cacophony of the Present.'

When Ernest Bloch conducted a program of his works in New York in May 1917, the critic of the New York *Evening Post* bracketed him with Schoenberg as futurists trying to 'distract attention from their creative shortcomings by pelting the ears of the hearers with cacophonies.' He said that 'Mr. Bloch's ideal of the Jewish music of the future is apparently the grotesque, hideous, cackling dispute of the Seven Jews in Richard Strauss's *Salome*.' Admitting that Ernest Bloch 'got plenty of applause,' he added, venomously, that the audience was 'largely of the Oriental persuasion.'

In his attempt to justify the obdurate tradition, Richard Aldrich wrote in the New York *Times* of November 15, 1915: 'Music that has been veiled to one generation has often been revealed to the next as a clear and intelligible advance. Will our grandchildren see it and smile indulgently at the bewildered listeners of 1915? The question is not really important; bewildered listeners of 1915 can only listen for themselves.'

Eight years later Aldrich wrote: 'The liberated music-maker and listener of the farthest advanced line are strangely uncritical persons. Whatever is presented to them as acrid ugliness or rambling incoherence is eagerly accepted as emanations of greatness and originality. It never occurs to them that it may be really simple, commonplace ugliness. . . . Is it only necessary to sound bad to be really good?'

Sometimes critics are fortunate enough to catch up with the musical future during their own lifetimes, and change their minds accordingly. The astute Philip Hale wrote disdainfully about Strauss's symphonic poem, *Don Juan,* in the Boston *Post* of November 1, 1891: 'Strauss uses music as the vehicle of expressing everything but music; for he has little invention, and his musical thoughts are of little worth. This symphonic poem is supposed to portray in music the recollections and regrets of a jaded voluptuary. Now, granting that music is capable of doing this, what do we find in this composition? There are recollections, not of Don Juan, but of Liszt and of Wagner. There are also regrets, but the regrets come from the hearers. Besides, Don Juan was more direct in his methods. His wooing was as sudden and as violent as his descent to the lower regions. According to Strauss, he was verbose, fond of turning corners, something of a metaphysician, and a good deal of a bore. When he made love, he beat upon a triangle, and when he was dyspeptic, he confided his woes to instruments that moaned in sympathy.'

Eleven years later, Philip Hale heard *Don Juan* again. This time, the music produced a vastly different impression on him—rivers of modernistic harmonies had gone over the dam in the meantime, and the perceptive ear had made the inevitable adjustments to a new mode of musical expression. Writing then in the Boston *Journal,* in its issue of November 2, 1902, Philip Hale responded enthusiastically to *Don Juan*: 'A daring, brilliant composition; one that paints the hero as might a master's brush on canvas. How expressive the themes! How daring the treatment of them! What fascinating, irresistible insolence, glowing passion!'

When Hugo Leichtentritt, a fine and liberal-minded scholar, heard Schoenberg's *Three Piano Pieces,* op. 11, for the first time in 1911, he wrote: 'I see in them complete dissolution of all that was heretofore regarded as musical art. It is possible that the music of the future will be like that, but I have no understanding of its beauty. Whether the pianist played the piece well or badly, I cannot judge, because in this music the listener cannot distinguish between right and wrong.'

In his treatise *Musical Form,* published in 1951, Leichtentritt revised his earlier judgment: 'These piano pieces have often been criticized as constructions which mock the laws of reason, the demands of the ear, as in fact "non-music," to which the usual reaction has been amused laughter and sneers. The following analysis will prove that these pieces are constructed not only sensibly, but strictly, logically, and concisely.'

Ill-starred prophecies abound in the annals of music criticism. '*Rigoletto* lacks melody,' wrote the *Gazette Musicale de Paris* in 1853; 'this opera has hardly any chance to be kept in the repertoire.' A correspondent of a London newspaper wrote in 1854: '*Lohengrin* has been given a few times . . . and I scarcely think it will be able to keep the stage for any length of time.' The Boston *Daily Advertiser* declared in 1874: 'It needs no gift of prophecy to predict that Berlioz will be utterly unknown a hundred years hence to everybody but the encyclopedists and the antiquarians.'

In their horror of the latest abomination, critics are often willing to forget and to forgive the trespasses of the musical sinners of the immediate past. By dint of an *argumentum ad deteriora* they hope to confound the newest monster through mock surrender to the monster of yesteryear. Thus, Chorley, the hater of Schumann, was willing to grant him some virtue, when confronted with the greater menace of Wagner. 'Dr. Schumann is as clear as Truth and as charming as Graces themselves,' he wrote, 'if he be measured against the opera composer who has been set up by Young Germany, at the composer's own instigation, as the coming man of the stage—I mean, of course, Richard Wagner.'

In 1893, Philip Hale described Brahms's First Symphony as 'the apotheosis of arrogance.' Thereupon, he drew a symbolic program of the score: 'The musicians are in a forest. The forest is dark. No birds are in this forest save birds that do not sing. . . . The players wander. They grope as though they were eyeless. Alarmed, they call to each other; frightened, they shout together. It seems that obscene, winged things listen and mock the lost. . . . Suddenly the players are in a clearing. They see close to them a canal. The water of the canal is green, and diseased purple and yellow plants grow on the banks of the canal. . . . A swan with filthy plumage and twisted neck bobs up and down in the green water. . . . And then a boat is dragged towards the players. The boat is crowded with queerly dressed men and women and children, who sing a tune that sounds something like the hymn in Beethoven's Ninth Symphony. . . . Darkness seizes the scene.'

The critic of the New York *Times* in the 1890's had his misgivings about Brahms, but when he was assigned to review a work by Strauss he was eager to concede that Brahms might be, relatively speaking, a charming composer. He wrote in an unsigned article of February 28, 1896: '*Till Eulenspiegel* is a horrible example of what can be done with an orchestra by a determined and deadly decadent. There was a time when Brahms was regarded as the Browning of music. Richard Strauss has made the symphonies of Brahms sound like Volkslieder.'

The Boston *Herald* wrote: '*Till Eulenspiegel* casts into the deepest shade the wildest efforts of the wildest follower of the modern school. It is a blood-curdling nightmare.'

The *Musical Courier* of January 29, 1902 said: 'Strauss's *Heldenleben* and *Thus Spake Zarathustra* are clear as crystal waters in comparison with Gustav Mahler's Fourth Symphony.'

When the Fourth Symphony of Sibelius was performed in America in 1913, the Boston *Journal* described it as 'a tangle of most dismal dissonances' which 'eclipses the saddest and sourest moments of Debussy.'

It is not clear why the mild music of Vincent d'Indy impressed some critics half a century ago as being worse than Strauss. The New York *Sun* thought so: 'Even *Ein Heldenleben* becomes as the croon of a cradle song besides d'Indy's Second Symphony.'

Then came Debussy. The New York *World* reported on March 22, 1907: 'New York heard a new composition called *The Sea,* and New York is probably still wondering why. The work is by the most modern of modern Frenchmen, Debussy. . . . Compared with this, the most abstruse compositions of Richard Strauss are as primer stories to hear and to comprehend.'

The New York *Sun,* reviewing the same performance, makes a similar concession to the relative agreeableness of Strauss vs. Debussy: 'Debussy out-Strausses Strauss. *The Sea* and all that's in that painted mud-puddle was merely funny when it fell to whistling Salome's own shrill trill.'

After listening to Varèse's symphonic work *Arcana,* Paul Schwers of the *Allgemeine Musikzeitung* was eager to welcome Schoenberg:

'Great Arnold Schoenberg, your famous *Five Orchestral Pieces* are gloriously vindicated! They are the utterances of pure classicism beside this barbarous monstrosity.' Conversely, Olin Downes invoked the gentle muse of Varèse to exorcise Schoenberg. 'How we would have been thrilled by some good red-blooded, rousing tune of Edgar Varèse!' he exclaimed upon hearing Schoenberg's *Variations for Orchestra.*

Unfamiliar music impresses a prejudiced listener as a chaos of random sounds. No wonder that to some critics the labor spent on rehearsing a modern piece appears a waste of effort. César Cui, who was a professional music critic as well as a composer, wrote after hearing a performance of *Sinfonia Domestica*: 'Put blank music sheets before the conductor and the players. Let the musicians play anything they wish and let the conductor conduct anything he wishes, giving cues and indicating the time, tempo, and the intensity of sound at random. Perhaps, the result would be even more remarkable in its genius than Strauss himself.'

The same procedure was suggested to conductors of Liszt's music by a London critic in *Era* of February 25, 1882: 'The conductor wields his baton, but the effect is not a bit more agreeable than if each performer threw down the notes and played at random with all his might and energy. . . . Let the conductor give instructions to each player to produce every discordant sound that is in the range of his particular instrument, and let the cacophony continue for half an hour under the title of *Lunacy* or *Moonstruck.*'

In all fairness to these particular prophets, it must be said that ultra-modern music of the mid-twentieth century made their nightmares come true. In 1948, a Paris radio engineer launched a 'musique concrète,' in which random sounds and noises are recorded and presented as a new method—we should call it the 'aleatory method'—of composition. The American composer John Cage later rationalized the idea by writing music according to a system of throwing Chinese dice.

Music critics often complain that modern works cause them actual physical pain. August Spanuth described Schoenberg's Chamber Symphony as a 'Chamber-of-Horrors' Symphony. Huneker wrote: 'Schoenberg mingles with his music sharp daggers at white heat, with which he pares away tiny slices of his victim's flesh.' Louis Elson suggested that a more fitting title for Debussy's *La Mer* should be 'Le Mal de Mer.' The urbane Percy A. Scholes reported in the London *Observer* of May 13, 1923 that hearing Béla Bartók play his piano works made him suffer more than at any time in his life 'apart from an incident or two connected with "painless" dentistry.'

When pain becomes unendurable, music critics themselves take part in the audible protest against the offending work. At a Vienna performance of Schoenberg's Second String Quartet, Ludwig Karpath pleaded, by way of extenuation for his own breach of professional decorum, a physiological necessity of crying out for relief.

René Brancour, the Paris critic, offered no apologies for his part in a public demonstration against the brassy importunities of Milhaud's symphonic suite *Protée*. 'I was in the first rank of objectors,' he wrote in *Le Ménestrel* of October 28, 1920, 'and a zealous, but otherwise courteous police officer was prepared to deliver me to the secular arm entrusted with the expulsion of heretics.' Brancour was saved from this indignity by the intercession of a similarly minded colleague who persuaded the officer to let Brancour remain in the hall.

On the other hand, the critic of the *Berliner Morgenpost* took it upon himself to defend the right of a modern composer to compose as he pleased. When a riot broke out at the second Berlin performance of Schoenberg's *Pierrot Lunaire*, on October 7, 1922, he rose from his seat and belabored the disturbers of the peace as 'ungebildete Lausejungen.'

Just as all good people are in favor of virtue, so music critics are unanimously in favor of melody. Berlioz, Brahms and Liszt were all charged at one time or another with willful neglect of melodic writing. 'Non seulement M. Berlioz n'a pas d'idées mélodiques, mais lorsqu'une idée lui arrive, il ne sait pas la traiter,' opined the ineffable Scudo, the French writer, who ended his career in an insane asylum.

Hanslick described the Wagnerian melody as 'formlessness elevated to a principle.' The Boston *Traveler* lamented in 1882: 'Brahms might afford occasionally to put a little more melody into his work, just a little now and then for a change.' Another Bostonian wrote: 'If the fair and ingenious Scheherazade related her stories as confusedly and unmeaningly, not to say cacophonously, as Rimsky-Korsakov has related them musically, the Sultan would have ordered her to be bowstrung, or to have her head lopped off after the second or third night.' The Boston *Gazette* of January 5, 1879 said this about *Carmen:* 'Of melody, as the term is generally understood, there is but little.'

The *Gazette Musicale de Paris* declared in 1847: 'There has not yet appeared an Italian composer more incapable than Verdi of producing what is commonly known as a melody.'

In 1907 the New York *Post* dismissed Debussy in these words: 'Debussy's music is the dreariest kind of rubbish. Does anybody for a moment doubt that Debussy would write such chaotic, meaningless, cacophonous, ungrammatical stuff, if he could invent a melody?'

Arthur Pougin, who, as the editor of the supplement to the *Biographie Universelle des Musiciens,* had described the score of *Die Meistersinger* as a collection of 'absolutely indecipherable puzzles,' and who lived to witness the rise of Debussy, wrung his hands at the monstrosities of *Pelléas et Mélisande:* 'What adorable progressions of consecutive triads, with the inevitably resulting fifths and octaves! What a collection of dissonances, sevenths, and ninths, ascending even by disjunct intervals!'

Hanslick was horrified by a 'monstrous edifice of fifths—E, B, F♯, D, A, and E' in Liszt's *Mephisto Waltz.* The American critic W. F. Apthorp was racked by 'the most ear-flaying succession of chords' in *Tosca.*

George Templeton Strong, the magnificent reactionary whose diary reflecting the New York scene in the middle of the nineteenth century was published in 1952, was naturally anti-Berlioz, anti-Liszt and anti-Wagner. With an uncommon gift for an imaginative phrase, he described the introduction to *Lohengrin* as 'two squeakinesses with a brassiness between them.' He said that Wagner wrote like an 'intoxified' pig, and Berlioz like a tipsy chimpanzee. Liszt's Piano Concerto in E♭ was to him 'catarrhal or sternutatory.' He heard in it 'a graphic instrumentation of a fortissimo sneeze' and 'a protracted, agonized bravura on the pocket handkerchief.'

Anti-modern critics are, of course, aware of the historical fact that the musical classics of today were the unmelodious monsters of yesterday, and they like to disassociate themselves from their short-sighted predecessors. Raphaël Cor, the compiler of the extraordinary symposium of impatient vituperation published in 1910 under the pointed title, *Le Cas Debussy,* took cognizance of the fact that Wagner had, like Debussy, been assailed for the unmelodiousness of his music: 'Let no one interpose that the same criticism was once directed against Wagner, for the Wagnerian melody eluded his adversaries, whereas the music of Monsieur Debussy, according to his own admission, contains no trace of melody.'

In a spirit of good-humored raillery at the Debussyan rage at the Paris Conservatory, Erik Satie drew a table of 'commandements du catéchisme du Conservatoire' in which the students were enjoined: 'Thou shalt not be melodious!' And he wittily deified Debussy as *Dieu*bussy:

> *Dieu*bussy seul adoreras
> Et copieras parfaitement—
> Mélodieux point ne seras
> De fait ni de consentement.*

Charles Villiers Stanford, who was in his prime a Wagnerian modernist, was distracted by the novel modernism of the incipient twentieth century. In protest against the musical depredations of Debussy and Strauss, he concocted a rather heavy-footed *Ode to Discord,* stuffed it with unresolved dissonances and whole-tone scales, and presented it to the London public on June 9, 1909. Stanford described his score as a 'chimerical bombination in four bursts' (with a learned reference to the line 'Chimaera bombinans in vacuo' from Erasmus) and dedicated it to the Amalgamated Society of Boiler Makers. The orchestration included a 'hydrophone' and a 'dreadnaught drum' measuring eight feet nine inches across. There was an aria which apostrophized in mock-solemn verse:

> Hence, loathed Melody!
> Divine Cacophony, assume
> The rightful overlordship in her room,
> And with Percussion's stimulating aid,
> Expel the Heavenly but no longer youthful Maid!

* Satie signed these verses Erit Satis, i.e., This Will Be Enough; they were published posthumously in *La Semaine Musicale* of November 11, 1927.

New music always sounds loud to old ears. Beethoven seemed to make more noise than Mozart; Liszt was noisier than Beethoven; Strauss, noisier than Liszt; Schoenberg and Stravinsky, noisier than any of their predecessors.

Reviewing the first London performance of the Ninth Symphony, the *Musical Magazine and Review* made this philosophical observation: 'Beethoven finds from all the public accounts that noisy extravagance of execution and outrageous clamor in musical performances more frequently ensures applause than chastened elegance or refined judgment. The inference, therefore, that we may fairly make, is that he writes accordingly.'

After the first Boston performance of the Ninth Symphony, the Boston *Daily Atlas* reported that the last movement 'appeared to be an incomprehensible union of strange harmonies,' and sought explanation of Beethoven's decline in his deafness: 'the great man upon the ocean of harmony, without the compass . . . the blind painter touching the canvas at random.'

Robert Browning, who loved Rossini, was outraged by the noisiness of Verdi's operas. He wrote in wrathful verse:

> Like Verdi, when, at his worst opera's end
> (The thing they gave at Florence, what's its name),
> While the mad houseful's plaudits near out-bang
> His orchestra of salt-box, tongs, and bones,
> He looks through all the roaring and the wreaths
> Where sits Rossini patient in his stall.

The loudness of Wagner's music was lampooned in hundreds of contemporary caricatures, variously representing him as conducting a siege of Paris or driving a nail into the listener's ear. Yet, in computable quantity of decibels, Wagner's noisiest orchestral interludes fall far below a German military march.

One of the characters in Oscar Wilde's novel *The Picture of Dorian Gray* points out conversational advantages of Wagner's music: 'I like Wagner's music better than anybody's. It is so loud that one can talk the whole time without other people hearing what one says.'

A poem entitled 'Directions for Composing a Wagner Overture,' published in an American newspaper in the 1880's, ends with this quatrain:

For harmonies, let wildest discords pass:
Let key be blent with key in hideous hash;
Then (for last happy thought!) bring in your Brass!
And clang, clash, clatter—clatter, clang and clash!

In 1924 a bewildered subscriber to the Boston Symphony concerts contributed these lines upon hearing Stravinsky's *Le Sacre du Printemps*:

Who wrote this fiendish Rite of Spring,
What right had he to write the thing,
Against our helpless ears to fling
Its crash, clash, cling, clang, bing, bang, bing?

The last lines of the anti-Wagner and anti-Stravinsky poems are practically identical. It is safe to assume that the author of the anti-Stravinsky poem regarded Wagner's music as a thing of beauty.

A fairly accurate time-table could be drawn for the assimilation of unfamiliar music by the public and the critics. It takes approximately twenty years to make an artistic curiosity out of a modernistic monstrosity; and another twenty to elevate it to a masterpiece.* Not every musical monstrosity is a potential musical masterpiece, but its chances of becoming one are measurably better than those of a respectable composition of mediocre quality.

One musical curiosity that was not destined to become an immortal masterpiece was the *Network of Noises* by the Italian futurist Luigi Russolo. When he conducted it in Milan on April 21, 1914, the excitable audience actually threatened bodily harm to the futurist offenders. A skirmish followed, as a result of which eleven members of the audience had to be hospitalized, but the futurists suffered only minor bruises. Who remembers now these excitements? The Italian futurists seem to have a brilliant future behind them.

When a modern composer is not accused of noise making, he is assailed for the annoying tenuousness of his musical speech. Camille Bellaigue, a musical reactionary blessed with a gift of elegant prose, conceded that Debussy's orchestra makes little noise,

* With what precision the law of a forty-year lag in the integral acceptance of a modern masterpiece operates, was demonstrated by the wild cheers that greeted Stravinsky at the performance of *Le Sacre du Printemps* in Paris on May 8, 1952, thirty-nine years after its première. Pierre Monteux, who conducted both performances, in 1913 and in 1952, remarked: 'There was just as much noise the last time, but of a different tonality!'

but said that it is 'a nasty little noise' ('un vilain petit bruit').

The London *Times* of April 28, 1924 compared Ravel's music to the work of 'some midget or pygmy, doing clever but very small things within a limited scope' with an 'almost reptilian cold-bloodedness.'

Anti-modernist critics who prepare their reviews in advance, but fail to attend a concert, ought to make sure that the performance of the offending music has actually taken place. Leonid Sabaneyev, the Moscow critic, published in 1916 a damning review of the announced première of Prokofiev's *Scythian Suite.* He did not go to the concert and did not know that the work was taken off the program at the last moment. Sabaneyev was forced to resign from his paper as a result of this indiscretion, but he refused to make amends to the composer.

Under similar circumstances, H. E. Krehbiel of the New York *Tribune* was much more of a gentleman. In his review of a New York concert of Russian music, Krehbiel indignantly attacked Prokofiev for the 'musical bestiality' of *Hircus Nocturnus,* a composition by Sergei Vasilenko. The next day, Krehbiel published a note of apology, blaming the dim light in the hall for his failure to read the composer's name on the program, and good-naturedly congratulated Prokofiev for not having written the score.

Non-Acceptance of the Unfamiliar in music extends to unsymmetrical rhythms as well as atonal melodies and dissonant harmonies. The celebrated Hanslick seriously suggested, upon hearing Tchaikovsky's *Pathétique,* that the 5/4 meter of the *Allegro con grazia* might well have been arranged in 6/8, thus sparing the annoyance to both listener and player.

In *La Revue des Deux Mondes* of July 1, 1892, Camille Bellaigue gives a satirical description of the musical notation of the future. Little did he realize how prophetic was the tableau presented by him! 'Let us wait a few years,' he wrote, 'and there will be no sense to study the laws of harmony, nor those of melody, which are set down only to be violated. The key signatures will no longer carry the necessary sharps or flats, these guardians of tonality. A piece of music will be no more in 3/4 or 12/8 than in C major or D minor. Caprice will become the rule, and chance, the law. The musical speech, disarticulated, deprived of grammar and syntax, devoid of logic, without proper notation, without punctuation, will meander aimlessly, and lose itself in the chaos of infinite melopoeia and errant modulation.'

In his 'Reminiscences of a Quinquagenarian,' published in *The Proceedings of the Musical Association of London* for the year 1910, George Bernard Shaw offers some illuminating remarks on the growth of musical tolerance: 'It is not easy for a musician of today to confess that he once found Wagner's music formless, melodyless, and abominably discordant; but that many musicians, now living, did so is beyond all question. . . . The technical history of modern harmony is a history of growth of toleration by the human ear of chords that at first sounded discordant and senseless to the main body of contemporary professional musicians.'

When Varèse presented his early symphonic work *Bourgogne* in Germany, it was met with obtuse hostility by the critics. Varèse reported the event to Debussy, declaring that he was not in the least concerned about this reception. In his reply Debussy made some penetrating remarks about the public and the critics. He wrote to Varèse on February 12, 1911: 'Vous avez parfaitement raison de ne pas vous alarmer de l'hostilité du public. Un jour viendra ou vous serez les meilleurs amis du monde. Mais dépêchez-vous de perdre l'assurance que la critique de chez nous est plus clairvoyante qu'en Allemagne. Et ne perdez pas de vue qu'un critique aime rarement ce dont il a à parler. Souvent même, il apporte un soin jaloux à ne pas savoir du tout de quoi il est question! La critique pourrait être un art si on pouvait la faire dans des conditions de libre jugement nécessaires. Ça n'est plus qu'un métier. . . . Il faut dire que d'ailleurs les soi-disant artistes ont beaucoup aidé à cet état de choses.'*

In the minds of righteous reactionaries, musical modernism is

* 'You are perfectly justified in not being alarmed by the hostility of the public. The day will come when you will be the best of friends in the world. But you had better give up your belief that our critics are more perspicacious than those in Germany. Also, do not forget that a critic seldom likes what he has to describe. Sometimes he makes a special effort not to know what he is talking about! Criticism could be an art if it were practiced under the necessary conditions of free judgment. But it is now no more than a trade. It must be said in passing that the so-called artists have contributed a great deal to this state of affairs.'

often associated with criminality and moral turpitude. Operas dealing with illicit love have been consistently assailed for the immorality of their librettos. In an inflammatory editorial published in the New York *Evening Journal* of January 21, 1907, William Randolph Hearst vesuviated: 'Many crimes have been committed in the name of music. Men of genius have exhausted their ingenuity, degraded the human voice and all musical instruments by causing them to describe murders and every kind of loathsomeness. But it is left for *Salome,* this latest opera, combining the musical genius of Strauss and the vile conception of Oscar Wilde, to produce a so-called work of art and show to the people a great singer in a scene that can be best compared to a hen trying to swallow a toad. . . . In a public performance, a woman is made to declare a desire to bite the swollen lips of a severed head, "as one would bite a ripe fruit." . . . If that is art, will somebody set to music that department of Armour's packing house in which they make the sausages?'

The London *Times* devoted a special 'leader' in its issue of August 7, 1856 to the iniquities of *La Traviata,* attacking the opera as 'public representation of prostitution' in the 'brothels and abominations of modern Paris, of the Boulevards as they exist in the year 1856.' The writer issued a solemn warning to 'the ladies of England to take heed of this matter,' lest their husbands and sons should be 'inoculated with the worst type of Parisian vice.'

In another 'leader' published four days later, the *Times* renewed its 'indignant protest against this exhibition of harlotry upon the public stage.' The article continued: 'An unfortunate young person who has acted the part of a public prostitute . . . coughs her way through three acts, and finally expires on the stage in a manner which, however true to nature, ought to be revolting to the feelings of the spectators. . . . Next season we trust to hear no more such abominations.'

The *Music Trade Review* of London declared in 1878: 'If it were possible to imagine his Satanic Majesty writing an opera, *Carmen* would be the sort of work he might be expected to turn out.'

The London theatrical paper *Figaro* published this comment on *Carmen* in 1884: 'Carmen is a *fille de joie* of the very worst type, passing from man to man without a particle of scruple. The libretto revels in immorality of the most flagrant kind. No sooner do the factory girls, smoking real cigarettes, come on the stage than the evil spirit of Carmen asserts itself. The *Habanera,* replete in sensuality, is made still more telling by the attitude and the open gestures of the shameless girl.'

Die Walküre elicited some protests on the part of London moralists in 1882. 'The thirty minutes devoted to the indecent presentation of a brother and sister's incestuous love,' ran one comment, 'is rather too much for Anglo-Saxon ideas of propriety, and that this part of the opera was not prohibited after the first performance is unaccountable to a number of highly moral journals.'

A British reviewer had this to say after the London première of Puccini's *Tosca*: 'Those who were present were little prepared for the revolting effects produced by musically illustrating the torture and murder scenes of Sardou's play. The alliance of a pure art with scenes, so essentially brutal and demoralizing, results in a contrast that produced a feeling of nausea. There may be some who will find entertainment in this sensation, but all true lovers of the gentle art must deplore with myself its being so prostituted. What has music to do with a lustful man chasing a defenseless woman, or the dying kicks of a murdered scoundrel?'

To proper Anglo-Saxons, including music critics, Paris has always been an alluring and a shocking symbol of profligacy, the navel of immorality. In reviewing the first American performance of Charpentier's opera *Louise,* H. E. Krehbiel wrote in the New York *Tribune* of January 4, 1908:

'This opera is Parisian in its immorality. Coupled with its story, which glorifies the licentiousness of Paris and makes mock of virtue, the sanctity of the family tie and the institutions upon which social stability and human welfare have ever rested and must forever rest, the music may also be set down as immoral. . . . To the intellectual and moral anarchism universally prevalent among the peoples of Western culture, which desires to have idealism outraged, sacred things ridiculed, high conceptions of beauty and duty dragged into the gutter, and ugliness, brutality and bestiality placed upon a pedestal, it makes a strong appeal.'

The erotic naturalism of Shostakovitch's opera *Lady Macbeth of Mzensk* was denounced, in a policy-making article in the Moscow *Pravda,* as a neurotic product of bourgeois decadence. It also shocked some listeners and critics at the opera's production in New

York. W. J. Henderson wrote in the New York *Sun* of February 9, 1935:

'*Lady Macbeth of Mzensk* is a bed-chamber opera. We see much of the coarse embraces of the two sinners mumbling and fumbling about in bed with the side of the house removed so we shall miss nothing. For their first embraces the composer has written music which for realism and brutal animalism surpasses anything else in the world. Here indeed we can indulge in superlatives. Shostakovitch is without doubt the foremost composer of pornographic music in the history of the art. He has accomplished the feat of penning passages which, in their faithful portrayal of what is going on, become obscene. And to crown this achievement he has given to the trombone a jazz slur to express satiety, and this vulgar phrase, rendered tenfold more offensive by its unmistakable purpose, is brought back in the last scene to help us to understand how tired the lover is of his mistress. The whole scene is little better than a glorification of the sort of stuff that filthy pencils write on lavatory walls.'

The custodians of public morals were profoundly shocked by the rise of syncopated music in America at the turn of the century. The *Musical Courier*, in an editorial entitled 'Degenerate Music,' published in its issue of September 13, 1899, took note of the new peril: 'A wave of vulgar, filthy and suggestive music has inundated the land. Nothing but ragtime prevails, and the cake-walk with its obscene posturings, its lewd gestures. . . . Our children, our young men and women, are continually exposed to the contiguity, to the monotonous attrition of this vulgarizing music. It is artistically and morally depressing, and should be suppressed by press and pulpit.'

The Most Reverend Francis J. L. Beckman, Archbishop of Dubuque, told the National Council of Catholic Women at Biloxi, Mississippi, on October 25, 1938: 'A degenerated and demoralizing musical system is given a disgusting christening as "swing" and turned loose to gnaw away the moral fiber of young people. . . . Jam sessions, jitterbugs and cannibalistic rhythmic orgies are wooing our youth along the primrose path to Hell!'

In Russia, American popular music was damned as 'a rhythmically organized chaos of deliberately ugly neuro-pathological sounds.' American jazz band leaders were described in Soviet publications as 'jazz bandits.'

Maxim Gorky, to whom American dance music was a capitalist perversion, reported his impression of a jazz band concert in these words: 'An idiotic little hammer knocks drily: one, two, three, ten, twenty knocks. Then, like a clod of mud thrown into crystal-clear water, there is wild screaming, hissing, rattling, wailing, moaning, cackling. Bestial cries are heard: neighing horses, the squeal of a brass pig, crying jackasses, amorous quacks of a monstrous toad. . . . This excruciating medley of brutal sounds is subordinated to a barely perceptible rhythm. Listening to this screaming music for a minute or two, one conjures up an orchestra of madmen, sexual maniacs, led by a man-stallion beating time with an enormous phallos.'

Sir Richard R. Terry saw in jazz a challenge to the white race. He wrote in *Voodooism in Music:* 'The White races just now are submerged in a spate of negroid sentiment. Hot Jazz, Fox Trots and Black Bottoms occupy the young folk; Negro Spirituals send the adults into tears; the Crooner wails his erotic inanities every night over the Radio. We have reached the stage of a spineless acceptance of all these phenomena. . . . We may see no paganism in what we deem mere harmless amusements, but the observant onlooker cannot fail to see that in the not too far distant future the Catholic Church will be standing as the one barrier in the path of the pagan advance.'

Jazz was assailed as the work of Satan by the English composer and theosophist Cyril Scott: 'After the dissemination of jazz, which was definitely put through by the Dark Forces, a very marked decline in sexual morals became noticeable. Whereas at one time women were content with decorous flirtation, a vast number of them are now constantly preoccupied with the search for erotic adventures, and have thus turned sexual passion into a species of hobby.'

In dance, art, literature, and in politics, the psychological phenomenon of Non-Acceptance of the Unfamiliar operates as forcefully as in music. The good old Waltz was excoriated in Rees's Cyclopedia, published in London in 1805: 'Waltz is a riotous German dance of modern invention. Having seen it performed by a select party of foreigners, we could not help reflecting how uneasy an English mother would be to see her daughter so familiarly treated, and still more to witness the obliging manner in which the freedom is returned by the females.'

When the Tango invaded Europe in 1913, there were outcries of shock and consternation from the press, the pulpit, and the throne. In his message of January 1, 1914, the Archbishop of Paris threatened excommunication to Tango addicts: 'We condemn the dance of foreign origin known as the Tango, which by its lascivious nature offends morality. Christians ought not in conscience to take part in it. Confessors must in the administration of the sacrament of penance enforce these orders.' Cardinal O'Connell of Boston declared: 'If this Tango-dancing female is the new woman, then God spare us from any further development of the abnormal creature.'

To vindicate the honor of his country, the Ambassador of Argentina in Paris was compelled to state formally that the Tango was 'a dance peculiar to the houses of ill fame in Buenos Aires, and is never cultivated in respectable gatherings.'

The suggestive posturings of modern ballet roused the moralists as much as lasciviousness in opera. When Diaghilev presented Debussy's *L'Après-midi d'un faune* with Nijinsky to the Parisian public in 1912, there was an outcry in the reactionary wing of the Paris press. Calmette, the editor of *Le Figaro,* refused to publish a customary account of the production on the ground that its animal realism *à la russe* was a breach of decency. Diaghilev issued a statement in protest, and said, among other things, that Nijinsky's interpretation of the faun had received high praise from the sculptor Rodin. To this, Calmette replied that Rodin himself was guilty of exhibiting obscene sketches in a building formerly occupied by a church. Calmette's moral sense did not deter him, however, from publishing, for political purposes, the intimate correspondence between the French Minister Caillaux and Mme. Caillaux before their marriage. One day, Mme. Caillaux broke into Calmette's office and shot him dead, for which impulsive act she was duly acquitted by a sympathetic Paris jury.

When Isadora Duncan danced, barefoot, before a Boston audience, in October 1922, the then Mayor Curley forthwith issued an order barring her from further appearances. Miss Duncan figuratively shook the Boston dust off her bare feet, and declared (to a New York reporter) that 'all Puritan vulgarity centers in Boston.' She added that 'to expose one's body is art; to conceal it is vulgar.'

Modernist painters have been attacked as viciously as modern composers. The French publication *L'Artiste* declared in its issue of May 1874: 'Monsieur Cézanne is a madman afflicted with delirium tremens. . . . His weird forms are generated by hashish and inspired by a swarm of insane visions.'

Gasperini, a French anti-Wagnerite of a century ago, draws a parallel between the Music of the Future and a putative Art of the Future. How could he foresee that, a mere half-century later, his caricature of modern art would turn out to be an excellent description of the technique of distortionism and angular transposition? Here is what he wrote, as quoted in *Le Ménestrel* of August 20, 1865: 'Do you wish to know what the Music of the Future will be like? Let us suppose that a sculptor, finding nature little to his taste, would fashion a statue to suit his fancy. What would he then do? Exactly the opposite of what had been done before him. In place of a mouth parallel to the chin, he would chisel a perpendicular mouth; in place of the nose, he would put a cheek; and in place of the generally accepted two eyes, a single eye in the middle of the forehead. He would then proudly lift his head and exclaim: This is the Sculpture of the Future!'

Leo Stein reminisced dyspeptically about his sister Gertrude and their mutual friend Picasso: 'They are in my belief turning out the most Godalmighty rubbish that is to be found.'

Albert Wolff, the French art critic, wrote in 1874: 'Just try to explain to Monsieur Renoir that the torso of a woman is not a mass of decomposing flesh, its green and violent spots indicating the state of complete putrefaction of a corpse.'

The *Churchman* delivered this judgment in 1886: 'Degas is nothing but a peeping Tom, behind the coulisses, and among the dressing-rooms of the ballet dancers, noting only travesties on fallen debased womanhood, most disgusting and offensive. It demands no unusual penetration to detect on these walls that satanic and infernal art whose inspirations are verily set on fires of Hell.'

John Burroughs, the American naturalist, wrote in *Current Opinion* in 1921: 'I have just been skimming through an illustrated book called *Noa Noa* by a Frenchman, Paul Gauguin, which describes, or pretends to describe, a visit to Tahiti. Many of his figures are distorted, and all of them have a smutty look, as if they had been rubbed with lampblack or coal dust. When the Parisian becomes a degenerate, he is the worst degenerate of all—a refined, perfumed degenerate.'

The psychological drama of the *fin de siècle* outraged the moralists. William Winter, the American drama critic, wrote in the New York *Tribune* of February 6, 1900: 'There is no surer sign of mental and moral obliquity than a taste for decadent literature and art—the morbid trash of such authors as Ibsen, Pinero and Maeterlinck. No man who is in good health ever bestows attention upon stuff of that kind. He would just as soon haunt a slaughterhouse to smell the offal.'

Walt Whitman was the recipient of lashing invective. 'Walt Whitman is as unacquainted with art as a hog with mathematics,' wrote *The London Critic* in 1855. 'The chief question raised by *Leaves of Grass*,' commented the New York *Tribune* in November 1881, 'is whether anybody—even a poet—ought to take off his trousers in the market-place.'

As in the arts and literature, so in social mores there is always an attitude of shock at the new ways of the world. In his amusing history of manners, *Learning How to Behave,* Arthur Schlesinger, Sr., quotes this from an old book of etiquette: 'We think the prospects for the future happiness of that young girl are small, who will be seen in public with a gentleman who is smoking.' Worse things were in the offing. 'Ladies no longer affect to be disgusted by the odor of tobacco, even at table,' revealed an etiquette book published in 1887. And finally, in a later edition, came this shocking news: 'Women, and women in America—in certain sets—do smoke.'

The horrendous secret in Wolf-Ferrari's opera *Secret of Suzanne* is that Suzanne indulges surreptitiously in cigarette smoking. Her husband, finding an ash tray with a cigarette in it, suspects that Suzanne had been entertaining a gentleman friend. He is both appalled and relieved to find that the mysterious cigarette had been smoked by Suzanne herself. There is a happy ending.

As late as 1923, American males in some regions regarded women who smoked as creatures of evil deserving death for their transgressions. The following story appeared in the New York *Times* of November 12, 1923:

SLAYS BRIDE WHO HAD PACK OF CIGARETTES

CLARKSBURG, W. VA.—When pretty Luella Mae Hedge, a bride of five months, refused to tell how she came to have a package of cigarettes, her husband, Okey Hedge, shot her dead. Hedge said he was maddened at finding the package of cigarettes in her pocketbook and at her taunting laugh when he questioned her on the subject.

In politics, Non-Acceptance of the Unfamiliar is demonstrated every time liberal legislation is debated. Daniel Webster, John Adams and James Madison all joined hands against universal suffrage, decrying the rule by 'King Numbers,' and the political power of the 'ring-streaked and speckled population of our towns and cities.' Women's suffrage aroused even greater protests. An editorial in *Harper's Magazine* for November 1853 made use of a musical metaphor, to carry its anti-suffragist argument: 'This unblushing female socialism defies alike the Apostles and the Prophets. Nothing could be more anti-biblical than letting women vote. . . . Instead of that exquisitely harmonized instrument which comes from the right temperament of the sexual relations, it would make human life a tuneless monochord, if not, in the end, a chaos of all harsh and savage dissonance.'

The obscurantist opposition to progressive ideas in science is often made in the name of rational thinking and logic. Fromundus of Antwerp advanced what he must have deemed an unanswerable argument against the rotation of the earth: 'Buildings and the earth itself would fly off with such rapid motion that men would have to be provided with claws like cats to enable them to hold fast to the earth's surface.'

Melanchton wrote in *Elements of Physics:* 'The eyes are witnesses that the heavens revolve in the space of twenty-four hours. But certain men, either from the love of novelty, or to make a display of ingenuity, have concluded that the earth moves. It is a want of honesty and decency to assert such notions publicly, and the example is pernicious.'

Scipio Chiaramonti declared: 'Animals, which move, have limbs and muscles; the earth has no limbs or muscles; therefore, it does not move.'

Dr. John Lightfoot, Vice-Chancellor of the University of Cambridge, announced, as a result of his study of the Scriptures, that 'heaven and earth were created all together, in the same instant, on October 23, 4004 B.C. at nine o'clock in the morning.' When geological and paleontological evidence began to pile up tending to show that things existed before October 23, 4004 B.C., the fundamentalists proffered an ingenious explanation in a pamphlet, *A Brief and Complete Refutation of the Anti-Scriptural Theory of Geologists,* published in London in 1853: 'All the organisms found in the depths of the earth were made on the first of the six creative days, as models for the plants and animals to be created on the third, fifth, and sixth days.'

Cardinal Manning declared that Darwin's theory was 'a brutal philosophy,—to wit, there is no God, and the ape is our Adam.' Disraeli coined a famous phrase when he said: 'The question is this: Is man an ape or an angel? I, my Lord, am on the side of the angels.'

Dr. Nicolas Joly of Toulouse ridiculed Pasteur. 'It is absurd to think,' he declared, 'that germs causing fermentation and putrefaction came from the air; the atmosphere would have to be as thick as pea soup for that.'

Bishop Berkeley argued fervently against the rationality of differential calculus. In his paper, *The Analyst, or a Discourse Addressed to an Infidel Mathematician,* he wrote: 'The further the mind analyseth and pursueth these ideas the more it is lost and bewildered; the objects, at first fleeting and minute, soon vanishing out of sight. Certainly, in any sense, a second or third fluxion seems an obscure Mystery. The incipient celerity of an incipient celerity, the nascent augment of a nascent augment, i.e., of a thing which hath no magnitude. . . . And what are these fluxions? The velocities of evanescent increments. And what are these same evanescent increments? They are neither finite quantities, nor quantities infinitely small, nor yet nothing. May we not call them the ghosts of departed quantities?'

Einstein's famous formula which underlies the release of atomic energy was ridiculed as meaningless in a book by Samuel H.

Guggenheimer, *The Einstein Theory Explained and Analyzed:* 'It is well to note here an example of the danger of relying too much on mathematical abstraction, afforded by the formulation of Einstein's application of his transformations to problems of additions of energy to moving masses. He tells us that the kinetic energy of a mass, *m,* is no longer given by the expression

$$m\frac{v^2}{2}$$

but, according to the Lorentz transformation, by the expression

$$\frac{mc^2}{\sqrt{1-\frac{v^2}{c^2}}}$$

where v is the velocity of m and c the velocity of light. In other words, the energy, for all ordinary velocities, becomes mc^2, meaning the mass multiplied by the square of the velocity of light. This is certainly a meaningless expression unless the c value be eliminated by making it unity, and is so felt to be by the Professor.'

Prospects of controlled release of atomic energy were deemed negligible as late as 1931, as appears from Frank Allen's book *The Universe,* published in that year. 'Should some method be devised,' he wrote, 'whereby the proper energy could be released, which at present cannot be done, and, indeed, seems quite beyond the range of possibility . . . the experimenter, his laboratory, and even his city would forthwith be swept to destruction.'

The forced acceptance of formerly untenable theories is illustrated by the following story. At the opening lecture on chemistry in the 1890's, the professor wrote in large letters on the extreme left corner of the wall-size blackboard: ELEMENTS ARE NOT TRANSMUTABLE. It so happened that after the lecture the janitor propped up a bookshelf against the blackboard, covering the inscription. Several years elapsed, and radium was discovered. The professor announced a special lecture on atomic transmutation. He needed the entire blackboard for his formulas, and ordered the obstructing bookshelf removed. The words, chalked down in the days of intransmutability, were revealed to the students who read with amazement: ELEMENTS ARE NOT TRANSMUTABLE.

Even the harmony of the spheres seems to have gone modern, if the classical-minded astronomers are to be believed. The New York *Times* of August 27, 1950 brought modern music into play in its account of the new radio telescope that registers the static electricity of distant galaxies: 'If this be the music of the spheres, it is more like the cacophonies of modernistic composers than the harmonies that the ancient Greeks extolled.'

The first musical Schimpflexicon, limited to anti-Wagnerian outbursts, was compiled by Wilhelm Tappert, and published in 1877 under the interminable title, *Ein Wagner-Lexicon, Wörterbuch der Unhöflichkeit, enthaltend grobe, höhnende, gehässige und verleumderische Ausdrücke welche gegen den Meister Richard Wagner, seine Werke und seine Anhänger von den Feinden und Spöttern gebraucht worden sind, zur Gemütsergötzung in müssigen Stunden gesammelt.*

The assorted entries in the *Wagner-Lexicon* give an idea of what the critics can do to a man they really hate. The virulence, the animus seething in the inflamed breast of the invective-hurling, foaming-at-the-mouth vilifier, find their culmination in the verbal implosion in a most unlikely tome—a treatise on the Spanish theater by the German historian J. L. Klein. Wrote he:

'The wild Wagnerian corybantic orgy, this din of brasses, tin pans and kettles, this Chinese or Caribbean clatter with wood sticks and ear-cutting scalping knives. . . . Heartless sterility, obliteration of all melody, all tonal charm, all music. . . . This revelling in the destruction of all tonal essence, raging satanic fury in the orchestra, this diabolic, lewd caterwauling, scandal-mongering, gun-toting music, with an orchestral accompaniment slapping you in the face. . . . Hence, the secret fascination that makes this music the darling of the feeble-minded royalty, the plaything of the camarilla, of the court flunkeys covered with reptilian slime, and of the blasé hysterical female court parasites who need this galvanic stimulation by massive instrumental treatment to throw their pleasure-weary frog-legs into violent convulsions . . . the diabolical din of this pig-headed man, stuffed with brass and sawdust, inflated, in an insanely destructive self-aggrandizement, by Mephistopheles' mephitic and most venomous hellish miasma, into Beelzebub's Court Composer and General Director of Hell's Music—Wagner!'

This tirade bids fair to excel, in sheer intensity of vituperative logorrhea, the American classic of vilification, delivered by W. C.

Brann of Waco, Texas, against a newspaper editor: 'I can but wonder what will become of the editor of the Los Angeles *Times* when the breath leaves his feculent body and death stops the rattling of his abortive brain. He cannot be buried in the sea lest he poison the fishes. He cannot be suspended in mid-air, like Mahomet's coffin, lest the circling worlds, in their endeavor to avoid contamination, crash together, wreck the universe and bring about the return of chaos and Old Night. The damn scoundrel is a white elephant on the hands of the Deity, and I have some curiosity to know what He will do with him.'

Why do music critics, who are in private life, most of them, the mildest of creatures, resort so often to the language of vituperation?

Philip Hale may have provided an answer to this psychological paradox, when he commented, in the Boston *Journal* of January 14, 1893, upon Hanslick's tirade against Tchaikovsky's Violin Concerto (Hanslick said the Concerto stank to the ear): 'I think that the violence of Dr. Hanslick was as much inspired by the desire to write a readable article as by any just indignation.'

HOW THE LEXICON WAS PUT TOGETHER AND WHO HELPED

Material for the present Schimpflexicon has been gathered by dint of persistent digging in the massed files of music magazines and newspapers in America and abroad. Of course, serendipity played its role – some of the liveliest specimens of musical invective were found while looking for something else.

The following libraries and collections were the richest sources: the Music Department of the Boston Public Library; the archives of the Boston Symphony Orchestra; the New York Public Library; and the Carl Van Vechten Collection at Fisk University. To the librarians of these institutions and to many contributors from libraries and private collections in Europe and America, sincere thanks are due. In the editorial shaping up of the material, Ruth Stoneridge and Robert Beckhard were of great help.

To preserve the documentary value of the quotations, the reviews from French and German sources are given in the original languages as well as in translation. The separate entries under each composer's name are arranged chronologically to establish the proper historic perspective.

A special feature of the book is the Invecticon (this neologism was suggested by Mr. Beckhard). It is an index of invectives in alphabetical order, from Aberration to Zoo. Thus, under 'excruciating cacophony' we find a reference to Chopin; under 'lunatic' to Berlioz, Liszt and Strauss; under 'demented eunuch,' 'charlatan,' and 'communist' to Wagner; under 'obscene' to Tchaikovsky; under 'Mal de Mer' to Debussy; under 'Massacre du Printemps' to Stravinsky; under 'ordure' to Bartók; under 'Chamber-of-Horrors Symphony' to Schoenberg; under 'monstrous' and 'ugly' to Beethoven and practically everybody else.

NICOLAS SLONIMSKY

LEXICON

OF

MUSICAL

INVECTIVE

Critics kind—never mind!

Critics flatter—no matter!

Critics blame—all the same!

Do your best—damn the rest!

CONAN DOYLE: *Through the Magic Door*

BARTÓK If the reader were so rash as to purchase any of Béla Bartók's compositions, he would find that they each and all consist of unmeaning bunches of notes, apparently representing the composer promenading the keyboard in his boots. Some can be played better with the elbows, others with the flat of the hand. None require fingers to perform nor ears to listen to. . . . The productions . . . of Bartók [are] mere ordure.

(Frederick Corder, 'On the Cult of Wrong Notes,' *Musical Quarterly*, New York, July 1915)

-:-

The bulk of the Bartók Violin Sonata seemed to me the last word (for the present) in ugliness and incoherence. It was as if two people were improvising against each other.

(Ernest Newman, London *Sunday Times*, March 26, 1922)

-:-

I suffered more than upon any occasion in my life apart from an incident or two connected with 'painless dentristry.' To begin with, there was Mr. Bartók's piano touch. But 'touch,' with its implication of light-fingered ease, is a misnomer, unless it be qualified in some such way as that of Ethel Smyth in discussing her dear old teacher Herzogenberg—'He had a touch like paving-stone.' I do not, by the way, believe that Mr. Bartók would resent this simile. What I am describing is, I believe, a deliberate part of his intentions, and he will probably feel no more aggrieved at my denying him 'touch' than would be the village blacksmith if I refused it to him in some description of his musical performance with his two-stone hammer upon his red-hot horseshoe. If Bartók's piano compositions should ever become popular in this country, there will have to be established a special Anti-Matthay School to train performers for them, and I believe that it will be found that piano manufacturers will refuse to hire out pianos for the recitals of its alumni, insisting that these shall always be bought outright, and the remains destroyed on conclusion. . . The Bartók tone is, I take it, a symbol of adherence to the 'no-sentiment' school of modern music, and, as a matter of fact, many passages in Bartók's compositions might disqualify him for membership of that school were they less thunderously delivered, since some of his little two-note and three-note motives could easily become rather plaintive in their querulous repetitions. . . It appears to me that the Bartók system of composition and performance is one of the most rigid-minded, rigid-muscled ever invented; that in shunning sentiment Bartók has lost beauty, that in shunning rhetoric he has lost reason.

(Percy A. Scholes, *The Observer*, London, May 13, 1923)

-:-

Béla Bartók has done it. He has achieved [in his First Piano Concerto] one of the great desires of the modernists, in turning things upside down. . . . He has made big music sound small. . . . He has converted the grand orchestra into a mere mandolin. . . . He has gone after beauty with hammers and sticks. . . . In time, the object doubtless will be even better attained. If not Bartók, then someone else, will compel a 120-man orchestra, everybody blowing, scraping and smiting at full bent, to sigh as thinly as a rubbed goblet and to twang as faintly as a jew's harp. For out go not only melody and harmony, but also the timbre of violin, the volume of the trombone and the shading of the piano.

(*Christian Science Monitor*, Boston, February 16, 1928)

-:-

Mr. Bartók is old enough to know better. We managed to live through his Piano Concerto. We read Dr. Gilman's notes with respect, listened to a few of the masterminds afterwards, and in our own unimportant opinion, this work from first to last was one of the most dreadful deluges of piffle, bombast and nonsense ever perpetrated on an audience in these environs. . . One of our handsome young managers asserted during Bartók's Concerto that he was rushing home to drink thirty quarts of bitter champagne.

(H. Noble, *Musical America*, New York, February 18, 1928)

-:-

Mr. Bartók elected to play his composition dignified by the title *Concerto for Pianoforte and Orchestra.* Note the ommission of key. Ultra-moderns cannot be bothered with such trifling designations. . . . Bartók plays the piano part from memory. How does he do it? And would it make any difference if memory failed and different notes were substituted for those written in the score? Perhaps the unaccountable chaos of sound was caused by an incorrect distribution of the parts to the musicians. . . Is Bartók making fun at our expense? If so, the laugh is on us. . . It has been said that the Concerto is based upon folk tunes. They have been successfully concealed. Only tonal chaos arises from the diabolical employment of unrelated keys simultaneously. It is like a mystic maze. The guide alone knows the way out. . . He is in music's no man's land, and ingress and egress have been deliberately protected by heavily charged barbed wire. From the vantage point of his own planning, he hurls gas bombs in the direction of friend and foe indiscriminately. The tonal grenades burst with alarming detonation. If you emerge from the conflict without suffering from shell shock, you may consider that you have been a favorite of the gods.

(Cincinnati *Enquirer*, February 26, 1928)

-:-

The opening *Allegro* took me straight back to childhood and gave me in turn the rusty windlass of a well, the interlinking noises of a goods train that is being shunted, then the belly-rumblings of a little boy acutely ill after a raid on an orchard, and finally the singular alarmed noise of poultry being worried to death by a Scotch terrier. The second movement gave me continuously and throughout its short length the noise of a November wind in telegraph poles on a lonely country road. The third movement began with a dog howling at midnight, proceeded to imitate the regurgitations of the less-refined or lower-middle-class type of water-closet cistern, modulating thence into the mass snoring of a Naval dormitory around the dawn—and concluded inconsequently with the cello reproducing the screech of an ungreased wheelbarrow. The fourth movement took me straight back to the noises I made myself, on wet days indoors, at the age of six, by stretching and plucking a piece of elastic. And the fifth movement reminded me immediately and persistently and vividly of something I have never thought of since the only time I heard it: the noise of a Zulu village in the Glasgow Exhibition—a hubbub all the more singular, because it had a background of skirling Highland bagpipes. Both noises emerged in this final movement of this Fourth Quartet of Béla Bartók.

(From a letter written by Alan Dent, quoted in *The Later Ego* by James Agate, London, 1951)

BEETHOVEN Die Zweite Symphonie ist ein krasses Ungeheuer, ein angestochener, sich unbänding windender Lindwurm, der nicht ersterben will und selbst verblutend im Finale noch mit aufgerecktem Schweife wütend um sich schlägt.

(*Zeitung für die Elegente Welt,* Vienna, May 1804)

[Beethoven's Second Symphony is a crass monster, a hideously writhing wounded dragon, that refuses to expire, and though bleeding in the Finale, furiously beats about with its tail erect.]

-:-

Vor kurzem wurde die Ouvertüre zu Beethovens Oper *Fidelio* gegeben, und alle parteilosen Musikkenner und Musikfreunde waren darüber volkommen einig dass so etwas Unzusammenhängendes, Grelles, Verworrenes, das Ohr Empörendes schlechterdings noch nie in der Musik geschrieben worden. Die schneidensten Modulationen folgen aufeinander in wirklich grässlicher Harmonie und einige kleinliche Ideen vollenden den unangenehmen, betäubenden Eindruck.

(August von Kotzebue, *Der Freimütige,* Vienna, September 11, 1806)

[Recently there was given the overture to Beethoven's opera *Fidelio,* and all impartial musicians and music lovers were in perfect agreement that never was anything as incoherent, shrill, chaotic and ear-splitting produced in music. The most piercing dissonances clash in a really atrocious harmony, and a few puny ideas only increase the disagreeable and deafening effect.]

-:-

Beethoven, souvent bizarre et baroque . . . tantôt prend le vol majestueux de l'aigle; tantôt rampe dans les sentiers rocailleux. Après avoir pénétré l'âme d'une douce mélancolie, il la déchire aussitôt par un amas d'accords barbares. Il me semble voir renfermer ensemble des colombes et des crocodiles.

(*Tablettes de Polymnie,* Paris, 1810)

[Beethoven, who is often bizarre and baroque, takes at times the majestic flight of an eagle, and then creeps in rocky pathways. He first fills the soul with sweet melancholy, and then shatters it by a mass of barbarous chords. He seems to harbor together doves and crocodiles.]

Opinions are much divided concerning the merits of the Pastoral Symphony of Beethoven, though very few venture to deny that it is much too long. The *Andante* alone is upwards of a quarter of an hour in performance, and, being a series of repetitions, might be subjected to abridgment without any violation of justice, either to the composer or his hearers.

(*The Harmonicon,* London, June 1823)

-:-

Beethoven is not only still numbered amongst the living, but is at a period of life when the mind, if in *corpore sano,* is in its fullest vigor, for he has not yet completed his fifty-second year. Unfortunately, however, he is suffering under a privation that to a musician is intolerable—he is almost totally bereft of the sense of hearing; insomuch that it is said he cannot render the tones of his pianoforte audible to himself. . . . The Sonata, op. 111 consists of two movements. The first betrays a violent effort to produce something in the shape of novelty. In it are visible some of those dissonances the harshness of which may have escaped the observation of the composer. The second movement is an *Arietta,* and extends to the extraordinary length of thirteen pages. The greater portion of it is written in 9/16, but a part is in 6/16, and about a page in 12/32. All this really is laborious trifling, and ought to be by every means discouraged by the sensible part of the musical profession. . . . We have devoted a full hour to this enigma, and cannot solve it. But no sphinx ever imagined such a riddle as the 12/32 time presents. Here we find twelve demisemiquavers, and eight double-demisemiquavers in one bar; twelve demisemiquavers and twelve double-demisemiquavers in another, etc., and all without any appearance of a misprint! The general practice of writing notes apparently very short, then doubling their length by the word *Adagio,* is one of the abuses in music that loudly cries for reform; but the system of notation pursued in this *Arietta* is confusion worse confounded, and goes on, as we have before stated, to the extent of thirteen pages; and yet the publishers have, in their title, deemed it necessary to warn off all pirates by announcing the Sonata as copyright. We do not think they are in much danger of having their property invaded.

(*The Harmonicon,* London, August 1823)

Beethoven's compositions more and more assume the character of studied eccentricity. He does not write much now, but most of what he produces is so impenetrably obscure in design and so full of unaccountable and often repulsive harmonies, that he puzzles the critic as much as he perplexes the performer.

(*The Harmonicon,* London, April 1824)

-:-

We find Beethoven's Ninth Symphony to be precisely one hour and five minutes long; a fearful period indeed, which puts the muscles and lungs of the band, and the patience of the audience to a severe trial. . . . The last movement, a chorus, is heterogeneous. What relation it bears to the symphony we could not make out; and here, as well as in other parts, the want of intelligible design is too apparent.

(*The Harmonicon,* London, April 1825)

-:-

The merits of Beethoven's Seventh Symphony we have before discussed, and we repeat, that . . . it is a composition in which the author has indulged a great deal of disagreeable eccentricity. Often as we now have heard it performed, we cannot yet discover any design in it, neither can we trace any connection in its parts. Altogether, it seems to have been intended as a kind of enigma—we had almost said a hoax.

(*The Harmonicon,* London, July 1825)

-:-

Its length [of Beethoven's Ninth Symphony] alone will be a never-failing cause of complaint to those who reject monopoly in sounds. While we are enjoying the delight of so much science and melody, and eagerly anticipating its continuance, on a sudden, like the fleeting pleasures of life, or the spirited young adventurer, who would fly from ease and comfort at home to the inhospitable shores of New Zealand or Lake Ontario, we are snatched away from such eloquent music, to crude, wild and extraneous harmonies. . . . The chorus that immediately follows is in many places exceedingly imposing and effective, but then there is so much of it, so many sudden pauses and odd and almost ludicrous passages for the horn and bassoon, so much rambling and vociferous execution given to the violins and stringed instruments, without any decisive effect or definite meaning—and to crown all, the deafening boisterous jollity of the concluding part, wherein, besides the usual allotment of triangles, drums, trumpets, etc., all the known acoustical missile instruments I should conceive were employed . . . that they made even the very ground shake under us, and would, with their fearful uproar, have been sufficiently penetrating to call up from their peaceful graves the revered shades of Tallis, Purcell, and Gibbons, and even of Handel and Mozart, to witness and deplore the obstreperous roarings of modern frenzy in their art. . . . Beethoven finds from all the public accounts, that noisy extravagance of execution and outrageous clamor in musical performances more frequently ensures applause than chastened elegance or refined judgment. The inference therefore that we may fairly make, is that he writes accordingly.

(*Quarterly Musical Magazine and Review,* London, 1825)

-:-

Muss nicht jeder, je teurer ihm Beethoven und seine Kunst ist, desto inniger wünschen dass doch recht bald die Vergessenheit den versöhnenden Schleier werfen möge über solcher Verirrung seiner Muse, durch welche er den besungenen Gegenstand, die Kunst, und sich selber entweiht.

(Gottfried Weber on Beethoven's *Wellington's Victory,* in *Cæcilia,* Berlin, No. 10, 1825)

[Should not everyone, the dearer Beethoven and his art are to him, the more fervently wish that oblivion might very soon draw an expiatory veil on such an aberration of his muse, through which he has desecrated the glorified object, Art, and himself.]

(Beethoven showed his anger at this, in a marginal note scrawled in his copy of *Cæcilia*: 'O du elender Schuft! Was ich *scheisse,* ist besser als du je gedacht!')

-:-

Beethoven's Eighth Symphony depends wholly on its last movement for what applause it obtains; the rest is eccentric without being amusing, and laborious without effect.

(*The Harmonicon,* London, June 4, 1827)

-:-

It is not surprising that Beethoven should, occasionally, have entertained blasé notions of his art; that he should have mistaken noise for grandeur, extravagance for originality, and have supposed that the interest of his compositions would be in proportion to their duration. That he gave little time to reflection, is proved most clearly by the extraordinary length of some movements in his later symphonies. . . . His great qualities are frequently alloyed by a morbid desire for novelty; by extravagance, and by a disdain of rule. . . . The effect which the writings of Beethoven have had on the art must, I fear, be considered as injurious. Led away by the force of his genius and dazzled by its creations, a crowd of imitators has arisen, who have displayed as much harshness, as much extravagance, and as much obscurity, with little or none of his beauty and grandeur. Thus music is no longer intended to soothe, to delight, to 'wrap the senses in Elysium'; it is absorbed in one principle—to astonish.

(Letter to Editor in the *Quarterly Musical Magazine and Review*, London, 1827)

-:-

The *Heroic Symphony* contains much to admire, but it is difficult to keep up admiration of this kind during three long quarters of an hour. It is infinitely too lengthy. . . If this symphony is not by some means abridged, it will soon fall into disuse.

(*The Harmonicon*, London, April 1829)

-:-

Beethoven mystified his passages by a new treatment of the resolution of discords, which can only be described in words by the term, 'resolution by ellipsis,' or the omission of the chord upon which the discordant notes should descend. . . Many of his passages also appear confused and unintelligible, by a singular freedom in the use of diatonic discords or discords of transition; many instances appear of passages by contrary motion, each carrying their harmonies with them.

(*Musical World*, London, March 1836)

-:-

Beethoven, this extraordinary genius, was completely deaf for nearly the last ten years of his life, during which his compositions have partaken of the most incomprehensible wildness. His imagination seems to have fed upon the ruins of his sensitive organs.

(William Gardiner, *The Music of Nature*, London, 1837)

Il y a 24 parties d'employés dans l'explosion qui marque le passage du *Scherzo* au *Finale* de la symphonie en *ut* mineur. . . Je parle des 50 mesures du *Scherzo* qui précèdent l'*Allegro.* Il y a là une mélodie étrange qui en se combinant avec l'harmonie plus étrange encore d'une double pédale à la basse, un *sol* et un *ut,* produit une sorte de miaulement odieux et des discordances à déchirer l'oreille la moins sensible.

(A. Oulibicheff, *Nouvelle Biographie de Mozart,* Moscow, 1843)

[There are 24 parts participating in the explosion which marks the transition from the *Scherzo* to the *Finale* in the C minor Symphony of Beethoven. I speak of the 50 measures of the *Scherzo* that precede the *Allegro.* There is a strange melody, which, combined with even a stranger harmony of a double pedal point in the bass on G and C, produces a sort of odious meowing, and discords to shatter the least sensitive ear.]

-:-

The *Missa Solemnis* was generally regarded as an incomprehensible production, the depths of which (if they really were depths) it was impossible to fathom. This opinion I confess I adopted. After poring for hours over the ponderous pages, the only result was an absolute bewilderment among its mazes.

(London *Morning Chronicle,* quoted in the *Musical Times,* London, October 1845)

-:-

Beethoven a donné l'extension de six morceaux dans son treizième quatuor . . . Le premier de ces morceaux, remarquable par la recherche d'une harmonie étrange, par le retard fatigant des résolutions d'accords, par une sorte de haine systematique de la conclusion des parcelles de phrases de mélodies par la cadence parfaite, témoigne d'une imagination usée qui ne trouvait plus de chant. . . La cinquième et la sixième partie abondent surtout en ces ajournements inédits de terminaison. Au dire ingénieusement pittoresque d'un de nos premiers compositeurs, dont chacun admire la belle musique instrumentale, la pensée de Beethoven, dans le finale du treizième quatuor, est semblable à une pauvre hirondelle qui voltige incessamment, à vous fatiguer l'œil et l'oreille, dans un appartement hermétiquement fermé.

(H. Blanchard, *Revue et Gazette Musicale de Paris,* April 15, 1849)

[Beethoven extends his Quartet No. 13 to six movements. The first of these movements is remarkable for its search of strange harmonies, for the tiresome delay in the resolution of chords, for a sort of systematic hatred of ending a fragment of a melodic phrase by a perfect cadence, all of which is evidence of worn-out creative ability no longer capable of finding melodies. The fifth and the sixth movements in particular abound in these curious delays in concluding a phrase. To quote an ingeniously picturesque saying of one of our foremost composers whose fine instrumental music is admired by everyone, Beethoven's imagination in the Finale of this quartet suggests a poor swallow flitting incessantly in a hermetically sealed compartment to the annoyance of our eyes and our ears.]

-:-

If the best critics and orchestras have failed to find the meaning of Beethoven's Ninth Symphony, we may well be pardoned if we confess our inability to find any. The *Adagio* certainly possessed much beauty, but the other movements, particularly the last, appeared to be an incomprehensible union of strange harmonies. Beethoven was deaf when he wrote it. . . It was the genius of the great man upon the ocean of harmony, without the compass which had so often guided him to his haven of success; the blind painter touching the canvas at random. We can sincerely say that rather than study this last work for beauties which do not exist, we had far rather hear the others where beauties are plain.

(*Daily Atlas*, Boston, February 6, 1853)

-:-

Quand on est Beethoven, on fait tout ce qu'on peut faire, mais encore faudra-t-il que deux et deux fassent quatre. . . . Mettez deux scorpions et un pigeon à la clef si c'est votre opinion, mais n'y mettez pas ce qu'il n'y aura plus dans les mesures. . . Vous tous qui comprenez cela, expliquez-nous à nous, comment dans la seconde variation en 6/16, peut-il avoir six double-croches, à chaque mesure, plus six triples croches? . . . La démence du génie intéresse; le spectacle de toute autre, fréquente malheureusement, en musique de piano, n'est que déplorable.

(W. de Lenz on Sonata, op. 111, in *Beethoven et ses trois styles*, Paris, 1855)

[When one is Beethoven, it is possible to do anything, but still two and two must make four. Put two scorpions and a pigeon in the signature if this is your whim, but do not put there what is not in the measure. . . You who understand this, explain to us, how can there be, in the second variation in 6/16, six sixteenth-notes in each measure plus six thirty-second notes? The madness of a genius is of interest; but the spectacle of madness in others, which is unfortunately frequent in piano music, is merely deplorable.]

-:-

Beethoven ne fut pas l'homme de la fugue, et il ne le fut jamais moins que dans ce cauchemar— *Rudis indigestaque moles!*

(W. de Lenz on the Finale of Sonata, op. 106, in *Beethoven et ses trois styles,* Paris, 1855)

[Beethoven was not a man of the fugue, and he was never less so than in this nightmare—*a raw and undigested mass!*]

-:-

Ici, vous avez un fragment de 44 mesures, où Beethoven a cru devoir suspendre l'*habeas corpus* de la musique en la dépouillant de tout ce qui pourrait ressembler à de la mélodie, à de l'harmonie et à un rythme quelconque. . . Est-ce de la musique, oui ou non? Si l'on me répondait par l'affirmative, je dirais. . . que cela n'appartient point à l'art que j'ai l'habitude de considérer comme la musique.

(A. Oulibicheff, *Beethoven, ses critiques et ses glossateurs,* Paris, 1857, on the transition to the last movement of the Fifth Symphony)

[Here you have a fragment of 44 measures, where Beethoven deemed it necessary to suspend the habeas corpus of music by stripping it of all that might resemble melody, harmony and any sort of rhythm. . . . Is it music, yes or no? If I am answered in the affirmative, I would say that this does not belong to the art which I am in the habit of considering as music.]

-:-

Dans les symphonies précédentes, les traces de la troisième manière de Beethoven se réduisent . . . à quelques accords faux, à des intervalles de seconde superposés, à l'oubli de la préparation et de la résolution pour les dissonances. . . Dans la symphonie en *la,* la chimère monte en grade. . . Regardez par exemple la déplorable conclusion de l'*Andante*. Regardez et pleurez. . . . Conçoit-on le *fa dièze* et le *sol dièze* accompagnés avec l'accord de *la* mineur. . . . Conçoit-on le musicien qui a eu le triste courage de flétrir ainsi son propre chef-d'œuvre, de jeter le plus pur de son génie et de son âme aux griffes immondes de la chimère, comme on jette un os à un chien. . . C'est dans le dernier mouvement que la figure de la chimère se complète par l'ajoutage de la laideur mélodique à la laideur harmonique. . . . Lorsque j'entendis, pour la première fois, cette harmonie écorchante, j'éprouvai une crispation, et un vers de La Fontaine me revint en mémoire: *On vous sangla la pauvre drille.*

(A. Oulibicheff, *Beethoven, ses critiques et ses glossateurs*, Paris, 1857)

[In the preceding symphonies, the traces of the third style of Beethoven are limited to a few wrong chords, superimposed intervals of a second, the failure to prepare and to resolve dissonances. In the Seventh Symphony, the fantasm mounts. Look, for instance, at the deplorable ending of the *Andante*. Look, and weep! Can one imagine F sharp and G sharp accompanied by a chord of A minor! Can one imagine a musician who has the sad courage to debase in this way his own masterpiece, to throw the purest part of his genius into the hideous claws of the chimera, as one throws a bone to a dog. It is in the last movement that the figure of the chimera is completed by adding melodic ugliness to harmonic ugliness. When I heard this flayed harmony, I experienced a shudder, and a line of La Fontaine came back to my memory: *On vous sangla le pauvre drille*—and they whipped the poor devil!]

-:-

Beethoven avait pris goût aux dissonances anti-euphoniques, parce qu'il entendait peu et confusément. . . Les assemblages de notes les plus monstrueux finirent par résonner, dans sa tête, comme des combinaisons admissibles et bien sonnantes.

(A. Oulibicheff, *Beethoven, ses critiques et ses glossateurs*, Paris, 1857)

[Beethoven took a liking to uneuphonious dissonances because his hearing was limited and confused. Accumulations of notes of the most monstrous kind sounded in his head as acceptable and well-balanced combinations.]

Parmi les signes nouveaux qui viennent modifier le style de Beethoven . . . ce signe qui rappelle celui de Caïn . . . n'est rien moins que la violation des règles fondamentales et les plus élémentaires de l'harmonie, les accords faux, les agglomérations de notes intolérables à quiconque n'est pas absolument dépourvu d'oreille et qui arrachèrent à l'élève de Beethoven l'exclamation dont on se souvient: *Es klingt ja infam falsch!*

(A. Oulibicheff, *Beethoven, ses critiques et ses glossateurs,* Paris, 1857)

[Among new signs which bring about changes in Beethoven's style, this sign that is like the sign of Cain, is nothing less than a violation of fundamental laws and of the most elementary rules of harmony—wrong chords, and agglomerations of notes intolerable to anyone who is not completely deprived of the auditory sense, and which elicited a memorable exclamation from a Beethoven pupil: 'But it sounds damnably false!']

-:-

Ich . . . gestehe frei dass ich den letzten Arbeiten Beethovens nie habe Geschmack abgewinnen können. Ja, schon die vielbewunderte IX. Sinfonie muss ich zu diesen rechnen . . . deren 4. Satz mir so monströs und geschmacklos und in seiner Auffassung der Schillerschen Ode so trivial erscheint dass ich immer noch nicht begreifen kann wie ihn ein Genius wie der Beethovensche niederschreiben konnte. Ich finde darin einen neuen Beleg zu dem, was ich schon in Wien bemerkte, dass es Beethoven an ästhetischer Bildung und an Schönheitssinn fehle.

(Louis Spohr, *Selbstbiographie,* Cassel, 1861)

[I confess freely that I could never get any enjoyment out of Beethoven's last works. Yes, I must include among them even the much-admired Ninth Symphony, the fourth movement of which seems to me so ugly, in such bad taste, and in the conception of Schiller's Ode so cheap that I cannot even now understand how such a genius as Beethoven could write it down. I find in it another corroboration of what I had noticed already in Vienna, that Beethoven was deficient in esthetic imagery and lacked the sense of beauty.]

The whole orchestral part of Beethoven's Ninth Symphony I found very wearying indeed. Several times I had great difficulty in keeping awake. . . It was a great relief when the choral part was arrived at, of which I had great expectations. It opened with eight bars of a commonplace theme, very much like Yankee Doodle. . . As for this part of the famous Symphony, I regret to say that it appeared to be made up of the strange, the ludicrous, the abrupt, the ferocious, and the screechy, with the slightest possible admixture, here and there, of an intelligible melody. As for following the words printed in the program, it was quite out of the question, and what all the noise was about, it was hard to form any idea. The general impression it left on me is that of a concert made up of Indian war-whoops and angry wildcats.

(Quoted from a Providence, R. I., newspaper in *The Orchestra*, London, June 20, 1868)

-:-

Beethoven always sounds to me like the upsetting of bags of nails, with here and there an also dropped hammer.

(From John Ruskin's letter to John Brown, dated February 6, 1881)

-:-

We heard lately in Boston the Ninth Symphony of Beethoven. The performance was technically most admirable. . . But is not worship paid this Symphony mere fetishism? Is not the famous Scherzo insufferably long-winded? The Finale . . . is to me for the most part dull and ugly. . . . I admit the grandeur of the passage 'und der Cherub steht vor Gott' and the effect of 'Seid umschlungen Millionen!' But oh, the pages of stupid and hopelessly vulgar music! The unspeakable cheapness of the chief tune, 'Freude, Freude!' Do you believe way down in the bottom of your heart that if this music had been written by Mr. John L. Tarbox, now living in Sandown, N. H., any conductor here or in Europe could be persuaded to put it in rehearsal?

(Philip Hale, *Musical Record*, Boston, June 1, 1899)

BERG Alban Berg, one of Schoenberg's pupils, somehow persuaded a singer to immolate himself in singing his songs. They demanded a range of something like three octaves, including a desperate falsetto and a downward progression which no singer on earth could have made to sound like anything but a wail. 'Over the border of the All,' he sang, 'you look meditatingly out,' and a few wheezes and groans from the orchestra accompanied the announcement. The following notes could not be heard for laughter. Schoenberg, who conducted, turned around and said: 'I beg those who cannot remain quiet to leave the hall.' Then he began all over again—'Over the borders of the All.' Somehow he got through it.

(Dispatch from Vienna, Boston *Evening Transcript*, April 17, 1913)

-:-

Zum Bersten krampfhaft aufgeblähter Kehlkopf der Muse . . . Berg macht ein gequältes misstönendes Gackern, ein Hexenbreugel an abgehackten Orchesterlauten . . . misshandelten Menschenkehlen, tierischen Aufschreien, Brüllen, Röcheln und allen übeln Geräuschen. . . Berg ist ein Brunnenvergifter der deutschen Musik.

(*Germania*, Berlin, December 15, 1925)

[Splitting the convulsively inflated larynx of the Muse, Berg utters tortured mistuned cackling, a pandemonium of chopped-up orchestral sounds, mishandled men's throats, bestial outcries, bellowing, rattling, and all other evil noises. . . Berg is the poisoner of the well of German music.]

-:-

Als ich gestern Abend die Staatsoper verliess, hatte ich das Gefühl, nicht aus einem öffentlichen Kunstinstitut zu kommen, sondern aus einem öffentlichen Irrenhaus. Auf der Bühne, im Orchester, im Parkett, lauter Verrückte. Darunter in geschlossenen Gruppen, in trotzigen Quadres die Stossgrupps der Atonalen, die Derwische Arnold Schönbergs. . . . *Wozzeck* von Alban Berg war die Kampfparole. Das Werk eines Chinesen aus Wien. Denn mit europäischer Musik und Musikentwicklung haben diese Massen-Anfälle von Instrumenten nichts zu tun. . . In Bergs Musik gibt es nicht die Spur einer Melodie. Es gibt nur Brocken, Fetzen, Schluchzer und Rülpser. Harmonisch ist das Werk indiskutabel, da alles falsch klingt. . . Der Verbrecher dieses Werkes . . . baut fest auf die Dummheit und Erbärmlichkeit seiner Mitmenschen und verlässt sich im übrigen auf den lieben Gott und die Universal Edition. . . Ich halte Alban Berg für einen musikalischen Hochstapler und für einen gemeingefährlichen Tonsetzer. Ja, man muss weitergehen. Unerhörte Geschehnisse verlangen neue Methoden. Man muss sich ernstlich die Frage vorlegen, ob und wieweit die Beschäftigung mit der Musik kriminell sein kann. Es handelt sich, im Bereich der Musik, um ein Kapitalverbrechen.

(Paul Zschorlich, *Deutsche Zeitung*, Berlin, December 15, 1925)

[As I left the State Opera last night I had a sensation not of coming out of a public institution, but out of an insane asylum. On the stage, in the orchestra, in the hall, plain madmen. Among them, in defiant squads, the shock troops of atonalists, the dervishes of Arnold Schoenberg. *Wozzeck* by Alban Berg was the battle slogan. A work of a Chinaman from Vienna. For with European music and musical evolution this mass onslaught of instruments has nothing in common. In Berg's music there is not a trace of melody. There are only scraps, shreds, spasms, and burps. Harmonically, the work is beyond discussion, for everything sounds wrong. The perpetrator of this work builds securely upon the stupidity and charity of his fellow-men, and for the rest relies on God Almighty and the Universal Edition. I regard Alban Berg as a musical swindler and a musician dangerous to the community. One should go even further. Unprecedented events demand new methods. We must seriously pose the question as to what extent musical profession can be criminal. We deal here, in the realm of music, with a capital offense.]

-:-

Nietzsche sagt einmal, es müsse Chaos sein, wo ein Stern geboren werden solle. Ein musikalisches Chaos herzustellen, ist Alban Berg unter Aufwendung grosser Verschmitztheit und mit Verbrauch erheblicher Mengen von Gehirnschmalz glücklich gelungen.

(Karl Krebs, *Tag*, Berlin, December 15, 1925)

[Nietzsche said once that there must have been chaos where a star was to be born. Alban Berg has luckily managed to reestablish chaos with the expenditure of great cunning and waste of a considerable quantity of brain fat.]

-:-

Alban Berg vermeidet krampfhaft jede natürliche Ausdruckweise;

das Abstruse ist seine ausschliessliche Domäne. . . Nichts darf stimmen oder im Sinne eines natürlich empfindenden Menschen gut klingen, alles muss rhythmisch kompliziert, harmonisch querständig und verschroben sein. . . Ob einer falsch singt oder spielt ist bei einem musikalisch so unsauberen Darstellungstil schlechterdings gleichgültig.

(Leopold Schmidt, *Neue Freie Presse,* Vienna, December 15, 1925)

[Alban Berg painstakingly avoids every natural manner of expression; the abstruse is his exclusive domain. . . Nothing must be in tune, or in the sense of people with normal perception, sound well; everything must be rhythmically complicated, harmonically queer and perverse. Whether one sings or plays wrong notes in such an insalubrious style, is utterly immaterial.]

-:-

Von den geradezu stimmörderischen Zumutungen an die Sänger, von den Ohrenmartern, welchen man die beklagenswerten Sänger und die Mitglieder des Staatsopernorchesters in Proben über Proben ausgesetzt hat, kann sich, wer der Dissonanzenorgie *Wozzecks* nicht beigewohnt hat, keine Vorstellung machen.

(Adolf Diesterweg, *Zeitschrift für Musik,* Berlin, January 1926)

[One cannot imagine, without having lived through the dissonant orgy of *Wozzeck,* the downright murderous demands on the voice, the ear torture to which the poor singers and the members of the State Opera Orchestra were subjected in rehearsal after rehearsal.]

-:-

The music of Alban Berg . . . is tenuous stuff, brainspun, labored and self-conscious, diluted with Schoenberg, who, in spite of his name, is no more beautiful than his pupil.

(Olin Downes, New York *Times,* October 29, 1926)

-:-

It is my private opinion that Mr. Berg is just a bluff. But even if he isn't, it is impossible to deny that his music (?) is a soporific, by the side of which the telephone book is a strong cup of coffee.

(Samuel Chotzinoff, New York *Post,* April 5, 1935)

As absolute music, Berg's *Lulu* has no value whatever. It is not intellectually profound; it is not imposing in structure; it has no outward evidence of inner spiritual motivation. It is just labored and ugly, apparently aimless, and surely futile. It meanders and puffs and groans and grunts. It touches no responsive chord in the listener's heart, for it is seemingly without heart. And probably that is desired, for emotion or sentiment is abhorrent to the true modernist in music. Squalid and repulsive realism is his ideal.

(W. J. Henderson, New York *Sun*, April 5, 1935)

-:-

What was plainly to be heard in the vocal solos [of *Lulu*] was that Schoenbergian whooping and scooping, an entirely ugly, unfertile, unvocal and inexpressive style which has nothing to do with the functions of the voice or with the natural unfoldment of melody. It was very hard to sing and so unpleasant to the ear. . . To us Mr. Berg and his ilk are becoming tedious, rather childish and distasteful. Isn't it time that we say 'enough' to music which bluffs itself and will bluff us, too, if we allow it to do so? Who wants to be such a dupe of an artistic deception?

(Olin Downes, New York *Times*, April 5, 1935)

-:-

After a second performance of the excerpts from *Lulu*, this reviewer is moved to remark that he considers them involved trash, as he did at the first hearing, and a score that will not outlast the decade that gave it birth. . . Rapine, suicide, murder, the prevailing flavor of a highly diseased eroticism are, perhaps, just so much promising material for a musical Freud or Krafft-Ebing to work upon.

(Olin Downes, New York *Times*, November 29, 1935)

-:-

In Berg's opera *Wozzeck* nothing sings and nothing dances. Everything screams hysterically, weeps drunken tears, jitters, spasmodically wriggles, and writhes in epileptic convulsions. The classical forms of passacaglia, fugue and sonata are used as objects of savage modernistic mockery. . . All is calculated to stun the human ear and to insult the esthetic sense of any normal and healthy human being.

(V. Gorodinsky, *Music of Spiritual Poverty*, Moscow, 1950)

BERLIOZ Ses rares mélodies sont dépourvues de mètre et de rythme; et son harmonie, assemblage bizarre de sons peu faits pour se rencontrer, ne mérite pas toujours ce nom. Selon moi, ce que fait M. Berlioz n'appartient pas à l'art que j'ai l'habitude de considérer comme de la musique, et j'ai la certitude la plus complète que les conditions de cet art lui manquent.

(F.-J. Fétis, *Biographie Universelle des Musiciens,* Brussels, 1837)

[His rare melodies are deprived of meter and rhythm; and his harmony, a bizarre assemblage of sounds, not easily blended, does not always merit this name. I believe that what Monsieur Berlioz writes does not belong to the art which I customarily regard as music, and I have the complete certainty that he lacks the prerequisites of this art.]

-:-

The rumor of Paganini's benefaction to Berlioz made us anxious to ascertain the real amount of ideas in the compositions of this Beethoven redivivus. We have spent a long morning over his *Sinfonie Fantastique* arranged for the pianoforte by Liszt, and are enabled, without undue haste or presumption, to state our opinion that he stands very low in the scale of composers. . . This enormous *Sinfonie* is a Babel, and not a Babylon of music.

(H. F. Chorley, *The Athenaeum,* London, March 23, 1839)

-:-

Berlioz, musically speaking, is a lunatic; a classical composer only in Paris, the great city of quacks. His music is simply and undisguisedly nonsense. He is a kind of orchestral Liszt, than which I could name nothing more intensely disagreeable.

(*Dramatic and Musical Review,* London, January 7, 1843)

-:-

We should rather be inclined to class Berlioz as a daring lunatic than a sound, healthy musician. . . M. Berlioz is utterly incapable of producing a complete phrase of any kind. When, on rare occasions, some glimpse of a tune makes its appearance, it is cut off at the edges and twisted about in so unusual and unnatural a fashion as to give one the idea of a mangled and mutilated body, rather than a thing of fair proportions. Moreover, the little tune that seems to exist in M. Berlioz is of so decidedly vulgar a character as to exclude the possibility of our supposing him possessed of a shadow of feeling.

(Unidentified London newspaper, 1843)

-:-

Berlioz is fantastic in the structure of his movements—unmeaningly so—and this (to say nothing of his crude and baseless method of harmonization, and his defiance of rule and common sense in part writing), renders his music necessarily tiresome and unattractive to a polite ear.

(*Musical Examiner*, London, June 1, 1844)

-:-

Non seulement M. Berlioz n'a pas d'idées mélodiques, mais lorsqu'une idée lui arrive, il ne sait pas la traiter, car il ne sait pas écrire. Nous disons que M. Berlioz ne sait pas écrire, c'est à dire qu'il ne sait pas déduire d'une idée mélodique toutes les conséquences qu'elle renferme.

(P. Scudo, *Critique et Littérature Musicales*, Paris, 1852)

[Not only does M. Berlioz not have any melodic ideas, but when one occurs to him, he does not know how to handle it, for he does not know how to write. We say M. Berlioz does not know how to write, that is, he cannot deduce from a melodic idea all the consequences that it entails.]

-:-

M. Berlioz accouple des instruments qui hurlent de se trouver ensemble; il tonne, il éclate sans éclairs et sans orage. . . M. Berlioz est bizarre et désordonné, parce qu'il manque d'inspiration et de savoir; il est violent, parce qu'il n'a pas de bonnes raisons à donner, et, s'il veut nous étourdir, c'est qu'il ne sait pas nous charmer. La science de M. Berlioz est une science abstraite, une algèbre stérile. . . . Sans idées mélodiques et sans expérience dans l'art d'écrire, il s'est jeté dans l'extraordinaire, dans le gigantesque, dans l'incommensurable chaos d'une sonorité qui énerve, brise l'auditeur sans le satisfaire. . . . Il n'y a dans ces étranges compositions que du bruit, du désordre, une exaltation maladive et stérile. . . . Il souffle, il piaffe, il se remue, il se démène comme un démon déshérité de la grace divine qui veut escalader le ciel à force d'orgueil et de volonté.

(P. Scudo, *Critique et Littérature Musicales*, Paris, 1852)

[Berlioz matches instruments that howl when they meet; he thunders, he rages without lightning and without storm. . . M. Berlioz is bizarre and ill-ordered, because he lacks inspiration and knowledge; he is violent, because he has no good reasons to offer; he wishes to stun us, because he does not know how to charm us. The science of Monsieur Berlioz is an abstract science, a sterile algebra. Without melodic ideas and without experience in the art of writing, he plunges into the extraordinary, into the gigantic, into the incommensurable chaos of a sonority that enervates, tires the listener without satisfying him. . . There is nothing in these strange compositions but noise, disorder, a sickly and sterile exaltation. He gasps, he prances, he fidgets, he behaves like a demon disinherited from divine grace who wants to scale the heavens by force of pride and will.]

-:-

Overture to *King Lear* by Berlioz, mere rubbish and rot. Shakespearean overtures by galvanized anthropoid Parisians are becoming a nuisance.

(George Templeton Strong's Diary, December 17, 1864)

-:-

I can compare *Le Carneval Romain* by Berlioz to nothing but the caperings and gibberings of a big baboon, over-excited by a dose of alcoholic stimulus.

(George Templeton Strong's Diary, December 15, 1866)

-:-

Of the Berlioz nonsense it is difficult to speak with patience. It is bad in itself, false, frightful. The third movement has an ugly *Ranz-des-vaches* running through it. The *Fantastic Symphony* is a nightmare set to music. The third movement ends with what the programme calls 'the sinking of the sun—a distant roll of thunder—solitude—silence.' The thunder is well imitated, and the silence is delicious.

(Review in an unidentified New York newspaper, November 28, 1868)

-:-

The Berlioz overture *Les Francs-Juges* . . . surprises us at intervals with a lively melodious motive such as Berlioz rarely suffers himself to be led away by. But then come the dreary deserts of sound, with vagrant discords running about them in the vain search after oases of resolved chords, getting lost and stopping bewildered, and wailing in misery until they are swallowed up in the barbaric blare of brass and the crash of drums and cymbals.

(New York *Tribune,* November 21, 1870)

-:-

Berlioz is, in our opinion, by far the least respectable of the composers of the new school. . . He has no breath of inspiration and no spark of creative genius. . . A knowledge of the principles of composition will no more make a composer than an acquaintance with etymology a poet. . . It needs no gift of prophecy to predict that he will be utterly unknown a hundred years hence to everybody but the encyclopedists and the antiquarians.

(Boston *Daily Advertiser,* October 29, 1874)

-:-

In the *Symphonie Fantastique,* a composer attempts suicide, all for love. Instead of dying from the opium he has taken, he merely sleeps when the beloved one comes to him in the guise of a melody. At one time this melody is cut short by the headsman's axe, the sleeper dreaming that he has killed the woman. . . It may be called a nightmare or the delirium tremens set to music. There is a limit to realism in music. We must protest against the idea of endeavoring to reproduce repulsive scenes by sound. There are enough great works by other composers that should find a place upon the program of the Harvard Symphony Concerts in lieu of this monstrosity.

(*Musical Record,* Boston, February 21, 1880)

-:-

If all bedlam were about to be let loose on earth, it does not seem as though any preparatory shock or foreboding could be more stupendous. What state of mind Berlioz was in when he conceived this music may never be known, but it may be imagined that if ever genius and insanity were found akin, it was at the time of the writing of *La Damnation de Faust.* If he was mad—a raving maniac at the time, as many profess to believe—then there was a method in his madness.

(Boston *Home Journal,* May 15, 1880)

To analyze or criticize so extraordinary a score (Berlioz's *Grand Requiem Mass,* recently performed at the Crystal Palace) would be impossible in a newspaper. Otherwise a pertinent inquiry might be allowed why the call to the Resurrection, the prayer for pity, to the tremendous King of Majesty, and the pathetic *Lachrymosa* should be accompanied by the hideous noise of trombones and ophicleides, of ten able-bodied men thwacking at kettledrums, of tubas and cornets, of double drums, cymbals and tam-tams. The tam-tam is not usually considered a celestial instrument and the din, which caused music lovers with delicate aural apparatus to close their ears, could not well have been greater if Berlioz had been trying to describe the casting out of that old serpent which deceiveth the whole world, and if the ancient reptile were energetically protesting against his punishment.

(*Figaro,* London, May 28, 1883)

-:-

In the finale, 'Bacchanale of the Brigands,' in Berlioz's symphony, *Harold in Italy,* the brigands seem to be holding a church sociable or a conference, and the way that the percussion section is let loose adds much to the percussedness of the proceedings.

(*Keynote,* New York, March 1, 1884)

-:-

Hector Berlioz's *Requiem* is an embodiment of the pomp and circumstance befitting death—the torchlight is there, the catafalque, the plumes and all the flummery, but the lament of the broken hearts that pervades the simpler *Requiem* services of Cherubini and Mozart are wanting. . . It is much as clever Albert Wolff says in his *Voyage à travers le monde* à propos of Wagner's operas, which require calcium and electric lights, steam and nitrate, with an audience imprisoned under lock and key in semi-darkness, whereas you could bring out and enjoy the beauties of *Don Giovanni* under the light of two tallow dips.

(New York *World,* November 20, 1885)

-:-

The final movement of the *Fantastic Symphony* is a dreary, cacophonous mess, an interminable galimatias.

(Boston *Home Journal,* December 1, 1890)

BIZET Se posant en novateur et rêvant dans son sommeil fiévreux d'arracher quelques rayons à la couronne du prophète Richard Wagner, M. Georges Bizet s'est lancé à corps perdu dans ce maelstrom sonore au risque d'y laisser ses ailes de néophyte et surtout les oreilles des auditeurs. . . . Je comprends que nous ayons beaucoup progressé dans l'art d'écouter des dissonances et de manger du piment sans sourciller. Je dirai même qu'en feuilletant toute l'œuvre de Wagner, j'ai trouvé bien des pages nuageuses, bien des audaces plus ou moins contestables, mais jamais, non jamais rien de semblable!

(Paul Bernard, *Revue et Gazette Musicale de Paris,* May 26, 1872)

[Posing as an innovator and dreaming in his feverish slumber to tear a few rays from the crown of the prophet Richard Wagner, M. Georges Bizet plunges head over heels into this sonorous maelstrom [*Djamileh*] at the risk of leaving there his apprentice's wings, and particularly the ears of the listeners. . . . I realize that we have made much progress in the art of hearing dissonances and eating pepper without blinking . . . I would even say, that going over all the works of Wagner, I have found plenty of nebulous pages, and more or less debatable audacities, but never, never anything like that!]

-:-

M. Bizet est un jeune musicien d'une grande et incontestable valeur qui produit de détestable musique . . . un de cette pléiade de compositeurs français qui ont abdiqué leur individualité pour se mettre à la remorque de Wagner. *Le Vaisseau-Fantôme* les traine dans le sillon de la *mélodie infinie* sur cette mer morte de la musique sans tonalité, sans rythme, sans carrure, insaisissable et horriblement énervante. M. Bizet et son patron ne changeront pas la nature humaine. Ils ne feront pas que les miaulements chromatiques d'un chat amoureux ou effrayé, entendus sur un accord formant double pédale ou accompagnés par autant d'accords de septième diminuée qu'il y a de notes dans ces miaulements, remplacent jamais, chez un auditeur sain d'esprit et d'oreille, une mélodie tonale, expressive, bien pondérée, d'un tour original, distinguée quoique naturelle et accompagnée d'accords *justes.*

(Oscar Comettant, *Le Siècle,* Paris, May 27, 1872)

[M. Bizet is a young musician of great and incontestable worth who writes detestable music, one of this group of French composers who have abdicated their individuality to place themselves in the harness of Wagner. The Flying Dutchman drags them into the path of endless melody on that Dead Sea of music without key, without rhythm, without stature, elusive and horribly enervating. M. Bizet and his master will not succeed in changing human nature. To the listener of sound mind and ear, these chromatic meows of an amorous or frightened cat—heard over a chord with a double pedal, or accompanied by as many diminished-seventh chords as there are notes in these meows— will never replace an expressive tonal melody, well pondered, of original turn, distinguished and yet natural, and accompanied by chords that are *correct*.]

-:-

Le cœur de M. Bizet, blasé par l'école de la dissonance et de la recherche, a besoin de se refaire une virginité. Cet opéra n'est ni scénique, ni dramatique. Ce n'est pas avec des détails d'orchestre, qu'on peut exprimer musicalement les fureurs et les caprices de Mlle. Carmen. Nourri des succulences harmoniques des chercheurs de la musique de l'avenir, Bizet s'est échauffé l'âme à ce régime qui tue le cœur!

(Oscar Comettant, *Le Siécle,* Paris, March 1875)

[The heart of M. Bizet, made callous by the school of dissonance and experimentation, needs to recapture its virginity. *Carmen* is neither scenic nor dramatic. One cannot express musically the savagery and the caprices of Mlle. Carmen with orchestral details. Nourished by the succulent harmonies of the experimenters of the music of the future, Bizet opened his soul to this doctrine that kills the heart.]

-:-

M. Bizet appartient à cette secte nouvelle dont la doctrine consiste à vaporiser l'idée musicale au lieu de la resserrer dans les contours définis. Pour cette école, dont M. Wagner est l'oracle, le motif est démodé, la mélodie surannée; le chant, soufflé et dominé par l'orchestre, ne doit être que son écho affaibli. Un tel système doit nécessairement produire des œuvres confuses. L'orchestration de *Carmen* abonde en combinaisons savantes, en sonorités imprévues et rares. Mais cette concurrence excessive faite aux voix par les instruments, est une des erreurs de l'école nouvelle.

(Paul de Saint-Victor, *Moniteur Universel,* Paris, March 1875)

[M. Bizet belongs to that new sect whose doctrine is to vaporize a musical idea instead of compressing it within definite contours. For this school, of which M. Wagner is the oracle, themes are out of fashion, melody is obsolete; the voices, strangled and dominated by the orchestra, are but its enfeebled echo. Such a system must inevitably result in the production of ill-organized works. The orchestration of *Carmen* abounds in learned combinations, in unusual and strange sonorities. But the exaggerated competition by the instruments against the voices is one of the errors of the new school.]

-:-

If it were possible to imagine His Satanic Majesty writing an opera, *Carmen* would be the sort of work he might be expected to turn out. After hearing it, we seem to have been assisting at some unholy rites, weirdly fascinating, but painful. It is difficult to say what ideas governed Bizet in setting the libretto but it is certain that a great portion of the music resembles that of the Venusberg in *Tannhäuser,* as being at once forbidding and alluring. But here the similarity ends. *Tannhäuser* is intensely human, but the *dramatis personae* in *Carmen* are no types of living beings. The characters evoke no interest in the spectators; nay, more, they are eminently repulsive. . . It is another *La Traviata,* with the redeeming features which may be discovered in that libretto carefully eliminated. The heroine is an abandoned woman, destitute not only of any vestige of morality, but devoid of the ordinary feelings of humanity—soulless, heartless and fiendish. Indeed, so repulsive was the subject of the opera, that some of the best artists of Paris declined to be included in the cast. In the introduction . . . we have a noisy, blatant theme, which starts off wildly without preface. . . Scarcely have we recovered from our surprise when the bright key of A gives way to F, and a jovial march is heard. This gives place as suddenly to a curiously chromatic, not to say ugly, phrase *andante,* breaking off upon a discord.

(*Music Trade Review,* London, June 15, 1878)

-:-

The only personage in *Carmen* who excites any interest is Don José, and that which he does excite he destroys by the brutal and foolish crime which is the climax and end of the work. We observe that in preliminary notices of the opera some stress is laid upon the fact that its composer is a son-in-law of Halévy. But apart from the physiological fact that genius does not descend to sons-in-law, what would a more direct connection between Bizet and the composer of *La Juive* have been likely to produce? . . . Be this as it may, *Carmen* must stand on its own merits—and those are very slender. It is little more than a collocation of couplets and chansons . . . and musically, is really not much above the works of Offenbach. As a work of art, it is naught.

(New York *Times,* October 24, 1878)

-:-

The composer of *Carmen* is nowhere deep; his passionateness is all on the surface, and the general effect of the work is artificial and insincere. Of melody, as the term is generally understood, there is but little. The air of the Toreador is the only bit of 'tune' in the opera, and this . . . scarcely rises above the vulgarity of Offenbach. The orchestration is in the Wagnerian school, though it lacks the richness and the flow of Wagner, and at times is so broken up and elaborated as to confuse by its fragmentary effect, rarely supporting the voice, but nearly always at odds with it. Bizet aimed at originality, and he undoubtedly obtained it, but he obtained monotony at the same time.

(Boston *Gazette,* January 5, 1879)

BLOCH M. Ernest Bloch est un 'révolutionnaire' et il le prouve. . . C'est un rébus indéchiffrable que cette musique de *Macbeth*, aussi bien au point de vue rythmique qu'au point de vue tonal. . . C'est non pas le caprice, mais l'incohérence à jet continu, par suite d'incessantes modifications dans la mesure. En un certain endroit je remarque cette succession: une mesure à 3/4, une mesure à quatre temps, une à 6/4 et une à quatre temps. . . Que devient l'unité rythmique, et que peut devenir, en de telles conditions, la sûreté de l'exécution? Quant aux successions harmoniques, elles ne sont pas moins extraordinaires, et l'on peut vraiment les qualifier de sauvages. . . La musique de M. Ernest Bloch semble la parodie de celle de M. Richard Strauss. . . C'est simplement du bruit pour le bruit.

(Arthur Pougin, *Le Ménestrel*, Paris, December 3, 1910)

[Mr. Ernest Bloch is a 'revolutionary,' and he proves it. This music for *Macbeth* is an indecipherable puzzle, from the rhythmic as well as tonal point of view. It is not merely capricious, but incoherent throughout, by virtue of incessant modifications of meter. In one place, I find the following succession: one measure in 3/4, one in 4/4; one measure in 6/4, and one in 4/4. What becomes of rhythmic unity, and how can accuracy of performance be attained under such conditions? As to harmonic progressions, they are no less extraordinary, and they may well be termed as savage. The music of Ernest Bloch seems to be a parody of Richard Strauss. It is simply noise for the sake of noise.]

-:-

Mr. Bloch's ideal of the Jewish music of the future is apparently the grotesque, hideous, cackling dispute of the Seven Jews in Richard Strauss's *Salome*. . . Nearly all of Bloch's music is hot in the mouth with curry, ginger and cayenne, even where one has a right to expect vanilla and whipped cream. . . The futurists have now taken to distracting attention from their creative shortcomings by pelting the ears of the hearers with cacophonies. It is the easiest thing to do. Even the mellifluous Mozart can be made to sound like Bloch or Schoenberg by simply changing all flats to sharps and all sharps to flats. Mr. Bloch seems to be really in need of such a method, for, with the keenest attention, the present writer, whom no real musical thought has ever escaped at a first hearing, could not find a single worthwhile melody in all the music he heard last night—a part of Bloch's symphony *Israel, Three Jewish Poems,* and an interminably long Hebrew rhapsody, called Salomon [*Schelomo*], for violoncello and piano, which does not reveal that monarch in all his glory. Mr. Bloch got plenty of applause from a large audience, largely of the Oriental persuasion.

(New York *Evening Post,* May 14, 1917)

-:-

The rambling cacophonies from Mr. Bloch's pen—the *Three Jewish Poems*—produced no effect except boredom. . . Are there not enough horrors assailing the world at present without adding those of unnecessary dissonances?

(New York *Evening Post,* January 11, 1918)

-:-

The funeral march from Bloch's *Three Jewish Poems* can be likened to the lugubrious sounds which mournfully assail the ears at the Wailing Wall in Jerusalem. Such a series of dissonant Jeremiads possibly never before resounded within the walls of the Academy.

(Brooklyn *Eagle,* January 26, 1918)

-:-

Bloch employs a rhythmic anarchy which effectively dispels the last remnant of logic his music might otherwise show. Since he has destroyed the harmonic order which makes intelligible rhythm possible, he is forced into all kinds of bizarre evasions. He does not maintain a given time signature for more than an average of two measures. . . The total result is a cacophony that makes Stravinsky sound like an eighteenth-century reactionary. This Bloch may justify, I suppose, by relating his scores to his conception of primitive Indian religion, of ancient Hebrew rebellion, or of modern scientific skepticism. . . To me, there is something monstrous about his gargantuan enterprise, something at once grotesque and pathetic.

(Edward Robinson, 'Bloch the Messiah,' *The American Mercury,* New York, December 1931)

BRAHMS In Brahms's First Symphony there appears to be a large quantity of mere surplusage, a strenuous iteration and reiteration, after the manner of one who is unable to utter his thought once and for all, or even to clear it up to his own satisfaction—an uneasy shifting of form, key and rhythm, and one or two bare spots of bald bathos.

(Boston *Evening Transcript*, January 4, 1878)

-:-

Johannes Brahms is a modern of the moderns, and his C minor Symphony is a remarkable expression of the inner life of this anxious, introverted, over-earnest age. . . . We venture to express a doubt that this work demonstrates its author's right to a place beside or near Beethoven.

(Boston *Daily Advertiser*, January 18, 1878)

-:-

The Brahms C minor Symphony sounds for the most part morbid, strained and unnatural; much of it even ugly. . . . Melody has become, by this time, a pretty vague term . . . but when it comes to an oboe and a clarinet making absolute speeches at each other (*vide*, for instance, a passage in the *Andante*), the listener's mind is at so great trouble to remember what the first has said, that it is impossible to appreciate whether the reply of the second is pertinent or not.

(W. F. Apthorp, Boston *Courier*, January 20, 1878)

-:-

The First Symphony of Brahms seemed to us as hard and as uninspired as upon its former hearing. It is mathematical music evolved with difficulty from an unimaginative brain. . . . How it ever came to be honored with the title of *The Tenth Symphony* is a mystery to us. . . . This noisy, ungraceful, confusing and unattractive example of dry pedantry before the masterpieces of Schubert, Schumann, Mendelssohn, Gade, or even of the reckless and over-fluent Raff! Absurd! . . . All that we have heard and seen from Brahms's pen abounds in headwork without a glimmer of soul. . . . It is possible that as we grow more familiar with this symphony it may become clearer to us, but we might pore over a difficult problem in mathematics until the same result was reached without arriving at the conclusion that it is a poetic inspiration.

(Boston *Gazette,* January 24, 1878)

-:-

I have studied the second movement of the Second Symphony of Brahms with the greatest attention. Well! I have not the faintest idea what the composer means. . . . It seems as if it were only by the greatest effort that Brahms could firmly fix his own conceptions. Whatever he writes, he seems to have to force music out of his brain as if by hydraulic pressure. . . . It would take a year to really fathom the Second Symphony, and a year of severe intellectual work, too. One would only like to be a little more sure that such labor would be repaid.

(W. F. Apthorp, Boston *Courier,* January 11, 1879)

-:-

We do not find ourselves at all alone in saying that the Second Symphony of Brahms does not improve upon acquaintance. There is a certain feebleness, a sugar-and-water character, in the subject matter of the themes; and when it comes to the working up, it is done with an unstinted use of contrapuntal means. There are obscure, unsatisfactory periods. This super-refined contrapuntal distillment has produced nothing better than a bad quality of spirit, which shows its effects upon the brain in the uncomfortable, distracting headache (*Weltschmerz, Katzenjammer*). It still refuses to reveal its meaning, and leaves us with the sense of having listened to something ugly and ungenial, which we would fain avoid hereafter. It is fragmentary and disjointed; the rhythm and the tempo and thoughts themselves are continually changing without warning and apparently without reason; and there is nothing like development or continuity.

(*Dwight's Journal of Music,* Boston, March 15, 1879)

-:-

The principal work of the evening was Brahms's Symphony in C minor. We think a better choice might have been made for an opening concert. . . It is poor in ideas, and the few that there are want originality. They do not warm us, they do not speak to our hearts' emotions. Everything is measured, cold and of aristocratic reserve. . . Three slow movements following each other become extremely tedious, and the most striking motif of the whole work, the leading theme of the last movement, is so much like the finale of Beethoven's Ninth Symphony that, as another writer has admirably remarked, it should be put in quotation marks.

(New York *Post,* November 8, 1880)

-:-

It would appear as though Brahms might afford occasionally to put a little more melody into his work—just a little now and then for a change. His Second Symphony gave the impression that the composer was either endeavoring all the while to get as near as possible to harmonic sounds without reaching them; or that he was unable to find any whatever.

(Boston *Traveler,* February 27, 1882)

-:-

Musical people, as a rule, have not as yet got 'educated' by the 'music of the future' up to the point where they may enjoy passage after passage bereft of all tonality by meandering through doors of modulation, around corners of accidentals, and through mazes of chromatics that lead nowhere in particular unless it be to the realm of giddiness. They long occasionally to come out into the sunlight or to emerge upon some scene where recognizable objects may be viewed, grouped or marshaled somewhat according to nature and the understood laws of unity and symmetry. There is so much of this ultra-modern kind of writing in the Brahms *Serenade,* op. 11, that, with its inordinate length, its total effect is wearisome. The general treatment in this *Serenade* is after Brahms's usual fashion, abstruse, intellectual. The work, on a first hearing at least, is largely unintelligible.

(Boston *Daily Advertiser,* October 31, 1882)

-:-

The First Symphony of Brahms seems to strive after the unattainable; it is full of irritant and restless discords; it has strange, climbing, grasping phrases which seem to be trying to drag down something which still glides upward from their reach; its pastoral motifs often break away in suggestion of storm and confusion; and strings are frequently urged to the very top of their compass, and at times, as in the first and last movements, a sort of Walpurgis Night sweeps down and whirls everything away in a rhythmic chaos.

(Boston *Daily Advertiser*, December 29, 1883)

-:-

There is in Brahms's C minor symphony an iteration and reiteration of mere fragmentary ideas . . . which makes it simply tiresome, and the opening movement is suggestive of the Lord Chancellor's song in *Iolanthe*. . . The orchestra did wonderfully good work in all this tiresome waste of endless harmony.

(Boston *Herald*, December 31, 1883)

-:-

Brahms' *Tragische Ouvertüre* erinnert uns lebhaft an die Geistererscheinungen in den Shakespeareschen Dramen, die den Mörder durch ihre Anwesenheit erschrecken, während sie den Umstehenden unsichtbar bleiben. Wir wissen zwar nicht, welchen Helden Brahms in seiner *Ouvertüre* gemordet. Nehmen wir an, Brahms sei der Macbeth und die *Tragische Ouvertüre* der verkörperte Mord durch den Geist des Banquo, den er soeben durch die ersten Niederstreiche, wie sie gleich Beilhieben niederfallen, mordet.

(Hugo Wolf, *Salonblatt*, Vienna, March 23, 1884)

[Brahms's *Tragic Overture* strongly reminds us of the appearances of ghosts in Shakespeare's dramas, who frighten the murderer by their presence while they remain invisible to those present. We do not know which hero Brahms has murdered in his *Tragic Overture*. Let us assume that Brahms is Macbeth, and the *Tragic Overture* is the murder embodied in the ghost of Banquo, whom he murders with the very first downbows, which fall like axe blows.]

-:-

Like the great mass of the composer's music, the Third Symphony of Brahms is painfully dry, deliberate and ungenial. . . The Finale we could not understand, and it ends in a quiet and unimpressive manner that makes it an anticlimax after the fuss and noisiness that precede it.

(Boston *Gazette*, November 8, 1884)

Die zweite Nummer war: Brahms' Klavierkonzert in B-dur, vom Komponisten selber gespielt. Wer dieses Klavierkonzert mit Appetit verschlucken konnte, darf ruhig einer Hungersnot entgegensehen; es ist anzunehmen, dass er sich einer beneidenswerten Verdauung erfreut und in Hungersnöten mit einem Nahrung-Aequivalent von Fenstergläsern, Korkstöpseln, Ofenschrauben u. dgl. mehr sich vortrefflich zu helfen wissen wird.

(Hugo Wolf, *Salonblatt*, Vienna, December 13, 1884)

[The second number was Brahms's Piano Concerto in B-flat major, played by the composer himself. Who can swallow this concerto with appetite, can calmly await a famine; it is to be assumed that he enjoys an enviable digestion, and in time of famine will be able to get along splendidly on the nutritive equivalent of window glass, cork stoppers, stove pipes, and the like.]

-:-

Les quatuors de Brahms pour instruments à cordes sont nuls, impossibles et ne supportent pas l'analyse. . . Il y a dans cette musique une lutte constante entre les instruments, lutte agaçante et qui fatigue; jamais un moment de repos pour l'esprit ni pour les doigts.

(Ch. Dancla, *Miscellanées Musicales*, Paris, 1884)

[Brahms's quartets for strings are meaningless, impossible and support no analysis. . . There is in this music a constant struggle among the instruments, an irritating and tiresome struggle; there is never a moment of rest for the spirit or for the fingers.]

-:-

Lovers of Brahms were much disturbed by large numbers of people leaving the hall between the movements of the C minor Symphony. . . . It must be admitted that to the larger part of our public, Brahms is still an incomprehensible terror.

(Boston *Evening Transcript*, November 16, 1885)

-:-

Auffallend ist der Krebsgang in dem Produzieren Brahms'. Zwar hat sich dasselbe nie über das Niveau des Mittelmässigen aufschwingen können; aber solche Nichtigkeit, Hohlheit und Duckmäuserei, wie sie in der E-moll Symphonie herrscht ist doch in keinem Werke von

Brahms in so beängstigender Weise an das Tageslicht getreten. Die Kunst, ohne Einfälle zu komponieren, hat entschieden in Brahms ihren würdigsten Vertreter gefunden. Ganz wie der liebe Gott versteht auch Herr Brahms sich auf das Kunststück aus nichts etwas zu machen. . . Genug des grausamen Spieles! Möge es Herrn Brahms genügen in seiner E-moll Symphonie die Sprache gefunden zu haben, die seiner stummen Verzweiflung den beredtesten Ausdruck verliehen: die Sprache der intensivsten musikalischen Impotenz.

(Hugo Wolf, *Salonblatt,* Vienna, January 31, 1886)

[The retrograde movement of Brahms's production is striking. True, he could never rise above the mediocre; but such nothingness, hollowness, such mousy obsequiousness as in the E minor Symphony had never yet been revealed so alarmingly in any of Brahms's works. The art of composing without ideas has decidedly found in Brahms one of its worthiest representatives. Like God Almighty, Brahms understands the trick of making something out of nothing. Enough of the hideous game! Let Brahms be content that in his E minor Symphony he has found a language which gives the most persuasive expression of his mute despair: the language of the most intensive musical impotence.]

-:-

I played over the music of that scoundrel Brahms. What a giftless bastard! It annoys me that this self-inflated mediocrity is hailed as a genius. Why, in comparison with him, Raff is a giant, not to speak of Rubinstein, who is after all a live and important human being, while Brahms is chaotic and absolutely empty dried-up stuff.

(Tchaikovsky's Diary, entry under October 9, 1886)

-:-

Brahms's Second Symphony was listened to attentively but did not arouse any enthusiasm. What work of Brahms ever did? Of course it is an exceedingly erudite work, so to speak, containing details which betray an honest and profound musical thinker; but it lacks grand, sweeping ideas, and is deficient in sensuous charm. The *Allegretto* is the most original movement of the four. It is marked 'grazioso,' yet it rather reminds one of the gambols of elephants than of a fairy dance. The greater part of the symphony was antiquated before it was written. Why not play instead Rubinstein's *Dramatic Symphony*, which is shamefully neglected here, and any one movement of which contains more evidence of genius than all of Brahms's symphonies put together, and would certainly be received with more favor by the audience?

(New York *Post*, November 1, 1886)

-:-

Etwas, wie die neue *Cello-Sonate* von Herrn Dr. Johannes Brahms, aufzuschreiben, drucken, aufführen zu lassen . . . und von solchem Wahnsinn nicht angesteckt zu werden, ist keine Kleinigkeit mehr—und meiner Treu! ich fange an, vor mir Respekt zu kreigen. Ja, was ist denn heutzutage Musik, was Harmonie, was Melodie, was Rhythmus, was Inhalt, was Form—wenn dieses Tohuwabohu in allen Ernste Musik sein will? Will aber Herr Dr. Johannes Brahms seine Anbeter mit diesem neuesten Werke mystifizieren, will er sich über ihre hirnlose Veneration lustig machen, dann freilich ist es etwas anderes und wir bewundern in Herrn Brahms den grössten Foppmeister dieses Jahrhunderts und aller künftigen Jahrtausende.

(Hugo Wolf, *Salonblatt*, Vienna, December 5, 1886)

[To write down, to print, to have performed anything like the new Cello Sonata by Herr Dr. Johannes Brahms and not to be infected by this madness is no longer a trifle—and upon my heart, I am beginning to acquire respect for myself. . . What is then nowadays music, harmony, melody, rhythm, meaning, form, when this rigmarole seriously pretends to be regarded as music? If Herr Dr. Johannes Brahms intends to mystify his admirers with this newest work, if he wants to make fun of their brainless veneration, then it is of course something else, and we marvel at Herr Brahms as the greatest bluffer of this century and of all future millennia.]

-:-

Of the four movements of Brahms's Fourth Symphony the first has at least a semblance of vitality in it; but like the other three movements, it is characterized by Brahms's besetting sin—a profuse lack of ideas.

(New York *Post*, December 13, 1886)

Taken as a whole, the four movements of Brahms's Fourth Symphony do not seem well balanced. The character of the first and second are so similar that one feels the lack of contrast. The third, on the other hand, is massive and noisy, with the brass going continually. . . As far as the invention, construction and treatment of the different motives and themes are concerned, there is the usual monotony of sound to be found more or less in all of Brahms's orchestral works. . . With Brahms, the basses and violins are playing almost the whole time, which means that the body of the work is moving like a broad stream in a compass of four to five octaves, with but few breaks.

(*Musical Courier,* New York, December 29, 1886)

-:-

We find in Brahms's Fourth Symphony little to commend to the attention of a music-loving public. . . The orchestration is, like most of Brahms, of a certain sameness, rather thick and of India-rubber-like stickiness. . . Brahms evidently lacks the breadth and power of invention eminently necessary for the production of a truly great symphonic work.

(*Musical Courier,* New York, January 19, 1887)

-:-

Die sympathie die Brahms unleugbar hier und da einflösst . . . war mir lange ein Rätsel: bis ich endlich, durch einen Zufall beinahe, dahinter kam, dass er auf einen bestimmten Typus von Menschen wirkt. Er hat die Melancholie des Unvermögens; er schafft nicht aus der Fülle, er durstet nach der Fülle.

(Friedrich Nietzsche, second postscript to *Der Fall Wagner,* 1888)

[The sympathy that Brahms undeniably inspires now and then, was for a long time a puzzle to me, until I finally, almost by accident, realized that he impresses one definite type of people. He has the melancholy of impotence; he creates not out of abundance; he yearns after abundance.]

-:-

In the Brahms C minor Symphony every note draws blood. It has been plausibly questioned whether Brahms's music will ever become popular. . . That it is not popular now and in Boston is pretty evident, for our audiences listen to it in a silence that speaks more of dismay than of veneration.

(Boston *Evening Transcript*, December 9, 1888)

-:-

Brahms takes an essentially commonplace theme; gives it a strange air by dressing it in the most elaborate and far-fetched harmonies; keeps his countenance severely; and finds that a good many wise-acres are ready to guarantee him as deep as Wagner, and the true heir of Beethoven. . . Strip off the euphuism from these symphonies and you will find a string of incomplete dance and ballad tunes following one another with no more organic coherence than the succession of passing images reflected in a shop window in Piccadilly during any twenty minutes in the day.

(George Bernard Shaw, *The World*, London, June 18, 1890)

-:-

The themes of the Piano Quartet, op. 26, of Brahms are dry, insipid, and of trifling importance. . . We see the man at work rather than the result of the labor. The digressions are like the paths in a labyrinth; they perplex the wanderer who seeks a resting place; his eyes fall everywhere upon covers of counterpoint; and if by chance he threads the maze and finds the center, it is too apt to prove a disappointment instead of a relief. For in this Quartet, the promises of Brahms are seldom kept; the fuss and fury of preparation leads to a weak performance, and a little mouse is the reward of a great groaning and sore travail.

(Philip Hale, Boston *Traveler*, December 31, 1890)

-:-

It is possible that Brahms's creations are the true type of the music of the future. No doubt Beethoven shocked the ears of the great majority of his listeners with equal facility; and as for Schumann, even the present generation is not yet wholly reconciled to his dissonances. But it is hard to believe that Brahms is the true prophet.

(Boston *Courier*, November 29, 1891)

Brahms's *Requiem* has not the true funeral relish: it is so execrably and ponderously dull that the very flattest of funerals would seem like a ballet, or at least a *danse macabre*, after it.

(George Bernard Shaw, *The World*, November 9, 1892)

-:-

To me it seems quite obvious that the real Brahms is nothing more than a sentimental voluptuary. . . He is the most wanton of composers. . . Only his wantonness is not vicious; it is that of a great baby . . . rather tiresomely addicted to dressing himself up as Handel or Beethoven and making a prolonged and intolerable noise.

(George Bernard Shaw, *The World*, June 21, 1893)

-:-

I do not like and I cannot like the C minor Symphony of Brahms. . . . I am willing to admit without argument that the Symphony is grand and impressive and all that. So is a Channel fog. . . This C minor Symphony seems to me the apotheosis of arrogance. . . Or let the Symphony be treated in symbolism: The musicians are in a forest. The forest is dark. No birds are in this forest save birds that do not sing. . . The players wander. They grope as though they were eyeless. Alarmed, they call to each other; frightened, they shout together. It seems that obscene, winged things listen and mock the lost. . . Suddenly the players are in a clearing. They see close to them a canal. The water of the canal is green, and diseased purple and yellow plants grow on the banks of the canal. . . A swan with filthy plumage and twisted neck bobs up and down in the green water of the canal. And then a boat is dragged towards the players. The boat is crowded with queerly dressed men and women and children, who sing a tune that sounds something like the hymn in Beethoven's Ninth Symphony. . . Darkness seizes the scene.

(Philip Hale, Boston *Journal*, October 6, 1893)

-:-

Brahms's C minor Symphony figured on the program. I have most carefully studied the score of this symphony, and have pored over the analytical program, but acknowledge my inability to grasp the work or to see why it was written. The composition reminded me of a visit to a sawmill in the Adirondack Mountains. Great logs of melodies were hauled up with superhuman power and noisily sawed into boards of phrases varying in length and thickness. Some of them were again reduced to shingles and laths of figures, to be finally stacked away in a colossal pile of a climax. . . Brahms despises the charm of mere beauty. His harmonies are abrupt and not luxurious, his melodies quaint or grim rather than beautiful. He is somewhat too manly a musical bully.

(Clarence Lucas, *Musical Courier*, New York, December 6, 1893)

-:-

After the weary, dreary hours spent in listening to the works of Brahms I am lost in wonder at the amount of devotion accorded him and the floods of enthusiasm with which he is overwhelmed. I endeavor to comfort myself with the thought that even though Brahms gives us nothing in the way of beautiful themes, lovely harmonies or refreshing modulations, his example in preserving those musical forms, which Wagner sought to destroy, might stimulate other composers to enliven the old symphonic molds with melodies of beauty and grace. But, no. What do we see instead? Mistaking Brahms's un-beauty for a new line of thought, his followers amuse themselves with seeking in what a variety of means they, too, can twist and torture a series of commonplace tones and chords.

(Edgar Stillman Kelley, San Francisco *Examiner*, May 9, 1894)

-:-

Owing to the misfortune of being a musician, I cannot appreciate Brahms, and least of all Brahms in E minor. . . There is no more intolerably dull symphony in the world than the E minor.

(J. F. Runciman, *Saturday Review*, London, November 6, 1897)

-:-

All I heard of the program was my especial aversion, Johannes Brahms, his Piano Concerto, op. 15, and the Piano Concerto, op. 83. Brahms seems to appeal to those curious folk whose minds are made in bits carelessly joined or not joined at all. Of the two concertos, the one in D minor is distinctly less abominable than the other, but neither contains much genuine music. The usefulness on this occasion was that the pianist was permitted to show how excellent a football player he would make. He thrashed the piano until one feared its legs would crumble under the mighty onslaught.

(J. F. Runciman, *Saturday Review*, London, December 3, 1898)

-:-

I push Brahms away contemptuously. . . His music is a noisy, reverberating void. . . He was a kind of musical Chadband. . . I by no means wish to call Brahms an idiot; he was something considerably more than that; but if a boy or a man, who is an idiot in all other respects can sometimes attain to an astonishing mastery of figures, surely it is not unfair to suppose that Brahms may have had this wonderful technical musical talent without any special brain power in other respects. . . Only once or twice was Brahms really expressive of an original emotion, and that emotion was the feeling of despondency, grief, melancholy, which was aroused in him by a sense of his own emotional impotence.

(J. F. Runciman, *Musical Record*, Boston, January 1, 1900)

-:-

The Brahms Sextet is a work built upon dry-as-dust elements. It is one of those odd compositions which at times slipped from the pen of Brahms, apparently in order to prove how excellent a mathematician he might have become, but how prosaic, how hopeless, how unfeeling, how unemotional, how arid a musician he really was. . . You feel an undercurrent of surds, of quadratic equations, of hyperbolic curves, of the dynamics of a particle. . . But it must not be forgotten that music is not only a science; it is also an art. The Sextet was played with precision, and that is the only way in which you can work out a problem in musical trigonometry.

(Vernon Blackburn, *Pall Mall Gazette*, London, February 28, 1900)

-:-

The weak despair of Brahms when he contemplated death . . . and the snivelling pessimism of some of his absolute music may be attributed justly to his constitutional defect. . . Page after page of his *Requiem* is saturated with indigo woe, and the consolatory words are set to music that is too often dull with unutterable dullness.

(Philip Hale, *Musical Record*, Boston, November 1, 1900)

-:-

Art is long and life is short: here is evidently the explanation of a Brahms symphony.

(Edward Lorne, *Fanfare*, London, January 1922)

BRUCKNER Die Rätsel die uns Bruckner aufgibt sind dunkel. . . Die Tongespenster machen es gar zu toll; als hätten Wolfsschlucht und Walpurgisnacht sich ein Rendezvous gegeben, so stampft und tobt, brüllt und wiehert alles wild durcheinander. Die Zukunft, welche ein solches zerrissenes, aus 100 Klüften widerhallendes Tonstück zu geniessen vermag, wünschen wir uns fern.

(Max Kalbeck, *Wiener Allgemeine Zeitung,* February 13, 1883)

[The puzzles that Bruckner presents to us are dim. . . The tonal ghosts are altogether too mad: it is as though a pack of wolves met on Walpurgis Night, such stamping and roaring, raging and screaming goes wildly on. If the future can relish such a chaotic piece of music, with sounds echoing from a hundred cliffs, we wish that future to be far away from us.]

-:-

The Third Symphony by one Anton Bruckner, a professor of harmony in the Vienna Conservatory, headed the program. A hearing of the work induces a feeling of surprise that any sane publisher should have accorded the score the dignity of print, that is only equalled by a natural wonderment on the part of the listener that anyone should punish an inoffensive audience by the infliction of its performance, for anything more inane and wearisome cannot well be conceived than this *olla podrida* of miscellaneous rubbish. . . The scoring is throughout puerile in the extreme, and the absence of intelligent construction or inventive ability completes the sum total of Herr Bruckner's musical imbecility.

(*Keynote,* New York, December 12, 1885)

-:-

Wirklich schaudern wir vor dem Modergeruch, der aus den Missklängen dieses verwesungssüchtigen Kontrapunktes in unsere Nasen dringt. Bruckners Phantasie ist so unheilbar erkrankt and zerrüttet dass etwas wie die Förderung einer Gesetzmässigkeit in Akkordfolge und Periodenbau überhaupt für sie nicht existiert. . . Bruckner komponiert wie ein Betrunkener!

(Gustav Dömpke, *Wiener Allgemeine Zeitung,* March 22, 1886)

[We recoil in horror before this rotting odor which rushes into our nostrils from the disharmonies of this putrefactive counterpoint. His imagination is so incurably sick and warped that anything like regularity in chord progressions and period structure simply do not exist for him. Bruckner composes like a drunkard!]

-:-

It is polyphony gone mad. There is nothing under the heavens, or on the earth, or in the waters under the earth like unto Bruckner's Seventh Symphony. . . The language of the orchestra is a sort of musical Volapuk. . . Everything is as cold as a problem in mathematics. Herr Bruckner realized and extended the acoustician Euler's belief that it is possible to figure out a sonata. He revels in discords. . . . The work is a failure. It may be beautiful in twenty-five years; it is not beautiful now. The music fell like lead upon the listeners, fully one-third of whom left the hall after the second movement.

(H. E. Krehbiel, New York *Tribune*, November 13, 1886)

-:-

The sole impression created by Bruckner's Seventh Symphony is that its composer, being without inspiration or individuality, has borrowed his materials from Wagner, and reproduced them in an intensely exaggerated and pretentious form. . . Bruckner seems to have made up his mind that, as he could not approach Wagner in his own particular field of opera, he would masquerade in the lion's skin elsewhere. Every feature in the imitation is grossly and absurdly overdone. . . His passion for mannerisms is so overwhelming that as in an earlier symphony he wrote such a number of silent bars that it was designated 'The Pause Symphony,' so in the Seventh Symphony he has adopted the contrapuntal device of inversion by contrary motion with a persistency that would be wearisome were its use not already nullified by the complexity and confusion which it creates. . . The extra trumpets, trombones, and contrabass tuba duly cooperated, and it may fairly be believed that the composer could not have desired a finer or noisier performance.

(*Musical Notes*, London, May 1888)

-:-

Alles fliesst unübersichtlich, ordnungslos, gewaltsam in eine grausame Länge zusammen. . . Es ist nicht unmöglich dass diesem traumverwirrten Katzenjammerstil die Zukunft gehört—eine Zukunft die wir nicht darum beneiden.

(Eduard Hanslick, on Bruckner's Eighth Symphony, *Neue Freie Presse*, Vienna, December 23, 1892)

[Interminable, disorganized, and violent, Bruckner's Eighth Symphony stretches out into a hideous length. . . It is not impossible that the future belongs to this nightmarish Katzenjammer style, a future which we therefore do not envy.]

-:-

Le programme nous apprend que la Symphonie qui a soumis la patience du public à une si rude épreuve, est dediée à Wagner qui embrassa l'auteur, M. Bruckner, l'assurant de la haute estime dans laquelle il tenait son œuvre. Certes, le baiser est de trop; l'estime suffisait. Si l'appréciation de Wagner était sincère, disons qu'elle fut une erreur. . . Les personnes qui ont entendu l'ouvrage sans trouver une seule occasion d'applaudir, ont constaté la débilité des formules dont il se compose, la sénilité des rythmes, l'insignifiance des sonorités, la correction lourde des développements, et la futilité de ce mouvement de polka qui agrémente si plaisamment le finale.

(*Le Ménestrel,* Paris, March 25, 1894)

[The program tells us that the symphony which put the patience of the audience to such a rude trial, is dedicated to Wagner, who embraced the composer, M. Bruckner, assuring him of the high esteem in which he held his work. The kiss was definitely superfluous; esteem sufficed. If Wagner's appreciation was sincere, we would say that it was an error. Those who heard the piece without having had a single occasion to applaud, noted the senility of rhythms, the insignificance of sonorities, the heavy correctness of development, and the futility of this polka movement which so pleasantly adorns the finale.]

-:-

Bruckner is the greatest living musical peril, a tonal Antichrist. The violent nature of the man is not written on his face—for his expression indicates the small soul of an average Kapellmeister; and yet he composes nothing but high treason, revolution and murder. His music may radiate the fragrance of heavenly roses, and yet be poisoned with the sulphur of Hell.

(An unidentified critic quoted in G. Engel, *The Life of Anton Bruckner,* New York, 1931)

CHOPIN In Aufsuchung ohrzerreissender Dissonanzen, gequälter Uebergänge, schneidender Modulationen, widerwärtiger Verrenkungen der Melodie und des Rhythmus, ist Chopin ganz unermüdlich. . . Alles, worauf man nur verfallen kann, wird hervorgesucht, um den Effect bizarrer Originalität zu erzeugen, zumal aber die fremdartigsten Tonarten, die unnatürlichsten Lagen der Accorde, die widerhaarigsten Zusammenstellungen in Betreff der Fingersetzung. . . Aber es verlohnt wahrlich nicht der Mühe, dass ich der verdrehten Mazureks des Herrn Chopin wegen so lange Philippiken halte . . . Hätte Herr Chopin diese Composition einem Meister vorgelegt, so würde dieser sie ihm hoffentlich zerrissen vor die Füsse geworfen haben, was wir hiermit symbolisch thun wollen.

(L. Rellstab, *Iris*, Berlin, July 5, 1833)

[In search of ear-rending dissonances, torturous transitions, sharp modulations, repugnant contortions of melody and rhythm, Chopin is altogether indefatigable. All that one can chance upon, is here brought forward to produce the effect of bizarre originality, especially the strangest tonalities, the most unnatural chord positions, the most preposterous combinations in regard to fingering. But it is not really worth the trouble to hold such long philippics for the sake of the perverse Mazurkas of Herr Chopin. Had he submitted this music to a teacher, the latter, it is to be hoped, would have torn it up and thrown it at his feet—and this is what we symbolically wish to do.]

-:-

Wo Field lächelt, macht Herr Chopin eine grinsende Grimasse; wo Field seufzt, stöhnt Herr Chopin; Field zuckt die Achseln; Herr Chopin macht einen Katzenbuckel. Field thut etwas Gewürz an seine Speise; Herr Chopin eine Hand voll Cayenne Pfeffer. . . Ferner hat Herr Chopin wieder nicht versäumt sich die fremdesten Tonarten zu wählen, B moll, H dur, und freilich auch Es dur; aber in dieser letztern Tonart denn auch so moduliert, dass man in einem wahren Irrgarten zu sehen glaubt. Wenn man Fields reizende Romanzen vor einen verzerrenden Hohlspiegel hielte, so dass aus jedem feineren Ausdruck ein grob aufgetragener wird, so erhält man Chopin Arbeit. Wir beschwören Herrn Chopin, der wahrlich nicht ohne Talent ist, zu Wahrheit und Natur zurückzukehren.

(L. Rellstab, *Iris*, Berlin, August 2, 1833)

[Where Field smiles, Mr. Chopin makes a snickering grimace; where Field sighs, Mr. Chopin groans; Field shrugs the shoulders, Mr. Chopin arches his back like a cat; Field adds spice to his meal; Mr. Chopin throws in a handful of pepper. Furthermore, [in his three Nocturnes, op. 9] Chopin has again not failed to choose the remotest keys, B flat minor, B major, and, of course, E flat major. But in this latter key he also has such modulations that one feels himself in a labyrinth. If one were to hold Field's charming romances before a crooked mirror, so that every finer expression is exaggerated, then one would get Chopin's handiwork. We beseech Mr. Chopin, who is really not without talent, to return to truth and nature.]

-:-

M. Frederic Chopin has, by some means or other which we cannot divine, obtained an enormous reputation but too often refused to composers of ten times his genius. M. Chopin is by no means a putter down of commonplaces; but he is, what by many would be esteemed worse, a dealer in the most absurd and hyperbolical extravagances. . . The entire works of Chopin present a motley surface of ranting hyperbole and excruciating cacophony. When he is not *thus* singular, he is no better than Strauss or any other waltz compounder. . . There is an excuse at present for Chopin's delinquencies; he is entrammeled in the enthralling bonds of that archenchantress, George Sand, celebrated equally for the number and excellence of her romances and her lovers; not less we wonder how she, who once swayed the heart of the sublime and terrible religious democrat Lammenais, can be content to wanton away her dreamlike existence with an artistical nonentity like Chopin.

(*Musical World*, London, October 28, 1841)

-:-

Chopin has hardly ever carried further his peculiar system of harmony than in his Third Ballade. Nothing but the nicest possible execution can reconcile the ear to the crudeness of some of the modulations. These, we presume, are too essentially part and parcel of the man, ever to be changed; but it is their recurrence, as much as the torture to which he exposes the poor eight fingers which will hinder him from ever taking a place among the composers who are at once great and popular.

(H. F. Chorley, *The Athenaeum*, London, December 24, 1842)

The novelty of the evening was Chopin's Piano Concerto in F minor. It is the first work on a large scale which Chopin has attempted. . . It is as that of one who has ventured into a new region and aims at eccentricities without producing any great effect. . . It was dry and unattractive.

(London *Times,* April 4, 1843)

-:-

We are aware that it would be unfair and injudicious to criticize the music of M. Chopin by the chaste models of Mozart or Clementi, or even of Beethoven. . . We do not doubt that much of the music of M. Chopin is destined to become fashionable, and as we cannot imagine the distinguishing features of modern pianoforte music to be further exaggerated than by himself, we may venture to hope for a return to the more wholesome taste by the time that our composer has had his day.

(*Dramatic and Musical Review,* London, October 28, 1843)

-:-

The wildness of both the melody and harmony of Chopin is, for the most part, excessive. . . We cannot imagine any musician, who has not acquired an unhealthy taste for noise, and scrambling, and dissonance, to feel otherwise than dissatisfied with the effect of either of the Third *Ballade,* or the *Grande Valse,* or the Eight Mazurkas.

(*Dramatic and Musical Review,* London, November 4, 1843)

-:-

M. Chopin increasingly effects the crudest modulations. Cunning must be the connoiseur, indeed, who, while listening to his music, can form the slightest idea when wrong notes are played—its difficulties to the eye being doubled by the composer's eccentricity of notation.

(H. F. Chorley, *The Athenaeum,* London, December 20, 1845)

-:-

Chopin was essentially a drawing-room composer. Away from his nocturnes and mazurkas, he became as trivial and incoherent as in those attractive trifles he was earnest and individual. The Concerto in E minor is for the most part a rambling series of passages, with one or two pretty motivi, with which but little is done.

(London *Times,* May 16, 1855)

COPLAND Copland's Piano Concerto shows a shocking lack of taste, of proportion. After thunderous, blaring measures in which one brass instrument vies with another in arrogant announcement, there are gentle purposeless measures for the piano, which is struck by fingers apparently directed at random, as a child amuses itself by making noises when it is restless in the room. Let us not forget that the leading English reviewers characterized Schumann's Symphony in B flat when they first heard it as belonging to the 'Broken Crockery School.' Our objection to Mr. Copland's broken crockery is that it is not of the first quality.

(Philip Hale, Boston *Herald,* January 29, 1927)

-:-

If there exists anywhere in the world a stranger concatenation of meaninglessly ugly sounds and distorted rhythms than Mr. Copland's Piano Concerto, Boston has been spared it. Since there must be a bit of jazz in all American music nowadays, Mr. Copland has his measures in that view, but as one young man in the audience remarked, 'No dance-hall would tolerate jazz of such utter badness.'

(Warren Storey Smith, Boston *Post,* January 29, 1927)

-:-

The jazz theme was a pretty poor pick, as those things go. But Mr. Copland surrounded it with all the machinery of sound and fury, and the most raucous modernistic fury at that. The composer-pianist smote his instrument at random; the orchestra, under the impassioned baton of Mr. Koussevitzky, heaved and shrieked and fumed and made anything but sweet moans until both pianist and conductor attained such a climax of absurdity that many in the audience giggled with delight. Mr. Copland was evidently seriously engaged in saying something of vital importance to himself, and played away, frantically aided and abetted by the orchestra, which made barnyard and stable noises in the intervals of proclaiming imposing Scriabinish fanfare.

(Samuel Chotzinoff, New York *World,* February 4, 1927)

-:-

Mr. Copland's Piano Concerto opens with a tremendous fracas. . . There are gargantuan dance measures, as of a herd of elephants engaged in jungle rivalry of the Charleston and dances further south. Rhythm runs away with rhythm and key shatters its sabre against key. . . A curious and puzzling performance, this Concerto.

(Pitts Sanborn, New York *Telegram*, February 4, 1927)

-:-

The Copland Piano Concerto is a harrowing horror from beginning to end. There is nothing in it that resembles music except as it contains noise—just as the words employed by Gertrude Stein may be said to resemble poetry because poetry consists of words, and so does her crazy clatter. Copland's music is not 'new music.' It seems to be dissonance for the sake of dissonance. It is of all sounds the most illogical, the most anti-human. The piano part of the composition is not played but merely happened upon at random, as it might be if the performer struck the keyboard with his elbows instead of his fingers.

(Editorial in the Boston *Evening Transcript*, February 5, 1927)

-:-

In American music, Aaron Copland is the great man for small deeds; a 'shrewd investor of pennies,' as Theodore Chanler describes him. A small, cool creative gift, but an ego of much frenetic drive, a devious personality with a feline *savoir faire*, with his fine commercial acumen and acute sense of the direction of today's wind, Aaron Copland is primarily a shrewd manager of *musique à succès*. He everlastingly changes his palette, his composing technique and his advertising technique. . . His is a flagrant example of composer by propaganda. Quite early this alert, suave businessman of music began to sway his esthetics with the claims of the day. . . Copland's *Short Symphony* I cannot describe more exactly than inane and rainy. . . A quite bewildering piece of creative impotence! . . . A feeble score is the *Appalachian Spring*: music anemic and insignificant. . . Copland cannot forget the coachmen's and wet nurses' dances, *Petrushka's* liveliest. His Appalachian peasants sound more like Appalachian Cossacks. . . Now, to the *magnum opus*, the loudly trumpeted *Lincoln Portrait*. . . After a short-lived attempt at the grand line, the *petit maître* appears in all his nakedness. We see pitifully clearly what the new dress of the king is. It is the dress of a compiler whose loud trumpets try to herald an imposing creator; the dress of a master of small deeds who has the audacity to trade in things sacred.

(Lazare Saminsky, *Living Music of the Americas*, New York, 1949)

COWELL Henry Cowell, in the suite for what he is pleased to term 'solo string and percussion piano' with chamber orchestra, has added to *materia musica* a darning-egg and a pencil, with which, together with more familiar implements, he assailed the innards of a grand piano. . . Many of the sounds which Mr. Cowell achieved last evening might be duplicated with a tack-hammer and any convenient bit of unupholstered furniture.

(Warren Storey Smith, Boston *Post,* March 12, 1929, under the caption: USES EGG TO SHOW OFF THE PIANO)

-:-

Von Cowell war gesagt, er habe Tongruppen geschaffen die auf dem Klavier mit Hilfe der Fäuste und des Unterarms gespielt werden! Warum so zaghaft? Mit dem Gesäss kann man viel mehr erreichen! Die musikalischen Insassen eines Irrenhauses schienen sich an diesem Abend ein Stelldichein gegeben zu haben.

(Paul Zschorlich, *Deutsche Zeitung,* Berlin, March 13, 1932)

[It is said about Cowell that he has invented tonal groups that can be played on the piano with the aid of fists and forearms! Why so coy? With one's behind one can cover many more notes! The musical inmates of a madhouse seem to have held a rendezvous on this occasion.]

-:-

Henry Cowells *Synchrony* beginnt mit einem läppischen Solo der gestopften Trompete. Die knochenerweichenden Triller dieser milch triefenden Einleitung lösten bei den Hörern unbezwingbare Heiterkeit aus. Im Programm heisst es, dass es dieses musikalischen *Selfmademans* besonderes Verdienst sei, sogenannte Tone-Clusters erfunden zu haben, die auf dem Klavier mit den Fäusten oder mit dem Unterarm 'gespielt' werden. Nun, ein gewaltiger Tonkleister war dieses kreischende und stampfende sogennante Stück Musik ohne allen Zweifel.

(Paul Schwers, *Allgemeine Musikzeitung,* Berlin, March 18, 1932)

[Henry Cowell's *Synchrony* begins with a silly little solo of the muted trumpet. The bone-softening trills of this milk-dripping introduction aroused irrepressible hilarity among the listeners. The program says that the particular distinction of this self-made man is the invention of so-called tone-clusters, which are 'played' on the piano with fists and forearms. Well, this screechy and banging piece of so-called music is beyond any doubt a mighty *Tonkleister.*]

DEBUSSY M. Claude Debussy is unknown so far as the great public is concerned. A *Faun's Afternoon* was certainly *fin-de-siècle* enough as a title. As a wit remarked, the next would no doubt be *The Five O'Clock of a Nymph*! The work itself is a curious fantasie, full of unprecise harmonies and fleeting phrases. . . There was a large and unimproved opportunity for some beautiful pastoral melodies. But then melody is not the fashion, of course.

(*Musical Courier*, New York, October 28, 1895)

-:-

Pelléas et Mélisande aura été une limite infranchissable, je crois, et méritera certainement de figurer, à titre de curiosité, dans toutes les bibliothèques de musique. M. Debussy consentera peut-être à renoncer à son système et à revenir à une conception plus saine de l'art musical.

(Eugène d'Harcourt, *Figaro*, Paris, May 1, 1902)

[*Pelléas et Mélisande* reaches a limit which cannot be transgressed, and I believe it will certainly be worthy of inclusion as a curiosity in all music libraries. Perhaps Debussy will consent to renounce his system and to return to a more sane conception of musical art.]

-:-

M. Debussy's score of *Pelléas and Mélisande* defies description, being such a refined concatenation of sounds that not the faintest impression is made on the ear. The composer's system is to ignore melody altogether; his personages do not sing, but talk in a sort of lilting voice to a vague musical accompaniment of the text. No solo, no detached phrase ever breaks the interminable flow cf commonplace sound. The effect is quite bewildering, almost amusing in its absurdity.

(*Era*, London, May 2, 1902)

-:-

Le rythme, le chant, la tonalité, voilà trois choses inconnues à M. Debussy et volontairement dédaignées par lui. Sa musique est vague, flottante, sans couleur et sans contours, sans mouvement et sans vie. . . . Quelle jolie série de fausses relations! Quelles adorables suites d'accords parfaits marchant par mouvement direct, avec les quintes et les octaves qui s'ensuivent! Quelle collection de dissonances, septièmes ou neuvièmes, montant avec énergie, même par intervalles disjoints! . . . Non, décidément, je ne serai jamais d'accord avec ces anarchistes de la musique!

(Arthur Pougin, on *Pelléas et Mélisande,* in *Le Ménestrel,* Paris, May 4, 1902)

[Rhythm, melody, tonality, these are three things unknown to Monsieur Debussy and deliberately disdained by him. His music is vague, floating, without color and without shape, without movement and without life. What a pretty series of false relations! What adorable progressions of triads in parallel motion, and fifths and octaves which result from it! What a collection of dissonances, sevenths and ninths, ascending with energy, even disjunct intervals! . . . No, decidedly, I will never agree with these anarchists of music!]

-:-

Ce n'est pas la moindre originalité de M. Debussy d'écrire une partition entière sans une phrase, que dis-je, sans une mesure de mélodie. . . Dans *Pelléas et Mélisande,* il ne saurait y avoir de leitmotive par la bonne raison qu' il n' y a pas de motifs du tout. . . Le rythme ne lui parait pas moins haïssable. En son art deux fois amorphe, l'abolition du rythme répond à la suppression de la mélodie. L'orchestre de M. Debussy parait grêle et pointu. S'il prétend caresser, il égratigne et blesse. Il fait peu de bruit, je l'accorde, mais un vilain petit bruit. Aucun n'est mieux qualifié que l'auteur de *Pelléas et Mélisande* pour présider à la décomposition de notre art. La musique de M. Debussy tend à la diminution et à la ruine de notre être. Elle contient des germes non pas de vie et de progrès mais de décadence et de mort.

(Camille Bellaigue, *Revue des Deux Mondes,* Paris, May 15, 1902)

[Not the least original trait of M. Debussy is to write an entire score without a phrase, without even a measure of melody. In *Pelléas et Mélisande* there cannot be any leitmotives for the good reason that there are not any motives at all. Rhythm is no less abhorrent to him. In his doubly amorphous art, the abolition of rhythm follows the suppression of melody. The orchestra of M. Debussy seems pockmarked and gaunt. When it pretends to caress, it scratches and hurts. It makes little noise, I concede, but it is a nasty little noise. No one is better qualified than the composer of *Pelléas et Mélisande* to preside over the decomposition of our art. The music of M. Debussy leads to the emaciation and ruin of our essence. It contains germs not of life and progress, but of decadence and death.]

-:-

The vocal parts of *Pelléas et Mélisande* are written without any attention being paid to the characteristics of the singing voice. In fact, the singers recite their roles to notes without the composer's having cared as to whether the sequence of these notes shall prove agreeable to the ear. Of melody there is not the slightest pretension. In fact, the same results would be obtained exactly if the singers were to declaim their parts instead of singing them, provided they kept the pitch of the voice quite distinct from the tonality of the orchestra. D'Harcourt says, 'Debussy has a horror of the common chord, and if by accident he uses it, it is nearly always in another tonality,' as if to say, 'this is a common chord, it is true, but you will admit that it doesn't sound like one.'

(*Musical Courier*, New York, May 28, 1902)

-:-

Through the intellectual refinement of a crazy pursuit for novelty, Debussy has arrived at the greatest negation of every doctrine. He disowns melody and its development, and despises the symphony with all its resources. The opinion of the best musical critics is unanimous in declaring *Pelléas et Mélisande* a work of musical decline. . . France may be still congratulated upon possessing Reyer, Massenet, Saint-Saëns, and Charpentier. They cannot certainly prevent the decline of the musical art; but they will delay it for a while.

(S. Marchesi, *Monthly Musical Record*, London, June 1902)

-:-

In Debussy's opera, *Pelléas et Mélisande*, consecutive fifths, octaves, ninths, and sevenths abound in flocks, and not only by pairs, but in whole passages of such inharmonious chords. . . Such progressions sound awful and as they come out in the strings, one gives an involuntary start, as when the dentist touches the nerve of a sensitive tooth.

(*Musical Courier*, New York, July 16, 1902)

I met Debussy at the Café Riche the other night and was struck by the unique ugliness of the man. His face is flat, the top of his head is flat, his eyes are prominent—the expression veiled and sombre—and, altogether, with his long hair, unkempt beard, uncouth clothing and soft hat, he looked more like a Bohemian, a Croat, a Hun, than a Gaul. His high, prominent cheek bones lend a Mongolian aspect to his face. The head is brachycephalic, the hair black. . . Richard Strauss via the music of Wagner, Liszt and Berlioz has set the pace for the cacophonists. Since his *Don Quixote* there has been nothing new devised—outside of China—to split the ears of diatonic lovers. . . Rémy de Gourmont has written of the 'disassociation of ideas.' Debussy puts the theory into practice, for in his peculiar idiom there seems to be no normal sequence. . . The form itself is decomposed. Tonalities are vague, even violently unnatural to unaccustomed ears. . . If the Western world ever adopted Eastern tonalities, Claude Debussy would be the one composer who would manage its system, with its quarter-tones and split quarters. Again I see his curious asymmetrical face, the pointed fawn ears, the projecting cheek bones—the man is a wraith from the East; his music was heard long ago in the hill temples of Borneo; was made as a symphony to welcome the head-hunters with their ghastly spoils of war!

(James Gibbons Huneker, New York *Sun*, July 19, 1903)

-:-

Debussy's *L'Après-midi d'un faune* was a strong example of modern ugliness. The faun must have had a terrible afternoon, for the poor beast brayed on muted horns and whinnied on flutes, and avoided all trace of soothing melody, until the audience began to share his sorrows. The work gives as much dissonance as any of the most modern art works in music. All these erratic and erotic spasms but indicate that our music is going through a transition state. When will the melodist of the future arrive?

(Louis Elson, Boston *Daily Advertiser*, February 25, 1904)

-:-

A vacuum has been described as nothing shut up in a box, and the prelude entitled *L'Après-midi d'un faune* may aptly be described as nothing, expressed in musical terms. The subject certainly affords opportunity for the exercise of the composer's imagination, but he appears to have come to the conclusion that the fortunate faun was not thinking about anything at all. . . The piece begins with a fragment of the chromatic scale played by the flute, manifestly selected with care to express nothing. After the flute has wobbled up and down with these fine semitones, the clarinet imitates its mild gambols, supported by the strings, which seem to take more interest in life. Presently the first violin gives out another theme, which begins with a suggestion of tenderness, but seems to grow frightened at venturing to suggest anything, and gets a bad attack of chromatics. . . I was glad when the end came.

(*Referee*, London, August 21, 1904)

-:-

Poor Debussy, sandwiched in between Brahms and Beethoven, seemed weaker than usual. We cannot feel that all this extreme ecstasy is natural; it seems forced and hysterical; it is musical absinthe; there are moments when the suffering Faun in Debussy's *Afternoon of a Faun* seems to need a veterinary surgeon.

(Louis Elson, Boston *Daily Advertiser*, January 2, 1905)

-:-

When we read the title of the first of the sea sketches by Debussy —*From Dawn till Noon*—we feared that we were to have a movement seven hours long. It was not so long, but it was terrible while it lasted. . . Frenchmen are notoriously bad sailors, and a Gallic picture of the sea is apt to run more to stewards and basins and lemons than to the wild majesty of Poseidon. We clung like a drowning man to a few fragments of the tonal wreck, a bit of a theme here, and a comprehensible figure there, but finally this muted-horn sea overwhelmed us. If this be Music, we would much prefer to leave the Heavenly Maid until she has got over her hysterics.

(Louis Elson, Boston *Daily Advertiser*, March 4, 1907)

-:-

The Sea is persistently ugly. . . It is prosaic in its reiteration of inert formulas. . . Debussy fails to give any impression of the sea. . . There is more of barnyard cackle in it than anything else.

(New York *Times*, March 22, 1907)

The Sea of Debussy does not call for many words of comment. The three parts of which it is composed are entitled *From Dawn till Noon, Play of the Waves,* and *Dialogue of the Wind and the Sea,* but as far as any pictorial suggestiveness is concerned, they might as well have been entitled *On the Flatiron Building, Slumming in the Bowery,* and *A Glimpse of Chinatown During a Raid.* Debussy's music is the dreariest kind of rubbish. Does anybody for a moment doubt that Debussy would not write such chaotic, meaningless, cacophonous, ungrammatical stuff, if he could invent a melody? . . . Even his orchestration is not particularly remarkable. M. Loeffler of Boston is far more original from this point of view.
(New York *Post,* March 22, 1907)

-:-

Debussy out-Strausses Strauss. *The Sea* and all that's in that painted mud-puddle was merely funny when it fell to whistling Salome's own shrill trill, till your ears rebelled and the sympathetic cold shivers ran down the orchestra's back. . . No instrument was allowed to utter its natural voice. . . *Dialogue of the Wind and the Sea* would have sounded as sweet if played backwards or upside down. The water had a certain ground swell. The wind—well, the old Irish song has that to rights:

I've lived a long time, Mary,
In this wide world, my dear;
But the wind to whistle a tune like that,
I never before did hear.

(New York *Sun,* March 22, 1907)

-:-

New York heard a new composition called *The Sea,* and New York is probably still wondering why. The work is by the most modern of modern Frenchmen, Debussy. . . Compared with this, the most abstruse compositions of Richard Strauss are as primer stories to hear and to comprehend.
(New York *World,* March 22, 1907)

-:-

We believe that Shakespeare means Debussy's ocean when he speaks of taking up arms against a sea of troubles. It may be possible, however, that in the transit to America, the title of this work has been changed. It is possible that Debussy did not intend to call it *La Mer,* but *Le Mal de Mer,* which would at once make the tone-picture as clear as day. It is a series of symphonic pictures of sea-sickness. The first movement is *Headache.* The second is *Doubt,* picturing moments of dread suspense, whether or no! The third movement, with its explosions and rumblings, has now a self-evident purpose. The hero is endeavoring to throw up his boot-heels!

(Louis Elson, Boston *Daily Advertiser,* April 22, 1907)

-:-

Debussy hat mit der Melodie endgültig abgerechnet. Er lässt uns in *Pelléas und Mélisande* drei und eine viertel Stunde hindurch nur Akkorde hören. Und was für Akkorde! Septimen–und Nonenakkorde, übermässige Dreiklänge und Akkorde die aus sechs verschiedenen Tönen bestehen. Alle diese hart nebeneinander ohne Verbindung. Es entstehen dadurch Querstände und Quintenparallelen in reicher Fülle. Die Partitur gleicht einem Raritätenkabinett von verzwickten Harmonien, einer Galerie harmonisierter Missgeburten. . . Die Musik sinkt herab zum Geräusch, das nur deshalb weniger unangenehm empfunden wird, weil es leise und diskret, halb verschwommen an unser Ohr dringt. Haarsträubende Schwierigkeiten werden den Sängern zugemutet. Das Orchester spielt *Fis-ais-e-g,* und der Sänger setzt *c* dazu ein. Solche Beispiele in Mengen.

(Hugo Schlemüller, *Signale,* Berlin, April 24, 1907)

[Debussy has definitely discounted all melody. In *Pelléas et Mélisande,* for three and a quarter hours, he lets us hear only chords. And what chords! Seventh-chords and ninth-chords, augmented triads and chords that consist of six different notes. All of these close together, without connection. This results in false relations and parallel fifths in rich profusion. The score resembles a curiosity shop of tangled harmonies, a gallery of harmonized abortions. The music degenerates into noise, which makes a less disagreeable impression only because it falls on our ears in soft and discreet half fading tones. Hair-raising difficulties are demanded from the singers. The orchestra plays F sharp, A sharp, E, G, and the singer puts in a C. Such examples are many.]

-:-

M. Claude Debussy . . . directed the first performance in England of his symphonic sketches, called collectively *La Mer.* . . As in all his mature works, it is obvious that he renounces melody as definitely as Alberich renounced love; whether the ultimate object of that renunciation is the same we do not know as yet. . . For perfect enjoyment of this music there is no attitude of mind more to be recommended than the passive unintelligent rumination . . . as long as actual sleep can be avoided. At all events, the practical result of this music is to make the musician hungry for music that is merely logical and beautiful.

(London *Times*, February 3, 1908)

-:-

Debussy's *Blessed Damozel* belongs to the world of the intangible. It offers almost nothing upon which the mind or the affections can fasten. It seems hardly worth while to spend so much labor and pains on being indefinite, but such is the kingdom of music these days. When music essays to rarefy itself to the extent of floating in the ether with disembodied spirits and voicing the anemic attachments of the vestal poesy of the Preraphaelite movement it finds itself in an atmosphere altogether too tenuous to sustain its life.

(New York *Sun*, December 6, 1908)

-:-

M. Debussy wrote three tonal pictures under the general title of *The Sea*. . . It is safe to say that few understood what they heard and few heard anything they understood. . . There are no themes distinct and strong enough to be called themes. There is nothing in the way of even a brief motif that can be grasped securely enough by the ear and brain to serve as a guiding line through the tonal maze. There is no end of queer and unusual effects in orchestration, no end of harmonic combinations and progressions that are so unusual that they sound hideously ugly.

(W. L. Hubbard, Chicago *Tribune*, January 30, 1909)

-:-

Debussys *Pelléas et Mélisande* wurde erbarmungslos niedergezicht, verhöhnt, ausgelacht. . . Es ist aber nicht unmöglich, dass ein andermal die Toten wieder erweckt werden. Gegen Maeterlincks delikate Poesie hat man ja hier nichts einzuwenden und vom Wesen der Komposition—dass man die Musik des vierten Aktes sehr wohl zum Texte des ersten und umgekehrt spielen, ja die Partitur auf den

Kopf oder vor den Spiegel stellen und so aufführen kann ohne ihren Eindruck wesentlich zu modifizieren—von alledem hat man hier noch keine Ahnung. Vielleicht lernt man es, wenn es zu spät ist, d. h. wenn diese Manier zu Komponieren Schule gemacht hat.

(F. Spiro, *Signale*, Berlin, April 21, 1909)

[Debussy's *Pelléas et Mélisande* was mercilessly booed, ridiculed and derided. But it is not impossible that the dead will be called back to life once more. No objections are raised here to Maeterlinck's delicate poetry. As to the nature of the composition, no one here has an inkling that it is quite feasible to play the music of the fourth act to the text of the first, and vice versa, or even turn the score upside down or put it in front of a mirror and perform it in this manner without an essential change in its effect. Perhaps, people will realize this when it will be too late, that is, when this style of composition will have established a school.]

-:-

La musique récente me fait l'effet d'une momie richement ornée, mais ne gardant l'apparence humaine qu'à grand renfort d'ingrédients. Ce n'est plus de la composition, c'est de la décomposition. La musique de Debussy a la grâce d'une jolie poitrinaire, aux regards languissants, aux gestes anémiés et dont la perversité a le charme de ce qui est frappé de mort. Une symphonie, un morceau, sont un organisme. L'organisme Debussyste rappelle celui des méduses dont la substance translucide s'irise brillamment aux rais du soleil à fleur de la vague, mais qui ne seront jamais que des protozoaires. . . Tout cela manque de nerf et de sang. J'ai la sensation d'une originalité déguisant une sorte d'impuissance.

(Alfred Mortier, *Rubriques Nouvelles*, Paris, December 1909)

[Recent music produces on me the effect of a richly adorned mummy which keeps human appearance only by great reinforcement of the ingredients. It is no longer composition, it is decomposition. The music of Debussy has the attractiveness of a pretty tubercular maiden, with her languorous glances, anemic gestures, whose perversity has the charm of one marked for death. A symphony, a piece of music, are organisms. A Debussyan organism reminds us of the jellyfish whose translucid substance lights up brilliantly at the touch of a sunlit wave, but which will never be anything but a protozoan. All this lacks fiber and blood. I have the sensation of originality covering up a kind of impotence.]

-:-

La Demoiselle élue de M. Claude Debussy, dont certains ont imaginé de faire chef d'école (!) . . . comprend un chœur et un long solo de voix récitante. . . Pas l'ombre de rythme: des harmonies vacillantes et fluides; pas même de nuances. Tout dans cette musique est indéterminé, vague, flottant, indécis, volontairement indéfini; musique amorphe, sans muscles et sans arêtes; musique grise, formant comme un brouillard sonore, que l'on voudrait percer pour voir s'il y a quelque chose derrière, mais que son opacité somnolente laisse impénetrable.

(Arthur Pougin, *Le Ménestrel,* Paris, April 9, 1910)

[*La Demoiselle élue* by Monsieur Claude Debussy whom some people intend to make the leader of a school (!) comprises a chorus and a long solo of vocal recitative. Not a shadow of rhythm; vacillating and fluid harmonies; not even any nuances. All in this music is indeterminate, vague, fleeting, indecisive, deliberately indefinite; formless music without muscle or backbone; gray music forming a sort of sonorous mist which one would like to pierce to see whether there is anything behind it, but whose somnolent opacity makes it impenetrable.]

-:-

La musique de M. Debussy qui prétend faire fi de tout élément mélodique, ne peut paraître qu'étrangement vaine, vide et inexistante . . . Qu'on n'objecte pas, que la même critique fût jadis adressée à Wagner, car ses adversaires étaient de ceux à qui la mélodie Wagnerienne échappait, alors que, de l'aveu même de M. Debussy, sa musique, à lui, n'en contient aucune trace. . . Elle déferle en petites notes vagues dont le va-et-vient berceur finit par nous donner comme une sensation de roulis. . . Cet art amorphe, si peu viril, semble fait tout exprés pour sensibilités fatiguées . . . quelque chose à la fois d'aigre et de douceâtre, qui éveille, on ne sait comment, une idée d'équivoque et de fraude . . . l'art minuscule que certains, naïvement, proclament l'art de l'avenir et qu'ils opposent, sans rire, à celui de Wagner. . . Il se réduit à une poussière musicale, une mosaïque d'accords. . . . art lilliputien pour une humanité des plus réduites.

(Raphaël Cor, 'M. Claude Debussy et le Snobisme Contemporain,' in *Le Cas Debussy*, Paris, 1910)

[The music of M. Debussy which professes to dismiss all elements of melody, apears strangely futile, vacuous and non-existent. Let no one object that the same criticism was once directed against Wagner, for the Wagnerian melody eluded his adversaries, whereas the music of M. Debussy, according to his own admission, contains no trace of melody. It splashes little vague notes whose lulling vibration ends by giving a sensation of sea-sickness. This amorphous art, so little virile, seems to be made specially for tired senses. It is something both bitter and sweetish, which evokes somehow the idea of falseness and fraud . . . a dimunitive art which some naively proclaim as the art of the future, opposing it, without a smile, to that of Wagner. . . It reduces itself to musical dust, a mosaic of chords . . . a lilliputian art for dwarfish humanity.]

-:-

'Quelle est l'importance réelle et quel est et doit être le rôle de M. Claude Debussy dans l'évolution musicale contemporaine?'—J'estime cette importance minime et je souhaite que le rôle le soit aussi. 'Représente-t-il une nouveauté féconde?'—Non. 'Une formule et une direction susceptibles de faire école, et doit-il-faire école en effet?'—Non, et encore non.

(A statement by Camille Bellaigue in reply to the questionnaire sent in 1909 by *La Revue du Temps Présent,* and published in *Le Cas Debussy*, Paris, 1910)

['What is the real importance and what is and ought to be the role of M. Claude Debussy in the contemporary evolution of music?'—I believe that this importance is infinitesimal, and I wish that his role would also be that. 'Does he represent a fertile innovation?' —No. 'A method and a direction susceptible to establish a school, and should he actually establish a school?'—No, and again no.]

-:-

M. Debussy ne ressemble à personne: déformateur musical et impressionniste; il correspond peut-être à quelque catégorie nerveuse difficile à désigner: mais voir en lui un chef d'école, une nouveauté et quoi que ce soit de profitable aux autres, c'est oublier que tous les chefs-d'œuvre se ressemblent parce qu'ils obéïssent aux mêmes règles de Palestrina à Wagner, de Bach à Berlioz et à Franck.

(A statement by Joséphin Péladan in reply to a questionnaire submitted by *La Revue du Temps Présent* in 1909, and published in *Le Cas Debussy,* Paris, 1910)

[M. Debussy is unlike anybody; he is a musical distorter and impressionist; he belongs, perhaps, to some nervous category difficult to designate; but to see in him the head of a school, an innovator, anything that may be beneficial to others, is to forget that all masterpieces resemble each other because they obey the same rules, from Palestrina to Wagner, from Bach to Berlioz and Franck.]

-:-

Debussy érige en principe l'absence de mélodie et de rythme, renonçant ainsi aux deux éléments constitutifs de la musique. Comme manifestation, d'une époque et de ses tendances, son œuvre mérite d'être prise en considération. Mais il n'y a pas moyen d'en tirer la moindre promesse pour l'avenir.

(A statement by Siegmund von Hausegger, in reply to a questionnaire sent out in 1909 by *La Revue du Temps Présent,* and published in *Le Cas Debussy,* Paris, 1910)

[Debussy elevates to a principle the absence of melody and rhythm, thus renouncing the two constituent elements of music. As a sign of our epoch and its tendencies, his work deserves consideration. But there is no way to derive from it the least promise for the future.]

-:-

Pelléas . . . cette poussière musicale prête à s'envoler au premier souffle, ces bégaiements, ces chuchotements, ces caresses furtives, ces frôlements où s'attardent des amants anémiés, qui ne peuvent se hausser jusqu'à la volupté et prennent leurs petits spasmes d'une seconde pour des transports d'amour et de passion. Les amoureux de M. Debussy semblent fatigués de naissance; on dirait qu'ils ont peur d'agir. . . Ce bêlements plaintifs, ces jérémiades, ces lamentations perpétuelles me causent une souffrance physique. . . L'amour de Pelléas me fait effet d'un traité de neurasthénie et d'impuissance.

(From a statement by A. Chéramy in reply to a questionnaire submitted in 1909 by *La Revue du Temps Présent,* and published in *Le Cas Debussy,* Paris, 1910)

[*Pelléas* . . . this musical dust about to fly off at a first breath, this stammering, this muttering, these furtive caresses, these contacts at which the anemic lovers pause, and, incapable of real passion, take their puny spasms of a second's duration for the ecstasies of love. The lovers of M. Debussy seem tired from birth; one might say that they are afraid to act. . . These plaintive bleatings, these jeremiads, these perpetual lamentations give me physical pain. The love of Pelléas produces the impression of a treatise on neurasthenia and impotence.]

-:-

Je crois qu'il y a une part énorme de snobisme et de bluff dans la réputation de ce musicien. . . . Moins que toute autre, la formule debussyste est susceptible de faire école. 'L'exemple a prouvé surabondamment qu'elle pouvait susciter les contrefaçons. Mais tous ces pasticheurs d'une manière où l'artifice joue déjà un si grand rôle n'ont abouti qu'à un art vide, froid, abstrait, et le plus mort qui ait paru depuis longtemps. Toute imitation préconçue est regrettable en art. Mais il n'en saurait être de plus vaine que celle de Debussysme.

(From a statement by Paul Flat in reply to a questionnaire submitted in 1909 by *La Revue du Temps Présent,* and published in *Le Cas Debussy,* Paris, 1910)

[I believe that there is an enormous amount of snobbism and bluff in the reputation of this musician. . . . The Debussyan formula is less than any other capable of creating a school. But this instance has proved abundantly that it can create counterfeit. However, all these makers of pastiche in a style in which artifice already plays such a great role have accomplished nothing but an art that is empty, cold, abstract, the deadest art that has appeared in a long time. All preconceived imitation is deplorable in art. But there is none that is so fruitless as the imitation in Debussysm.]

-:-

It would be impossible to conceive a finer vehicle of expression than that invented by Debussy through the simple yet original process of abolishing rhythm, melody and tonality from music and thus leaving nothing but atmosphere. If we could abolish from the human organization flesh, blood and bones, we should still have membrane. Membranous music is perhaps the fitting expression of *Pelléas et Mélisande.*

(James Gibbons Huneker, New York *Sun,* February 8, 1911)

-:-

Le *Prélude à l'Après-midi d'un faune* est d'une jolie sonorité, mais on n'y trouve pas la moindre idée musicale proprement dite; cela ressemble à un morceau de musique comme la palette, sur laquelle un peintre a travaillé, ressemble à un tableau. Debussy n'a pas créé un style; il a cultivé l'absence de style, de logique et de sens commun.

(Saint-Saëns in a letter to Maurice Emmanuel, dated August 4, 1920, published in *La Revue Musicale,* 1947)

[The *Prélude à l'Après-midi d'un faune* has pretty sonority, but one does not find in it the least musical idea, properly speaking; it resembles a piece of music as the palette used by an artist in his work resembles a picture. Debussy did not create a style; he cultivated an absence of style, logic, and common sense.]

-:-

At the Lexington Avenue Opera House I recently listened to an alleged opera called *Pelléas and Mélisande* in which a modern 'composer' has tried to realize in sounds and scenes the Maeterlinck play of that name. . . Dramatic action there was none, while music was reduced to a weaker Wagnerian orchestral comment—one long succession of puffs and snippets of melody and color . . . the same ridiculous awe-inspiring growlings and gruntings of the cellos and basses, the sudden stops, the long holdings of the chalumeau tones that Wagner has made us familiar with. The more inane the procedure of the music drama, the greater seemed the attention. People leaned forward and held their breath so as not to miss anything! . . . This crowning masterpiece of civilized European stupidity and lack of humor was holding them in a vice. The fake really worked.

(Carroll Brent Chilton, *The De-Assification of Music,* 'A Propagandist Magazine of One Number, Containing News of Importance to All Music Lovers, Especially to All Owners of Player Pianos,' New York, 1922)

Les Commandements du Catéchisme du Conservatoire

I. *Dieu*bussy seul adoreras
Et copieras parfaitement.
II. Mélodieux point ne seras
De fait ni de consentement.
III. De plan toujours tu t'abstiendras
Pour composer plus aisément.
IV. Avec grand soin tu violeras
Des règles du vieux rudiment.
V. Quintes de suite tu feras
Et octaves pareillement.
VI. Au grand jamais ne résoudras
De dissonance aucunement.
VII. Aucun morceau ne finiras
Jamais par accord consonnant.
VIII. Des neuvièmes accumuleras
Et sans aucun discernement.
IX. L'accord parfait ne désireras
Qu'en mariage seulement.
Ad Gloriam Tuam

I. Thou shalt adore God-Debussy only,
And copy him perfectly.
II. Thou shalt never be melodious
In fact or by condonement.
III. Thou shalt abstain from planning ever,
So as to compose with more facility.
IV. With great care thou shalt violate
The rules of the old primer.
V. Thou shalt use consecutive fifths
As well as consecutive octaves.
VI. Thou shalt never—oh never—
Resolve a dissonance in any manner.
VII. Thou shalt never end a piece
With a consonant chord.
VIII. Thou shalt accumulate ninth-chords
Without any discrimination.
IX. Thou shalt not desire a perfect concord
Except in marriage.
Ad Gloriam Tuam

(Satie signed these verses ERIT SATIS, i.e., This Will Be Enough; they were published posthumously in *La Semaine Musicale,* Paris, November 11, 1927)

FRANCK Les mélodies de M. Franck naissent pour se perdre aussitôt. . . Oh! l'aride et grise musique, dépourvue de grâce, de charme et de sourire. . . Les motifs eux-mêmes manquent le plus souvent d'intérêt: le premier, sorte de point d'interrogation musical, n'est guère au-dessus de ces thèmes qu'on fait développer par les élèves du Conservatoire. . . Le finale surtout de la symphonie en ré mineur nous a paru pénible. Il ramène avec rage les motifs des morceaux précédents.

(Camille Bellaigue, *Revue des Deux Mondes,* Paris, March 15, 1888)

[M. Franck's melodies are born to vanish at once. Oh, arid and gray music, devoid of grace, charm and smile! The motives themselves are in most cases uninteresting; the first, a sort of musical question mark, is hardly superior to those themes that are given for development to conservatory students. Particularly the Finale of the Symphony seemed painful to us. It furiously brings back the motives of the preceding movements.]

-:-

La Symphonie en ré mineur de César Franck se traine lentement, péniblement. Elle expose solennellement des phrases dont le principal mérite résulte de la gravité, du sérieux imperturbable avec lesquels on les présente. Cette musique est morose et fait naître pompeusement l'ennui. Le maître avait à dire ici très peu de choses mais il les proclame avec une conviction de pontife définissant le dogme.

(*Le Ménestrel,* Paris, November 26, 1893)

[The Symphony in D minor by César Franck drags slowly, painfully. It solemnly presents phrases whose chief merit comes from gravity, imperturbable seriousness with which they are given. This music is morose and pompously generates tedium. The maître had very little to say here, but he proclaims it with the conviction of the pontiff defining the dogma.]

-:-

The Franck Symphony is not a hilarious work . . . charcoal would make a white mark upon the Cimmerian darkness of its first movement. One hears the creaking of the machinery, one watches the development with no greater emotion than would be evoked by a mathematical demonstrator at the blackboard.

(Louis Elson, Boston *Daily Advertiser,* December 25, 1899)

GERSHWIN How trite and feeble and conventional the tunes are [in the *Rhapsody in Blue*]; how sentimental and vapid the harmonic treatment, under its disguise of fussy and futile counterpoint! . . . Weep over the lifelessness of the melody and harmony, so derivative, so stale, so inexpressive!

(Lawrence Gilman, New York *Tribune*, February 13, 1924)

-:-

An American in Paris is nauseous claptrap, so dull, patchy, thin, vulgar, long-winded and inane, that the average movie audience would be bored by it. . . This cheap and silly affair seemed pitifully futile and inept.

(Herbert F. Peyser, New York *Telegram*, December 14, 1928)

-:-

The honks have it. Four automobile horns, vociferously assisted by three saxophones, two tom-toms, rattle, xylophone, wire brush, wood blocks, and an ensemble not otherwise innocent of brass and percussion blew or thumped the lid off in Carnegie Hall when *An American in Paris* by George Gershwin had its first performance. . . . For those not too deeply concerned with any apparently outmoded niceties of art, it was an amusing occasion. . . They found the musical buffoonery of Gershwin's *An American in Paris* good fun in spite of, or perhaps because of its blunt banality and its ballyhoo vulgarity. . . To conceive of a symphonic audience listening to it with any degree of pleasure or patience twenty years from now, when whoopee is no longer even a word, is another matter. Then . . . there will still be Franck with his outmoded spirituality.

(Oscar Thompson, New York *Evening Post*, December 21, 1928)

-:-

Perhaps it is needlessly Draconian to begrudge Mr. Gershwin the song hits which he has scattered through his score [*Porgy and Bess*] and which will doubtless enhance his fame and popularity. Yet they mar it. They are its cardinal weakness. They are the blemish upon its musical integrity. Listening to such sure-fire rubbish as the duet between Porgy and Bess, 'You is my woman now,' . . . you wonder how the composer . . . could stoop to such easy and such needless conquests.

(Lawrence Gilman, New York *Herald Tribune*, October 11, 1935)

GOUNOD Le poème de *La Reine de Saba* est sans doute d'une déplorable indigence; mais l'insuffisance du poème ne saurait excuser le musicien. . . M. Gounod a le malheur d'admirer certaines parties alterées des derniers quatuors de Beethoven. C'est la source troublée d'où sont sortis les mauvais musiciens de l'Allemagne moderne, les Liszt, les Wagner, les Schumann, sans omettre Mendelssohn pour certaines parties équivoques de son style. Si M. Gounod a réellement épousé la doctrine de la mélodie continue . . . mélodie que l'on peut comparer à la lettre d'Arlequin: 'pour les points et les virgules, je ne m'en occupe pas; je vous laisse la liberté de les placer où vous voudrez,' M. Gounod serait irrévocablement perdu.

(P. Scudo, *La Revue des Deux Mondes,* Paris, March 15, 1862)

[The libretto of *The Queen of Sheba* is certainly of deplorably low quality; but the inadequacy of the libretto is no excuse for a musician. M. Gounod has the misfortune of admiring certain enharmonic progressions of the last quartets of Beethoven. This is the troubled waters from which came the bad musicians of modern Germany, the Liszts, the Wagners, the Schumanns, not omitting Mendelssohn in some ambiguous aspects of his style. If M. Gounod has really espoused the doctrine of endless melody . . . melody that one can compare to Harlequin's saying: 'I am not preoccupied with periods and commas, I leave it to you to place them where you please'—then, M. Gounod is irrevocably lost.]

-:-

Boito strains to paint heaven, Berlioz hell, Wagner the subterranean regions, and Gounod the Golgotha earthquake. Material imitation is the most rabid and rampant feature of the day. What next will the straining and presumptuous blunderers attempt? Monsieur Gounod possibly thinks that his music, too, is the music of the future. . . What is music coming to? Is it in its decline and fall? Fast going to the dogs in senile insanity, whose normal features are gross materialism and material grossness?

(*Musical Standard,* London, August 5, 1882)

HARRIS The *Overture From the Gayety and Sadness of the American Scene* by Roy Harris proved to be not only monumental but colossal—a colossal failure. Not only from the sound, but from the looks of things, it appeared that the musicians were imposed upon. To face the notes of such a music-less composition without becoming eligible for life membership in the booby hatch is a surprise to me.

(*The Citizen-News,* Hollywood, December 30, 1932)

-:-

Mr. Harris's *American Creed* invites kidding, as all of his programmatically prefaced works do. . . No composer in the world . . . makes such shameless use of patriotic feelings to advertise his product. One would think, to read his prefaces, that he had been awarded by God, or at least by popular vote, a monopolistic privilege of exposing our nation's deepest ideals and highest aspirations. And when the piece so advertised turns out to be mostly not very clearly orchestrated schoolish counterpoint and a quite skimpy double fugue (neither of which has any American connotation whatsoever), one is tempted to put the whole thing down as insincere and a bad joke.

(Virgil Thomson, New York *Herald Tribune,* November 21, 1940)

-:-

How blessed are they who are born deaf, and are spared the agony of listening to the hideous sounds of Symphony No. 3 by Roy Harris, just performed by the BBC Symphony Orchestra. Roy Harris should have stuck to truck driving instead of insulting music-lovers with his senseless noise.

(Letter to the Editor, *Radio Times,* London, June 12, 1942)

-:-

There was one deadly number, a clamorous and incoherent piece entitled *Cumberland Concerto* by Roy Harris. Harris had the gall to come out afterwards and take a bow.

(New York *Daily News,* November 12, 1951)

D'INDY The Entracte from *The Stranger* was one of the modern 'puzzle pieces.' We might suggest changing the title from the comparative to the superlative.

(Louis Elson, Boston *Daily Advertiser,* March 6, 1904)

-:-

The Second Symphony by d'Indy shows the work of a musical scientist who knows the orchestra thoroughly and takes daring liberties in progressions, cross harmonies and modulations, and juggles chromatics, ascending and descending, in a way to grieve the ear of the average concert attendant.

(Boston *Globe,* January 8, 1905)

-:-

D'Indy's symphony (????) is so unutterably shocking to us that we hesitate to express our frank opinion. It is evident that harmony books are now mere waste paper, that there are no more rules, that there is to be an eleventh commandment for the composer—'Thou shalt avoid all beauty.'

(Louis Elson, Boston *Daily Advertiser,* January 8, 1905)

-:-

The Second Symphony of d'Indy . . . is one long stretch of ugliness, a single piece of weird tonalities, hideous progressions, barren wastes of mechanism.

(Boston *Journal,* January 8, 1905)

-:-

Vincent d'Indy's Second Symphony is one of the works of the altogether utter modern school which hates all harmonies not afflicted with strabismus. It revels in fractured sevenths, dislocated ninths and unlucky thirteenths. When it cannot think of anything to do to make the blood curdle and the spine waggle, it snatches two minor seconds in different keys and incites them to murderous combat with one another. Proceedings of this sort administer galvanic shocks to the nerves and make people squirm in their seats so that at least they cannot go to sleep. . . People who do not like harmonies suggestive of rampant lemons and inebriated persimmons will not enjoy this Symphony.

(W. J. Henderson, New York *Sun,* January 13, 1905)

Wagner accused Berlioz of ciphering with notes, but Berlioz's works are the acme of poetry when compared with the musical arithmetic displayed in Vincent d'Indy's Second Symphony. Such music could at the best only produce a headache; it certainly could not soothe a heartache. . . There are certain formulas of ugliness which recur again and again in the Symphony. The skip of an upward seventh, the use of the augmented fifth (both with and without the seventh), the passages of major seconds, do not lose their ugliness by repetition, but they cease to surprise.

(Louis Elson, Boston *Daily Advertiser*, December 4, 1905)

-:-

There are those to whom the outgivings of the modern French musicians are as the preludings of a new birth of music, and to them Mr. d'Indy's Second Symphony presents the quintessence of a new and unfamiliar beauty. To most, it is an unmeaning cacophony, a striving after something not realized or unrealizable. . . There are passages of strange and fantastic cackle, in which the instruments are forced to unnatural utterance. . . The modern Frenchmen greatly affect the augmented intervals in harmony and strange dislocations of the sequence of tone and semitone in the melodic line. . . They wish to reconstitute our ears. . . But until they do, it is doubtful if Mr. d'Indy's Second Symphony will gain other than a painful and laborious access to its listeners.

(Richard Aldrich, New York *Times*, December 8, 1905)

-:-

Vincent d'Indy, stepfather of dissonance, fears a theme as something pernicious and vulgar. And the lengths! The stretches of barren, mincing tonal speech!

(*Town Topics*, Boston, December 14, 1905)

-:-

Mr. d'Indy's melodic and harmonic idioms belong to the outer extreme of that pungent world of dissonance in which Mr. Debussy dreams his operatic visions and Mr. Strauss makes orgies of song and story. . . Thrice blessed is he who can revel in this concourse of sour sounds. Even *Ein Heldenleben* becomes as the croon of a cradle song beside this.

(W. J. Henderson, New York *Sun*, December 10, 1909)

KRENEK Die Kunst, die Schubert als die Heilige besingt, die Königin sein sollte, zur Prostituirten erniedrigt wird. Und ein unaustilgbarer Makel bleibt an dem anhaften, der unter zynischer Verachtung ethischer und künstlerischer Urgesetze, um die er sich den Teufel kümmert, das Hohe in die Gemeinheit herabzerrt. Das hat Herr Krenek mit seinem *Jonny* zwar schon ausgiebig besorgt.

(Fritz Ohrmann, *Signale*, Berlin, December 12, 1928)

[The art that Schubert glorified as holy, that should be a Queen, is debased to a prostitute. An indelible stain remains on one who, in his cynical disdain of the prime laws of ethics and art, about which he does not give a damn, drags down the exalted to the common. Herr Krenek has fully accomplished it in his *Jonny Spielt Auf*.]

-:-

Krenek's Fourth Symphony is so removed from the listener's normal experience that one has a feeling of suddenly being transported to Mars not knowing whether to be amused or infuriated.

(John Briggs, New York *Post*, November 28, 1947)

-:-

Krenek's Fourth Symphony is a pseudo-masterpiece, with about as much savor to it as a pasteboard turkey.

(Virgil Thomson, New York *Herald Tribune*, November 28, 1947)

-:-

The American critic Olin Downes has observed once that Krenek belongs to the category of a new disillusioned civilization, whose creative process is dry, unromantic and emotionally sterile. In his monstrous operas, Krenek glorifies the vilest perversions of human nature, as in the idiotic *Sprung über den Schatten*. He modernizes the ancient story of Orestes by introducing American jazz, and in *Jonny Spielt Auf*, he cynically eliminates every living, warm human emotion. Here love is perverted into an animal, cattle-like concupiscence; there is nothing in it but filth, dirt, cold cruelty and sticky frog-like sexuality, combined with the dry rationalism of a biped calculating machine.

(V. Gorodinsky, *Music of Spiritual Poverty*, Moscow, 1950)

LISZT Liszt is a mere commonplace person, with his hair on end —a snob out of Bedlam. He writes the ugliest music extant.

(*Dramatic and Musical Review*, London, January 7, 1843)

-:-

Nous dirons fort peu de choses des compositions de M. Liszt. Sa musique est à peu près inexécutable pour tout autre que lui; ce sont des improvisations sans ordre et sans idées, aussi prétentieuses que bizarres.

(P. Scudo, *Critique et Littérature Musicales*, Paris, 1852)

[We shall say very little about M. Liszt's compositions. His music is all but unplayable by anyone but himself; it represents improvisations without order and without ideas, as pretentious as they are bizarre.]

-:-

It is well known that Richard Wagner has little respect for any music but his own . . . and that he is earnestly bent on upsetting all the accepted forms and canons of art . . . in order the more surely to establish his doctrines that rhythm is superfluous, counterpoint a useless bore, and every musician, ancient or modern, himself excepted, either an imposter or a blockhead. Now such rhodomontade may pass muster in the dreary streets of Weimar, where Franz Liszt reigns, like a musical King of Death, and quaffs destruction to harmony with beer and metaphysics, the Teutonic dilettanti have allowed their wits to go astray, and become dupes of the grossest charlatanism; but in England, where the beer and the philosophy are manufactured from more substantial and less deleterious stuff, it can hardly be.

(*Musical World*, London, January 20, 1855)

-:-

Turn your eyes to any one composition that bears the name of Liszt, if you are unlucky enough to have such a thing on your pianoforte, and answer frankly, if it contains one bar of genuine music. Composition indeed!—decomposition is the proper word for such hateful fungi, which choke up and poison the fertile plains of harmony, threatening the world with drought.

(*Musical World*, London, June 30, 1855)

Something about Faust by Liszt, rubbish that gave one a sensation like that produced by eating sour apples or chokecherries.

(George Templeton Strong's Diary, February 23, 1867)

-:-

For finale, Liszt's poème symphonique, *Lamento e Trionfo*. The *Lamento* was expressed by dreary phrases of the celli and double-basses that seemed suggestive of a cow in a strange lane seeking an abducted calf and seeking it in vain. The *Trionfo,* by crashing brass chords, illustrated by fantasias on the triangle, apparently descriptive of the triumphant hero with his hands in his pockets, jingling his pennies and his bunch of keys. A long rigmarole on fourth page of the program informed mankind that all this rubbish meant something about Tasso! The production of this trash and its endurance without audible protest disgraced the audience.

(George Templeton Strong's Diary, March 9, 1867)

-:-

We were afflicted by *Préludes,* poème symphonique by the miserable Liszt. They set my teeth on edge.

(George Templeton Strong's Diary, May 4, 1867)

-:-

The music of Liszt to Dante's Hell and Purgatory is to our thinking the worst that composers of this school can do. We are thankful to believe that in this symphony they have run their course to its very end and exhausted their power of perversion. Having lived through that hour of agony, during which the symphony lasted, and escaped with reason not overthrown, we can safely bid defiance to Liszt, Wagner, and their fellow madmen of the school of the future. . . It was like playing one of Beethoven's symphonies backward. . . The tortures of the damned were to be illustrated, and this congenial theme gave Liszt a famous excuse for unheard of bewilderment of his orchestra. . . It seemed as though Beelzebub, prince of devils, must have stood at the composer's right hand while he scored this work. . . The wonder is that Liszt's familiar spirit did not inspire him to compose for each class of instruments in a separate key. The effect of demoniac confusion and horror at which he aimed would then certainly have been attained, and his audience sent howling with anguish out of the house. . . The doors might then be closed on the audience, the orchestra tied down to their seats, and all the clergymen of the city invited to witness the result. . . . In fact, we know of nothing better calculated to call the obdurate to repentance than this work of Liszt's, for if any person could fully be brought to realize that his punishment hereafter would consist in being compelled forever to listen to the symphony that we heard for an hour on Saturday night, there is, we venture to say, no man living bold enough to contemplate unmoved such a doom, or who would not at once take measures to be rescued from so terrible a fate.

(New York *Sun*, April 4, 1870)

-:-

The Unfinished Symphony, by Schubert, may gain on further acquaintance. The orchestral part of a concerto by Liszt, very vile—a catarrhal or sternutatory concerto. One frequently recurring phrase is a graphic instrumentation of a fortissimo sneeze, and a long passage is evidently meant to suggest a protracted, agonized bravura on the pocket handkerchief. There were also coughs, snorts, and periods of choking. It's a great work!

(George Templeton Strong's Diary, November 4, 1870)

-:-

The worst of all, and positively devilish, was the *Mephisto Waltz.* . . . Such music is simply diabolical, and shuts out every ray of light or heaven from whence music sprang.

(*Dwight's Journal of Music,* Boston, November 5, 1870)

-:-

The Liszt Concerto is filthy and vile. It suggests Chinese orchestral performances as described by enterprising and self-sacrificing travelers. This may be a specimen of the School of the Future for aught I know. If it is, the future will throw the works of Haydn, Mozart and Beethoven into the rubbish bin.

(George Templeton Strong's Diary, November 19, 1870)

-:-

Liszt's orchestral music is an insult to art. It is gaudy musical harlotry, savage and incoherent bellowings.

(Boston *Gazette,* quoted in *Dexter Smith's Paper,* April 1872)

Both the Old and New Philharmonic Societies took a plunge into the 'Future,' the former by producing Liszt's symphonic poem, *Tasso,* the latter by giving a long selection from Wagner's *Lohengrin. . .* Neither Liszt nor Wagner gained much by Philharmonic patronage. The first was heard with an ear half-astonished, half-bewildered, as one listens to the outpouring of gibberish delivered with an air of an oracle and the pomp of an orator. The second simply wearied his audience, and in spite of occasional lapses into intelligibleness, acted upon them like water upon sugar. The atoms of the crowd lost cohesion and drifted out into the street.

(Quoted from an unidentified source in the *Musical World,* London, July 26, 1873)

-:-

Welch unwiderstehliche Aufgabe für die erotische Flagellanten–Musik der Liszt-Wagnerschen Schule! Liszt illustrirt die Lenausche Dorfschenke in einem ausgeführten Orchesterstück; dasselbe beginnt gleich mit so teuflischen Dissonanzen, dass dem Hörer eine Schlangenhaut über den Rücken läuft und die Zähne wehtun. Die Bässe spielen durch 24 Tacte die leere Quinte *e-h,* über welcher zuerst die Quinte *fis-cis,* dann *zusammen* die beiden Quinten *h-fis* und *d-a* angeschlagen werden und schliesslich, der grässliche Quinten-Aufbau *e-h-fis-d-a-e* sich erhebt! Liszt stellt einfach die musikalischen Naturgesetze auf den Kopf, und unfähig, aus eigenen Mitteln Schönes zu schaffen, ersinnt er mit Absicht das Hässliche.

(Eduard Hanslick, 1873)

[What an irresistible subject for erotic flaggelant music of the Liszt-Wagner School! *Mephisto Waltz* illustrates the village inn of Lenau in a full-fledged orchestral piece; it begins at once with devilish dissonances that send chills down the listener's spine, and give him a toothache. The basses play for 24 bars the empty fifth, E-B, over which is struck first the fifth, F♯–C♯, and then two fifths, B–F♯ and D–A *together;* and finally rises the monstrous edifice of fifths, E–B–F♯–D–A–E. Liszt simply turns all natural laws of music upside down. Incapable of creating the beautiful by his own means, he deliberately builds up the hideous.]

-:-

A complete novelty of the last Crystal Palace concert was provided in the shape of a Pianoforte Concerto in A major by Liszt. The Concerto consists of one movement only, but this includes within itself no less than seven changes of time and expression. . . A more chaotic effect could hardly have been produced had the notes been drawn, haphazard, out of the toy known as the musical kaleidoscope. Why was such trash allowed to figure in the program? Are instrumental soloists allowed to play whatever they choose?

(*Sporting News*, London, November 28, 1874)

-:-

Of the new German school . . . Liszt is one of the most defiant, his *Faust Symphony* being a monstrously exaggerated proof of the fact. . . . A very attentive and careful hearing of it disclosed to us little beyond a series of violent and spasmodic effects, in crude association and distorted contrast. . . Liszt has too often mistaken arrogant self-assertion for the prompting of genius, confused obscurity for metaphysical profundity, and an insolent contempt of all classical precedents of musical composition for an innate originality that we have hitherto failed to find in his works, otherwise than in a disagreeable and repugnant sense.

(*Daily News*, London, March 12, 1880)

-:-

Not even the weird fancy of Middle Age painters has conjured up anything equivalent in repulsiveness to the noises of Liszt. The instruments seem to have gone mad with one consent. . . If this *Faust* Symphony is music at all, it is music degraded. What has the heavenly maid done, in all her sweetness and benignity, that she should be galvanized into contortions that disgust and repel?

(*Musical World*, London, March 20, 1880)

-:-

Liszt's symphony to Dante's *Divina Commedia* deals with the Inferno, and infernal enough it is in confusion, noise and incoherence. . . . It appears to us that Liszt wasted much valuable time in committing this work to paper, as he could have saved his labor by instructing the orchestra to play for fifteen minutes anything that occurred to them at the moment, providing that they never relaxed from making the noisiest and most inharmonious charivari possible.

The only good that can be accomplished by such a composition is in adding a new terror to the hereafter of the wicked. From that point of view it may well deserve the title of the Music of the Future.

(Boston *Gazette,* November 22, 1880)

-:-

One is still a little timid of calling the Liszt *Faust* Symphony nonsense, for fear that it might turn out in the end to be a great, if misunderstood work. . . It seems too much like a sheer nothing, on the grandest possible scale. . . It may be the Music of the Future, but it sounds remarkably like the Cacophony of the Present.

(W. F. Apthorp, *Musical Review,* New York, December 23, 1880)

-:-

Bülow begann mit Liszts H-moll Sonate. . . Freilich lässt sich durch Worte keine Vorstellung von diesem musikalischen Unwesen geben. Nie habe ich ein raffinirteres, frecheres Aneinanderfügen der disparatesten Elemente erlebt, nie ein so wüstes Toben, einen so blutigen Kampf gegen alles was musikalisch ist. Anfangs verblüfft, dann entsetzt, fühlte ich mich doch schliesslich überwältigt von der unausbleiblichen Komik. . . Da hört jede Kritik, jede Diskussion auf. Wer *das* gehört hat und es schön findet, dem ist nicht zu helfen.

(Eduard Hanslick, 1881)

[Bülow began with Liszt's B-minor Sonata. It is impossible to convey through words an idea of this musical monstrosity. Never have I experienced a more contrived and insolent agglomeration of the most disparate elements, a wilder rage, a bloodier battle against all that is musical. At first I felt bewildered, then shocked, and finally overcome with irresistible hilarity. . . Here all criticism, all discussion must cease. Who has heard *that,* and finds it beautiful, is beyond help.]

-:-

All we can say is, that if the sounds given forth in Liszt's *Hungaria* were really heard in the Hungarian struggle, it was a wonder that the enemies of the Magyar race did not run away sooner, for we can hardly imagine any human beings of any race or color who could listen without terror and dismay to such unearthly sounds.

It is the peculiarity of Liszt . . . to place his passages in those portions of the particular instruments . . . where the most disagreeable sounds can be got. For example, the violinists are always capering and scraping nearly up to the bridge, where the tone is apt to resemble the forlorn wail of an amorous cat upon the tiles at midnight. If he has a passage for the bassoon, it is where the tone reminds one most naturally of the sigh of a prize pig at a cattle show. . . . The performers on the deeper stringed instruments must use their bows as timber men do their saws in cutting through the massive trunk of some monarch of the forest. The conductor wields his baton, but the effect is not a bit more agreeable than if each performer threw down the notes and played at random with all his might and energy. In fact, we cordially recommend the society to adopt the plan. Let the conductor . . . give instructions to each player to produce every discordant sound that is in the range of his particular instrument, and let the cacophony continue for half an hour under the title of *Lunacy* or *Moonstruck*.

(*Era*, London, February 25, 1882)

-:-

Liszt's Symphony to Dante's *Divina Commedia* was an infliction that we would gladly pass over in silence, were it not our imperative duty to register a protest against its insertion in a program designed for the gratification of intelligent amateurs. . . If we have been tempted to the verge of profanity, in speaking of this ludicrous exhibition of Liszt's pretentious incapacity and inordinate vanity, the blame rests with him. He also conveys a false impression, for, according to his musical teaching, Hell is preferable to Heaven, for it is at least amusing and ludicrous, whereas Heaven is unsufferably dull and uninteresting. . . We earnestly hope that so excellent an orchestra . . . will not again be subjected to the degradation of assisting in the promulgation of such pernicious rubbish.

(Boston *Courier*, February 25, 1882)

-:-

Liszt despises all system, all order, all coherence. Whatever comes uppermost in his singular mind is set down, and the result is chaos. . . . *Inferno*, the first movement of the Dante Symphony, is indeed infernal. We presume that Liszt intended to illustrate in music the tortures of the damned, and consequently the tones are nothing but a wild succession of the most fearful shrieks, groans, and yells that ever met the ear in a concert room. All the chords and passages that could by any possibility be written or played to express fiendish and discordant sounds are pressed into the service. The clank of steam hammers, the rattle of express trains, the howling of a hurricane, the roar of the ocean, the cries of wild beasts, are tame compared with the terrible uproar to be found in the score of Liszt.

(*Era,* London, April 29, 1882)

-:-

There is no doubt that Liszt has satisfactorily described the *Inferno.* Nothing so suggestive of unceasing torment and the wails of the damned has ever been written by mortal man. Let us hope the good Abbé will never go to a place where his own music is exceeded.

(Unidentified American newspaper, May 1882)

-:-

Liszt's *Faust* Symphony, intended to picture the conflicting emotions that struggle for mastery in the minds of Faust, rather suggests Hades and the jibes of torturing fiends, and the agonized sufferings of the victims. . . The enormous length of this incoherent and rambling tone-picture, bristling with the most excruciating dissonances, renders it exceedingly tiresome.

(Frederic Archer, *The Keynote,* New York, March 15, 1884)

-:-

Liszt's symphony to Dante's *Divina Commedia* is dedicated to Wagner, the first part being *Hell.* The business in hell was decidedly of an appalling character. The horrible chaos and noise can be compared to nothing but the upsetting of twenty thousand coal-scuttles; and the cries of the damned were everything that could be desired.

(Henry Labouchère, *Truth,* London, February 12, 1885)

-:-

Music will have fallen irrevocably into a condition of dry rot before such a composition as Liszt's Dante Symphony can be received at any higher value than that of a solemn travesty of all that is noble, beautiful and uplifting in the art. It is vulgar sensationalism run mad; a noisy tribute to bald orchestral effect. The whole work is a sombre farce in which the highest point of humor is reached in Liszt's attempt at fugal writing. The cacophony of the work is intolerable. It seems as though the composer had attempted to depict in music every moan and howl of pain ever heard by the human kind, from that caused by an agonizing colic to that produced by the woes of gout, interspersed now and then by a choice selection of the various shades of expression of which the voice of the nocturnal cat is capable.

(Boston *Gazette*, February 28, 1886)

-:-

I beg respectfully to suggest to Liszt and all 'musicians of the future,' get them carefully packed in air-tight boxes (like those awful preserved peas we are occasionally condemned to eat), and leave in their wills a stringent regulation that no rash hand shall bring them to light until at least 1966. We shall all be dead, then, my friend, and as for our decendants, *qu'ils s'arrangent!*

(*The Orchestra*, London, March 15, 1886)

-:-

Liszt's *Mephisto Waltz* is a hideous, incomprehensible jargon of noise, cacophony and eccentricity, musically valueless, and only interesting to ears that prefer confusion to meaning. . . It had about as much propriety on the program after Schumann and Handel as a wild boar would have in a drawing-room.

(Boston *Gazette*, November 20, 1887)

-:-

Liszt's bombast is bad; it is very bad; in fact there is only one thing worse in his music, and that is his affected and false simplicity. It was said of George Sand that she had a habit of speaking and writing concerning chastity in such terms that the very word became impure; so it is with the simplicity of Liszt.

(Philip Hale, Boston *Journal*, March 25, 1894)

MAHLER Strauss's *Heldenleben* and *Thus Spake Zarathustra* are clear as crystal waters in comparison with Gustav Mahler's Fourth Symphony. . . The Adagio, barring an abuse of organ point effects, is at first harmless enough; but suddenly we are introduced to a circus scene. This may be a not unwelcome diversion for some; but without wishing to be traditional or pedantic, we cannot but remark that for us, at that moment, it was a shock and an unpleasant one. From a business standpoint it might be advantageous to utilize portions of this adagio on the pleasure boats which travel up and down the Danube in the spring. The bands could easily master any difficulties forthcoming in such appropriate extracts, and the Viennese ladies, munching sweet cakes, sipping light wine and flirting with handsomely dressed officers, would no doubt very much enjoy a dainty accompaniment to their conversation.

(*Musical Courier*, New York, January 29, 1902)

-:-

The drooling and emasculated simplicity of Gustav Mahler! It is not fair to the readers of the *Musical Courier* to take up their time with a detailed description of that musical monstrosity, which masquerades under the title of Gustav Mahler's Fourth Symphony. There is nothing in the design, content, or execution of the work to impress the musician, except its grotesquerie. . . The writer of the present review frankly admits that . . . to him it was one hour or more of the most painful musical torture to which he has been compelled to submit.

(*Musical Courier*, New York, November 9, 1904)

-:-

It is a matter of extreme difficulty to detect tangible themes in the second movement of Mahler's Fifth Symphony, and it is an almost impossible task to follow them through the tortuous mazes of their formal and contrapuntal development. One has to cling by one's teeth, so to speak, to a shred of theme here and there, which appears for an occasional instant above the heavy masses of tone, only to be jumped upon immediately by the whole angry horde of instruments and stamped down into the very thick of the orchestral fray. The fighting grows so furious toward the finish that one is compelled to unclose one's teeth on the morsel of them, and lo and behold! it is seized upon, hurled through the screaming and frenzied ranks of the combatants, and that is the last seen or heard of the poor little rag of a theme.

(*Musical Courier*, New York, February 21, 1906)

-:-

Wenn Mahlers Musik jüdisch sprechen würde, wäre sie mir vielleicht unverständlich. Aber sie ist mir widerlich, weil sie *jüdelt.* Das heisst: sie spricht musikalisches Deutsch, aber mit dem Akzent, mit dem Tonfalle und vor allem auch mit der Geste des östlichen, des allzu östlichen Juden. . . Denn auch dem, den sie nicht gerade beleidigt, kann sie doch unmöglich etwas *sagen,* und man braucht von der künstlerischen Persönlichkeit Mahlers noch keineswegs abgestossen zu sein, um die völlige Leerheit und Nichtigkeit einer Kunst einzusehen, in der der Krampf eines ohnmächtigen Schein-Titanentums sich auflöst in das platte Behagen an gemeiner Nähmädel-Sentimentalität.

(Rudolf Louis, *Die Deutsche Musik der Gegenwart,* Munich, 1909)

[If Mahler's music would speak Yiddish, it would be perhaps unintelligible to me. But it is repulsive to me because it *acts* Jewish. This is to say that it speaks musical German, but with an accent, with an inflection, and above all, with the gestures of an eastern, all too eastern Jew. So, even to those whom it does not offend directly, it can not possibly communicate anything. One does not have to be repelled by Mahler's artistic personality in order to realize the complete emptiness and vacuity of an art in which the spasm of an impotent mock-Titanism reduces itself to a frank gratification of common seamstress-like sentimentality.]

-:-

Mahler had not much to say in his Fifth Symphony and occupied a wondrous time in saying it. His manner is ponderous, his matter imponderable.

(New York *Sun,* December 5, 1913)

A Modern Symphony

One Saturday at evening
The critic's work was done,
He sat within the Music Hall,
The concert had begun.
And by his side there might be seen
His little grandchild Wilhelmine.

Young Peterkin was also there
With program-book in hand,
And asked the critic to explain
What ailed the music-band.
What was the work that they had found
That was so big and full of sound.

The critic gazed upon the boy
That stood expectant by.
He knit his brows, he scratched his head,
He heaved a natural sigh.
'Tis some poor fellow's score, said he,
That wrote a monster symphonie.

With chords of ninths, elevenths, and worse,
And discords in all keys,
He turns the music inside out
With unknown harmonies.
But things like that, you know, must be
In every modern symphonie.

Great praise, the big brass tubas won,
And kettle-drums, I ween.
Why, 'twas a very ugly thing,
Said little Wilhelmine.
Nay, that you must not say, quoth he,
It is a famous symphonie.

(Louis Elson, Boston *Daily Advertiser,* February 28, 1914, with reference to Mahler's Fifth Symphony)

-:-

At the end of the first part of Mahler's Eighth Symphony, the *Veni Creator Spiritus,* I strolled about the lobby, absolutely disheartened and disillusioned. That these lovely old Latin iambics, filled with the breath of the Holy Spirit should be wrenched into rhythms, square and round, and yelled and shouted by hundreds of vociferous ladies and gentlemen, ponderously piled in superiorcumbent tiers, with a howling orchestra with additional instruments galore —seemed gross and irreverent. Dry Teutonic intricacies of melody and harmony seemed to instill a furor, with the accent on the *roar*.

(Charles Peabody, Boston *Daily Advertiser*, April 12, 1916)

-:-

If there is any music that is eminently a routine, reflective, dusty sort of musical art, it is certainly Mahler's five latter symphonies. The musical Desert of Sahara is surely to be found in these unhappy compositions. They are monsters of ennui, and by their very pretentiousness, their gargantuan dimensions, throw into relief Mahler's essential sterility. They seek to be colossal, and achieve vacuity.

(Paul Rosenfeld, *Musical Portraits*, New York, 1920)

-:-

Alas for the music of Mahler! What a fuss about nothing! What a to-do about a few commonplace musical thoughts, hardly worthy of being called ideas. Never was the poverty of his invention more apparent than in these songs, in which triviality is the dominant quality.

(L. A. Sloper, *Christian Science Monitor*, Boston, January 20, 1924)

-:-

If you are perverse enough to endure over an hour of masochistic aural flagellation, here's your chance! This grandiose Mahler 'Symphony of a Thousand' [Symphony No. 8], with all its elephantine forces, fatuous mysticism and screaming hysteria, adds up to a sublimely ridiculous minus-zero.

(R. D. Darrell, *Down Beat*, Chicago, June 4, 1952)

MILHAUD La symphonie de Mozart était remplacée par une *Suite Symphonique*(!) de M. Darius Milhaud, destinée à accompagner un *Protée* de M. Paul Claudel. Celui-ci demandait 'une musique Nouveau-Cirque pour illustrer le repas des phoques, une Bacchanale nocturne faite de silence' et autres belles choses. Plût aux dieux que le silence eût, en effet, remplacé ce tohu-bohu sans analogue, qui, peut-être, représentait les dits animaux dégurgitant leur dîner. Je ne ferai pas à cette piteuse insanité l'honneur d'une analyse. C'est bas, trivial et grossièrement tapageur. D'ailleurs, à part deux douzaines d'applaudisseurs, l'auditoire manifesta vertement son exaspération par des sifflets et des huées. Je me tins naturellement au premier rang des protestataires, et peu s'en fallut qu'un inspecteur zélé, mais d'ailleurs très courtois, ne me livrât au bras séculier chargé de l'expulsion des hérétiques. La courageuse intervention de notre éminent confrère, M. Paul Souday, affirmant avec énergie le droit indiscutable de l'auditeur à manifester son opinion, apaisa la maréchaussée.

(René Brancour, *Le Ménestrel,* Paris, October 28, 1920)

[The Mozart symphony, originally programmed, was replaced by a *Suite Symphonique* (!) by M. Darius Milhaud, written to accompany a *Proteus* by M. Paul Claudel who needed 'a score in the circus genre to illustrate a repast of seals, a nocturnal bacchanale of silence' and other beautiful things. Would it please the gods that silence should indeed replace this unprecedented turmoil which perhaps represented the said animals regurgitating their supper. I shall not honor this pitiful insanity by a description. It is low, trivial, and offensively noisy. Besides, apart from a couple of dozen applause makers, the audience vigorously manifested its exasperation by hissing and booing. Naturally I was in the first rank of objectors, and a zealous, but otherwise courteous, police officer was prepared to deliver me to the secular arm entrusted with the expulsion of heretics. Courageous intercession of my eminent colleague, M. Paul Souday, who energetically defended the incontestable right of a listener to express his opinion, pacified the constabulary.]

-:-

Wenn wir Ausländer bei uns zu Gaste haben, dann muss es doch ein anderer Typ sein, als dieser nach jeder Richtung hin impotente

Darius Milhaud, dessen blütig-dilettantische Machwerke ein Gefühl der Beschämung zurücklassen. . . *Schöpfung* . . . dieses Conglomerat quäkender gestopfter Trompeten, jaulender Saxophons, grunzender Posaunen—jeder der Instrumentengruppen natürlich in einer anderen Tonart, sodass der alte Regersche Witz wieder aufwacht: 'Machen die Leute dass so mit ihrem Munde?' 'Na, dös will i doch hoffen!' Die selbstquälerische Impotenz ist hier bis zu einem Grade gesteigert, dass jeder Laie die Diagnose auf hoffnungslos finden kann. . . Eine brutalere Selbstbeschuldigung der Versündigung am Geiste wahrer Kunst ist schwer aufzutreiben. . . Dies alles sind eben Dinge, die man doch in unseren Zeiten des Tierschutzes vor Misshandlungen vermeiden sollte.

(Max Chop, *Signale*, Berlin, November 13, 1929)

[If we must have foreigners as guests, then at least they should be of a different sort than this totally impotent Darius Milhaud, whose arch-amateurish handiwork leaves behind a sense of shame. *Création du monde* . . . this conglomeration of squeaking muted trumpets, howling saxophones, grunting trombones—each instrumental group naturally in a different key, so that the old witticism of Reger comes back to mind: 'Do people actually make this sort of noise with the mouth?' 'Well, at least I hope so!' The self-torturing impotence is here raised to such a degree that any layman can diagnose it as hopeless. A more brutal self-accusation of sinning against the spirit of true art is difficult to find. In our times of prevention of cruelty to animals, this sort of thing should really be prevented.]

-:-

Maximilien de M. Darius Milhaud fait le bruit le plus cruel. Il y a là un parti pris de rugosité hargneuse trop accusé et trop soutenu pour n'être point volontaire. Cette laideur—pour appeler un chat un chat—s'accompagne d'incohérence et de confusion.

(*Le Ménestrel*, Paris, January 1932)

[*Maximilian* of Darius Milhaud makes the cruelest of noises. There is a deliberate attitude of bilious asperity too obvious and too sustained to appear involuntary. This ugliness—to call a spade a spade—is accompanied by incoherence and confusion.]

-:-

Nous sommes venu à l'Opéra pour entendre une musique d'avant-garde, *Maximilien* de Darius Milhaud. Nous nous sommes cramponnés à notre fauteuil. Mais nous en avons été vidés par un tel ouragan de fausses notes que nous nous sommes retrouvés, à demi asommés, dans l'escalier d'étage, sans savoir comment nous avions bien pu dégringoler jusque là. . . L'auteur connait la grammaire, l'orthographe et la langue, mais il ne peut parler que l'esperanto et le volàpuk. C'est une conception de commis-voyageur communiste.

(P.-B. Gheusi, *Le Figaro*, Paris, January 7, 1932)

[We went to the Opera to hear music of the vanguard, *Maximilian* by Darius Milhaud. We clutched our chair. But we were hurled out of it by such a hurricane of wrong notes that we found ourselves, half dead, on the stairway, without knowing how we could fall down quite so far. The composer knows the grammar, the spelling and the language; but he can speak only Esperanto and Volapuk. It is a work of a Communist traveling salesman.]

-:-

M. Milhaud . . . unable to resign himself to making a career in normal conditions, seeing that his talent offered no originality, adopted an extraordinarily grim formula of writing in order to catch attention. . . *Maximilian* does not mark a new development. . . It is still the same system of accumulation of dissonant notes and of superpositions of tonality which deprives it of all logic and prevents a conductor from knowing whether the instrumentalists are playing their parts or not. In the presence of M. Milhaud, the orchestral musicians amused themselves by altering their parts in the course of a rehearsal and introducing ironical jokes without the composer or the conductor having the smallest possibility of noticing.

(Emile Vuillermoz, *Christian Science Monitor*, Boston, February 8, 1932)

MOUSSORGSKY *Boris Godunov* may be entitled Cacophony in Five Acts and Seven Scenes.

(Nicolas Soloviev, *Birzhevye Vedomosti,* St. Petersburg, February 11, 1874)

-:-

The overabundance of dissonances and the incompetence in handling vocal parts in *Boris Godunov* reach the point where the listener can not be sure of the composer's intentions and is unable to distinguish intentional wrong notes from the wrong notes of the performers.

(Hermann Laroche, *Golos,* St. Petersburg, February 11, 1874)

-:-

Musicians present at the performance of *Boris Godunov* were startled in a most disagreeable manner by the anarchy of the music in which different tonalities were mixed chaotically, by the outrageous agglomeration of unresolved discords, by constantly recurring consecutive fifths, in short, by a complete disregard of elementary rules of composition. . . Cross-relations, abuse of pedal points, insertion of alien notes into chords, harmonic progressions defying common sense—all this creates a heavy, unhealthy, sordid atmosphere in Moussorgsky's music. . . His resources are represented by a pot of mixed colors, which he tosses indiscriminately into the score with no concern for harmony or elegance of design. This crudity is a perfect proof of the composer's ignorance of the art of music.

(Alexander Famintzin, *Musikalnyi Listok,* St. Petersburg, February 15, 1874)

-:-

There are these chief defects in *Boris Godunov*: chopped recitative and looseness of musical discourse, resulting in the effect of a potpourri. . . These defects are the consequence of immaturity, indiscriminating, self-complacent, hasty method of composition.

(César Cui, *St. Petersburg Vedomosti,* February 18, 1874)

-:-

I have made a thorough study of *Boris Godunov*. . . I consign it from the bottom of my heart to the devil; it is the most insipid and base parody on music.

(Tchaikovsky in a letter to his brother Modest, dated Moscow, October 29, 1874)

Moussorgsky is a limited individual devoid of any desire of educating himself, blindly accepting the faith in the preposterous theories of his circle and in his own genius. Besides, his is a low nature, rough, crude and coarse. . . He is the very opposite of his friend Cui who sails in shallow waters, but is always well-mannered and elegant. Moussorgsky, on the other hand, flaunts his illiteracy and is proud of his ignorance. So he dashes off whatever comes, hit or miss. . . A sad spectacle!

(Tchaikovsky in a letter to Madame von Meck, dated January 5, 1878)

-:-

Moussorgsky is one of the most flagrant examples of mental chaos to which our intelligentsia has been reduced by our incompetent schooling. . . With his rudimentary technique of composition and a similarly underdeveloped mentality, Moussorgsky undertook to proclaim his new truths. . . As a result, he composed like Nozdrev's cook in Gogol's *Dead Souls*: if there happened to be an augmented fourth within reach, he would throw it in; if there were some scale passages in thirty-seconds available, he would pour them in, too; and he would spice his concoction with pedal points and enharmonic modulations—anything to make it boil, in the hope that something would come out of it in the end.

(Hermann Laroche, *Moscovskye Vedomosti,* December 29, 1888)

-:-

Une Nuit sur le Mont Chauve by Moussorgsky is as hideous a thing as we have ever heard . . . an orgy of ugliness and an abomination. May we never hear it again!

(*Musical Times,* London, March 1898)

PROKOFIEV One of the main attractions of the concert was the first performance of the *Scythian Suite* by a young composer, Prokofiev. If one would say that this music is bad, cacophonous, that no person with a differentiated auditory organ can listen to it, he would be told that this is a 'barbaric suite.' And the critic would have to retreat in shame. So I shall not criticize this music; quite to the contrary, I will say that this is wonderful barbaric music, the best barbaric music in the world. But when I am asked whether this music gives me pleasure or an artistic satisfaction, whether it makes a deep impression, I must categorically say: 'No!' The composer conducted himself with barbaric abandon.

(Leonid Sabaneyev in *News of the Season,* Moscow, December 25, 1916; the performance was canceled, and the above review was written by Sabaneyev before he found out that Prokofiev's Suite was never performed.)

-:-

Crashing Siberias, volcano hell, Krakatoa, sea-bottom crawlers. Incomprehensible? So is Prokofiev. A splendid tribute was paid to his *Scythian Suite* in Petrograd by Glazunov. The poor tortured classicist walked out of the hall during the performance of the work. No one walked out of Aeolian Hall but several respectable pianists ran out. The rest of the distinguished company listened attentively and almost everybody applauded furiously. These sophisticated listeners took no chances. Prokofiev might be the legitimate successor of Borodin, Moussorgsky, and Rimsky-Korsakov.

(*Musical America,* New York, November 20, 1918)

-:-

New ears for new music! The new ears were necessary to appreciate the new music made by Serge Prokofiev. . . As a composer, he is cerebral. . . The lyric themes are generally insipid. . . The Sonata, a second one, contains no sustained musical development. The finale of the work evoked visions of a charge of mammoths on some vast immemorial Asiatic plateau. . . Prokofiev uses, like Arnold Schoenberg, the entire modern harmonies. The House of Bondage of normal key relations is discarded. He is a psychologist of the uglier emotions. Hatred, contempt, rage—above all, rage—disgust, despair, mockery and defiance legitimately serve as models for moods.

(Richard Aldrich, New York *Times,* November 21, 1918)

The challenge to indignant protest against Mr. Prokofiev . . . was the so-called symphonic picture *Hircus Nocturnus*. Why do these Russians give us so much witch music? This new piece is sheerly bestial in its assaults upon the ear, fancy and intellectual decency... Mr. Prokofiev delights in rending our ears and outraging our sensibilities. 'The Blocksburg,' said one of Goethe's commentators, 'is the congregation of the evil ones, the collection of the rabble who perversely follow mistaken views of knowledge, will and power.' So are the composers who are mixing the elements of music in a witches' caldron and offering a hell-broth under the guise of an elixir of progress. If musicians and public had the courage of their convictions, they would send the brood packing.

(H. E. Krehbiel, New York *Tribune,* November 21, 1918; on the following day Krehbiel published, by way of retraction, this Note of Explanation and Apology: 'Indignation over the matter of Mr. Prokofiev's compositions . . . blinded the eyes of this reviewer to the fact that the ear-tearing, nerve-racking description of an orgy of witches (*Hircus Nocturnus*) was the creation of Vasilenko, not Mr. Prokofiev. The latter gentleman has artistic sins enough of his own to atone for, and ought not to have been saddled with those of another, whose name was overlooked in the dim light of the concert-room. We extend to him our apologies and simultaneously our congratulations that he is not the composer of the musical bestiality which we tried to scourge.')

-:-

As far back as the days of Hans von Bülow, the Russians were noted for their addiction to dissonantal din in music. The thing gradually came to be a sort of sport—as sportsmen have brought about the evolution of the ugliest possible bulldog, bestowing prizes on those that were most so. There is fierce competition among the composers for this award. The latest comer is always acclaimed by his friends as the worst ever. One of these worst evers was exhibited in Aeolian Hall yesterday afternoon. His name is Serge Prokofiev. . . He played his own compositions—presumably those which he considers his best—that is, futuristically speaking, his worst: four etudes, his second sonata, a prelude, a scherzo, a gavotte, and a *Suggestion diabolique*. . . The present writer has heard much more cruel things than Serge Prokofiev's compositions. Seldom, however, has he heard compositions so devoid of all musical interest. It is the same old story: 'When you have nothing new to say, camouflage your inability by pelting the hearer's ears with cacophonies.' The recipe for this sort of composition is as simple as that for boiling an egg. Write anything that comes into your head no matter how commonplace. Then change all the accidentals, putting flats in the place of sharps, and vice-versa, and the thing's done.

(New York *World,* November 21, 1918)

-:-

Every rule in the realm of traditional music writing was broken by Prokofiev. Dissonance followed dissonance in a fashion inconceivable to ears accustomed to melody and harmonic laws upon which their musical comprehension has been reared. There were times when the discords, the varying rhythms and the abrupt dynamic changes rent the air in indescribably chaotic fashion.

(New York *Sun,* November 21, 1918)

-:-

Mr. Prokofiev strikes me as a somewhat ribald and Bolshevist innovator and musical agitator. . . The human ear may in time become accustomed to anything, however weird and terrible. . . We are faced by the inevitable conclusion that music must in time recur to primal conditions—barbaric noise and rhythm without melody—which is unthinkable.

(Reginald De Koven, New York *Herald,* November 24, 1918)

-:-

Of the *Scherzo Humoresque* for four bassoons by Serge Prokofiev, we are grateful to be able to say as the old Latins said concerning money, 'non olet'; of a concerto composed and played by Mr. Prokofiev, even that phrase would be too complimentary. . . It was an example of bad language in music. . . The work itself and the manner in which Mr. Prokofiev played it, moved us to pity for the beautiful instrument which he belabored.

(H. E. Krehbiel, New York *Herald,* November 28, 1918)

-:-

Serge Prokofiev was starred both as composer and pianist; hadn't we better call him Fortissimist? . . . The first Piano Concerto of Prokofiev was in one movement, but compounded of many rhythms and recondite noises. . . The composer handled the keyboard—

handled is the right word—and the duel that ensued between his ten flail-like fingers was to the death; the death of euphony. The first descending figure—it is hardly a theme—is persistently affirmed in various nontonalities by the orchestra, the piano all the while shrieking, groaning, howling, fighting back, and in several instances it seemed to rear and bite the hand that chastised it. . . If this be the music of the future, then the music of the past has been mere aural titillation. . . There were moments when the piano and orchestra made sounds that evoked not only the downfall of empires, but also of fine crockery, the fragments flying in all directions. He may be the Cossack Chopin for the next generation—this tall, calm young man. The diabolic smiles press upon you as his huge hands, the hands of a musical primate, tear up trees and plow the soil. That fetching, old expression, 'Hell to pay and no pitch hot,' applies to Prokofiev: only he owns his Hades and has the necessary pitch in abundance. However, there is method in all these seething dissonances. . . There is a very definite pattern in the Concerto which will never be played by any one on earth, except Leo Ornstein, who is getting married this week. The human ear soon accommodates to such monstrous aberrations. . . Prokofiev wouldn't grant an encore. The Russian heart may be a dark place, but its capacity for mercy is infinite.

(James Gibbons Huneker, New York *Times*, December 11, 1918)

-:-

Mr. Prokofiev's pieces have been contributions not to the art of music, but to national pathology and pharmacopoeia. As such they were distinctly unwelcome, for Germany, since it came under the sway of moral and political degeneration, has provided quite as much musical *guano* as civilized soil could bear. . . This, we know, is plain talk, but it seems to be demanded in rebuke of a tendency to make a popular appeal with what we are constrained to call filthy music. . . We do not refer particularly to the pianoforte solos composed and played by Mr. Prokofiev, for they, we are sure, invite their own damnation, because there is nothing in them to hold attention. . . They pursue no esthetic purpose, strive for no recognizable ideal, proclaim no means for increasing the expressive potency of music. They are simply perverse. They die the death of abortions.

(H. E. Krehbiel, New York *Tribune*, December 12, 1918)

Prokofiev's mission in life would seem to be to make two dissonances grow where only one grew before. One gets an impression that the composer has found the construction of a chord containing all the notes of the chromatic scale the merest of child's play, and that he is casting about for some really difficult harmonic problem. Dissonance is piled on dissonance, and if there is anything he has not scored for, except the slapstick, it was not revealed. . . Yet there is a queer sort of half-sanity about the *Scythian Suite.* That is perhaps why the comments of the audience were so bitter. Suggestions were made all the way from playing the *Suite* out of doors during the armistice celebration to having it adopted as the national hymn of the Bolsheviki.
(*Musical America,* New York, December 14, 1918)

-:-

In these days when peace is heralded and the world is turning from dissonance to harmony, it comes as a shock to listen to such a program. Those who do not believe that genius is evident in superabundance of noise looked in vain for a new musical message in Mr. Prokofiev's work. Nor in the *Classical Symphony,* which the composer conducted, was there any cessation from the orgy of discordant sounds. As an exposition of the unhappy state of chaos from which Russia suffers, Mr. Prokofiev's music is interesting, but one hopes fervently that the future may hold better things both for Russia and listeners to Russian music.
(*Musical America,* New York, December 21, 1918)

-:-

The music of *The Love for Three Oranges,* I fear, is too much for this generation. After intensive study and close observation at rehearsal and performance, I detected the beginnings of two tunes. . . . For the rest of it, Mr. Prokofiev might well have loaded up a shotgun with several thousand notes of varying lengths and discharged them against the side of a blank wall.
(Edward Moore, Chicago *Tribune,* December 31, 1921)

-:-

What can Mr. Prokofiev's music do for the ear? Probably, for most of the listeners, it could do little but belabor it till insensibility set in, if it did set in, and further suffering was spared. There are a few, but only a very few, passages that bear recognizable kinship with what has hitherto been recognized as music. No doubt there are what pass for themes, and there is ingenuity of some kind in manipulating them; but it seldom produces any effect but that of disagreeable noise. . . The orchestra is a noble instrument, but it has seldom been put to so ignoble use as it is in *The Love for Three Oranges.*

(Richard Aldrich, New York *Times,* February 15, 1922)

-:-

Asked to hear the music of Prokofiev that is supposed to portray in tones 'all kinds of mechanism, from the steam hammer to the most highly delicate weaving machines,' with Russians vigorously at work, one might courteously decline the invitation, saying: 'I have been near a boiler factory, and riveters were making day hideous across the street from my house only last week.' Not only is the music of *Le Pas d'Acier* noisy, but the constant repetitions of raucous measures were soon monotonous, and Prokofiev for once seemed a boisterous bore. . . It has been said that *Le Pas d'Acier* may properly be called a Bolshevik ballet. The music by itself will not make converts to the Soviet cause.

(Philip Hale, Boston *Herald,* October 22, 1927)

-:-

In his new opera, *The Tale of a Real Man,* Prokofiev goes back to all the negative and repulsive usages present in his music of the period of reckless infatuation with modernistic trickery. Chaos, coarse naturalism, complete absence of melody, harmonic muddiness and bad taste, characterize this thoroughly vicious work.

(*Sovietskaya Musica,* Moscow, December 1948)

PUCCINI Those who were present at the performance of Puccini's opera *Tosca*, were little prepared for the revolting effects produced by musically illustrating the torture and murder scenes of Sardou's play. The alliance of a pure art with scenes so essentially brutal and demoralizing . . . produced a feeling of nausea. There may be some who will find entertainment in this sensation, but all true lovers of the gentle art must deplore with myself its being so prostituted. What has music to do with a lustful man chasing a defenseless woman or the dying kicks of a murdered scoundrel? It seemed an odd form of amusement to place before a presumably refined and cultured audience, and should this opera prove popular it will scarcely indicate a healthy or creditable taste.

(A London newspaper, July 13, 1900)

-:-

Doubtless Puccini is a very estimable and charming person; doubtless he works honestly for what he considers good art. Nevertheless he represents an evil art—Italian music, to wit—and his success would have meant the preponderating influence in England of that evil art. Wherefore, it has been my duty to throw back the score of *Tosca* at him. Puccini: may you prosper, but in other climes! Continue, my friend, to sketch in scrappy incidental music to well-known plays. But spare England: this country has done neither you nor your nation nearly so much harm as she has done other nations. Disturb not the existing peaceful relations!

(J. F. Runciman, *Saturday Review*, London, July 21, 1900)

-:-

In *La Bohème*, silly and inconsequential incidents and dialogues . . . are daubed over with splotches of instrumental color without reason and without effect, except the creation of a sense of boisterous excitement and confusion. In his proclamation of passion, Puccini is more successful so soon as he can become strenuous; but even here the expression is superficial and depends upon strident phrases pounded out by hitting each note a blow on the head as it escapes from the mouths of singers or the accompanying instruments.

(H. E. Krehbiel, New York *Tribune*, December 27, 1900)

-:-

Tosca is a 'melodrama' in the truest sense. The music is almost entirely subordinated to the drama. . . Distinction of style there is not; the composer is too eclectic. There is little, if any, thematic development; there is really no time for it. The rapidity of speech calls for rapidity in the score. The *parlando* is employed continually. It is as if a broken mirror was made to reflect and distort bits of sunlight; both eye and ear are often offended by the consecutive fifths, raw harmonic progressions and alterations of the tawdry with the solemn. But if the stream is not a deep one, it is both brawling and fugacious. Seldom does it, in its mad flight, pause long enough for a melodic eddy to form. So we get few set pieces or few prolonged melodies; indeed, the short bursts of sustained melody are generally formless. Here is the Wagner theory skeletonized, almost reduced to an absurdity.

(New York *Sun*, February 5, 1901)

-:-

At the first hearing much, perhaps most, of Puccini's *Tosca* sounds exceedingly, even ingeniously, ugly. Every now and then one comes across the most ear-flaying succession of chords; then, the instrumentation, although nearly always characteristic, is often distinctly rawboned and hideous; the composer shows a well-nigh diabolical ingenuity in massing together harsh, ill-sounding timbres. As for the harmony, Puccini, like some other of his countrymen—Arrigo Boito, for example—shows that his ear is far less sensitive to the unpleasant effect of cross-relations and illogical succession of chords than to that of harsh and complex dissonances. To my ear the most complex dissonant harmonies of Wagner or Richard Strauss—'chords' (so-called) of six or seven notes perhaps—have not half the rasp that some perfectly consonant triad-progressions have.

(W. F. Apthorp, Boston *Evening Transcript*, April 12, 1901)

RACHMANINOFF If there were a conservatory in Hell, and if one of its talented students was to compose a symphony based on the story of the Seven Plagues of Egypt, and if he had written one similar to Rachmaninoff's, he would have brilliantly accomplished his task and would have delighted the inhabitants of Hell.

(César Cui, St. Petersburg *News,* March 16, 1897)

-:-

Do people really love the crashing dissonances of a hundred instruments in such productions as the Symphony in E minor by Rachmaninoff, or do they simply go there because it is the thing to do? One could hardly escape the idea that the whole affair was some great mechanical contrivance for hypnotizing the audience with a complicated scheme of mechanical motion driven by some tremendous engine whose squeakings, and wheezings, and crashings were synchronously adjusted thereto. . . Rachmaninoff—no more for me!

(From a letter to the Editor, New York *Sun,* January 9, 1914)

-:-

Rachmaninoff's Second Piano Concerto is . . . a little too much like a mournful banqueting on jam and honey. . . In all the music of Rachmaninoff there is something strangely twice-told. From it there flows the sadness distilled by all things that are a little useless. . . He is still content with music that toys with the pianoforte. . . . He writes pieces full of the old astounding musical dislocation. . . . There was a day, perhaps, when such work served. But another day has succeeded to it. And so, Rachmaninoff comes amongst us like a very charming and amiable ghost.

(Paul Rosenfeld, *The New Republic,* New York, March 15, 1919)

-:-

Rachmaninoff's *Rhapsody on a Theme of Paganini* sometimes sounds like a plague of insects in the Amazon valley, sometimes like a miniature of the Day of Judgment . . . and for a change goes lachrymose.

(Pitts Sanborn, New York *World-Telegram,* January 14, 1936)

RAVEL In his String Quartet, M. Ravel is content with one theme which has the emotional potency of one of those tunes which the curious may hear in a Chinese theater, shrieked out by an ear-splitting clarinet. This theme serves him for four movements during which there is about as much emotional nuance as warms a problem in algebra. It is a drastic dose of wormwood and assafoetida.

(New York *Tribune*, December 12, 1906)

-:-

Who can unravel Ravel? We confess that we are puzzled at his upsetting of Mother Goose into French. If these *Esquisses enfantines* received their proper title, they would be labeled *Scenes from Second Childhood.* But since Richard Strauss paraded his monster baby in *Sinfonia Domestica,* children in music have not been as simple and artless as they once were.

(Louis Elson, Boston *Daily Advertiser,* December 27, 1913)

-:-

To hear a whole program of Ravel's works is like watching some midget or pygmy doing clever, but very small, things within a limited scope. Moreover, the almost reptilian cold-bloodedness, which one suspects of having been consciously cultivated, of most of M. Ravel's music is almost repulsive when heard in bulk; even its beauties are like the markings on snakes and lizards.

(London *Times,* April 28, 1924)

-:-

Ravel's *Bolero* I submit as the most insolent monstrosity ever perpetrated in the history of music. From the beginning to the end of its 339 measures it is simply the incredible repetition of the same rhythm . . . and above it the blatant recurrence of an overwhelmingly vulgar cabaret tune that is little removed, in every essential of character, from the wail of an obstreperous back-alley cat. . . Although Ravel's official biography does not mention it, I feel sure that at the age of three he swallowed a musical snuff-box, and at nine he must have been frightened by a bear. To both phenomena he offers repeated testimony: he is constantly tinkling high on the harps and celesta, or is growling low in the bassoons and double-basses.

(Edward Robinson, 'The Naive Ravel,' *The American Mercury,* New York, May 1932)

REGER Dem kleineren Ereignisse, das die Aufführung des Debussyschen Streichquartetts ohne Zweifel bedeutete, folgte am nächsten Tage ein grosses Ereignis, die erste Aufführung der *Sinfonietta* Max Regers, der mit Debussy das gemein hat dass er von den Wortführern der antiwagnerischen Reaktion als der eigentliche Mann der Zukunft auf den Schild erhoben wird. . . Einfach ist diese Sinfonietta ganz gewiss nicht. . . Reger hat ersichtlicher Weise einfach sein *wollen.* Aber es ist bei diesem Wollen geblieben; seine Absicht auszuführen ist er ausserstande gewesen. . . Von dem allgemeinen Eindruck, dass die *Sinfonietta,* auch im Vergleich mit andern Kompositionen Regers, kein inhaltlich bedeutendes Werk ist, dass ihre Tonsprache in wesentlichen darauf hinausläuft, durch tausend Künste des Kontrapunktes, der Harmonik und Modulation darüber hinwegzutäuschen . . . von diesem Allgemeineindruck macht nur das *Larghetto* eine Ausnahme. . . Wir haben hier viel weniger die unangenehme Empfindung, dass einer im guten Vertrauen auf die psychologische Tatsache der Suggestionswirkung . . . uns zum Narren halte.

(Rudolf Louis, *Münchener Neueste Nachrichten,* February 7, 1906)

[After the lesser event, that was undoubtedly signified by the performance of Debussy's String Quartet, followed on the next day the great event, the first performance of *Sinfonietta* by Max Reger, who has this in common with Debussy: that he has been nominated by the verbal leaders of the anti-Wagnerian reaction to carry the banner as the proper Man of the Future. . . This *Sinfonietta* is certainly not simple. . . Reger has manifestly wished to be simple. But it remained just wishing; he has been unable to carry out his intention. . . From a general impression that the *Sinfonietta,* even compared to other compositions by Reger, is not inherently a significant work, that its tonal language essentially depends on conjuring up the illusion of significance by a thousand contrapuntal tricks, the sole exception from this general impression is the *Larghetto.* We have here much less of the unpleasant sensation that someone, placing full faith in the psychological phenomenon of suggestive power, is taking us for fools.]

(This review provoked Reger to dispatch his famous scatological letter to the critic: 'Ich sitze in dem kleinsten Zimmer in meinem Hause. Ich habe Ihre Kritik vor mir. Im nächsten Augenblick wird sie *hinter* mir sein.'—'I am sitting in the smallest room of my house. I have your review before me. In a moment it will be behind me.')

It seems hardly worth while to spend so much labor and pains on being indefinite, but of such is the kingdom of music in these days as witness the monstrosity called a *Trio* by Max Reger performed with infinite devotion on Tuesday night. This pretentious rubbish will probably not be heard again in this enlightened town.

(New York *Sun,* December 6, 1908)

-:-

There is a story that a copy reader serving his novitiate was told by the editor to cut down an article one half. 'Which half shall I leave?' was the innocent inquiry that followed. If Reger's *Symphonic Prologue to a Tragedy,* after having been twice curtailed, had next been beheaded, then dismembered, and all of the fragments put away as things unpleasant to contemplate are generally disposed of, the revision would have been eminently satisfactory.

(H. E. Krehbiel, New York *Tribune,* November 12, 1909)

-:-

Rarely has the Queen's Hall been subjected to so great an acoustical shock as the dynamic force of Reger's 100th Psalm. It called to mind the famous remark of Grétry on a duet in Méhul's *Euphrosyne et Coradin*: 'It is enough to split the roof of the theater with the skull of the audience.'

(*Pall Mall Gazette,* London, May 23, 1911)

-:-

Regers Mathematic war eine Larve, eine Fratze. . . Reger war nicht hörbar, nur lesbar. Ich glaube selbst nicht dass er Ohren hatte. . . . Hier ist ein Mensch so ohne Zentrum, dass alles ganz unmittelbar vor sich geht. Hier schreibt nicht mehr die Hand, sondern . . .

(Walther Krug, *Die Neue Musik,* 1920; the dots, for an obscene word, are in the original)

[Reger's mathematics was a mask, a caricature. . . Reger could not be listened to; he could only be read. I do not even believe that he had ears. Here is a man so devoid of controlling centers that everything happens to him immediately. It is not his hand that writes but . . .]

This Reger is a sarcastic, churlish fellow, bitter and pedantic and rude. He is a sort of musical Cyclops, a strong, ugly creature bulging with knotty and unshapely muscles, an ogre of composition. In listening to these works with their clumsy blocks of tone, their eternal sunless complaining, their lack of humor where they would be humorous, their lack of passion where they would be profound, their sardonic and monotonous bourdon, one is perforce reminded of the photograph of Reger which his publishers place on the cover of their catalogue of his works, the photograph that shows something that is like a swollen, myopic beetle with thick lips and sullen expression, crouching on an organ-bench. There is something repulsive as well as pedantic in this art. His works are stereotyped, stale terribly quickly. . . They are like mathematical problems and solutions, sheer brain-spun and unlyrical works.

(Paul Rosenfeld, *Musical Portraits*, New York, 1920)

-:-

Reger's Quartet, op. 109 . . . looks like music, it sounds like music, it might even taste like music; yet it remains, stubbornly, not music. . . . Reger might be epitomized as a composer whose name is the same either forward or backward, and whose music, curiously, often displays the same characteristic.

(Irving Kolodin, New York *Sun*, November 14, 1934)

-:-

The Reger Piano Concerto is to our mind a most inflated, pretentious bag of wind, with a very heavily scored and somewhat brutally effective piano part. The orchestration, also, is swollen, thick and prevailingly in bad taste. Little bits of ideas are pretentiously and noisily bunched together, and they get nowhere. . . What incredibly bad taste, and poor invention!

(Olin Downes, New York *Times*, January 6, 1950)

RIEGGER Bei Wallingford Rieggers *Dichotomy* stürzten die wohwollenden Absichten unter dem Uebermass der Zumutungen zusammen. Es klang, als wenn eine Herde Ratten langsam zu Tode gepeinigt würde und dazwischen von Zeit zu Zeit eine sterbende Kuh stöhnte.

(Walter Abendroth, *Allgemeine Musikzeitung,* Berlin, March 25, 1932)

[With Wallingford Riegger's *Dichotomy,* the good intentions collapsed under the excess of demands. It sounded as though a pack of rats were being slowly tortured to death, and meanwhile, from time to time, a dying cow groaned.]

-:-

The concert closed with a wry and cryptic string quartet of Wallingford Riegger, at which point the sun disappeared behind a big dark cloud.

(Robert A. Hague, *PM,* New York, May 14, 1945)

-:-

Wallingford Riegger, indefatigable pursuer of dissonance as he is, was offered with a *Study in Sonority.* The title is innocent-sounding enough. But Mr. Riegger's designs upon the texture of music are not innocent, or mild, or bedtime stories for the unsophisticated. They make you think of the wolf: 'The better to eat you with, my dear!' And the title is a misnomer, for this is no mere study in sonorities. It is a haunted piece, with intervals and harmonies wholly of the composer's choice. It is for the individual to decide whether or not this 'choice' represents music.

(Olin Downes, New York *Times,* October 27, 1952)

RIMSKY-KORSAKOV *Sadko* von Rimsky-Korsakoff . . . ist Programm-Musik in verwegenster Bedeutung, ein Product der Verwilderung gepaart mit äusserster Blasiertheit. Solche Armuth des musikalischen Denkens bei solcher Frechheit der Instrumentirung ist uns selten vorgekommen. Die Elfen Mendelssohns, die Nixen Gades, Berlioz' Walpurgisnacht und Wagners Venusberg, das alles brodelt hier durcheinander in einem russischen Branntweinkessel. Herr von Korsakoff ist ein junger russischer Garde-Offizier, und wie fast alle russichen Garde-Offiziere, fanatischer Anhänger Richard Wagners. Der Stolz, auf heimischem Boden Aehnliches fabrizieren zu können, eine Art russischen Champagners, etwas sauer, aber viel stärker als der Original-Wagnersche, mag im Rechte sein zu Moskau und Petersburg. Allein in Wien, dürfen wir wohl noch protestiren gegen die Pflege solch wüsten Dilettantismus in unseren für die gute Musik gegründeten Concert-Instituten.

(Eduard Hanslick, 1872)

[*Sadko* by Rimsky-Korsakov is program music in its most unashamed form, a product of barbarism mated with utter cynicism. Such poverty of musical thought, and such impudence of orchestration, we have seldom heard. Mendelssohn's elves, Gade's mermaids, Berlioz's Walpurgis Night and Wagner's Venusberg, all this is boiling here in a Russian brandy kettle. Herr von Korsakov is a young Russian officer of the Guard, and like almost all Russian officers of the Guard, is a fanatic acolyte of Richard Wagner. The pride of being able to manufacture something similar on native soil, a sort of Russian champagne, a little sour, but much stronger than the Wagner original, might be justified in Moscow and St. Petersburg. But in Vienna, we still have a right to protest against the cultivation of such rank dilettantism in our concert organizations established for the cause of good music.]

-:-

Rimsky-Korsakoff kommandiert die äusserste Linke der jungrussischen Schule. Der Inhalt dieser Geschichten aus 1001 Nacht ist leider meinem Gedächtnisse entschwunden, und weder könnte ich mit Bestimmtheit sagen, was der Prinz Kalender eigentlich erzählt, noch endlich warum das Fest in Bagdad stattfindet. Nachdem die meisten Zuhörer sich offenbar in dem gleichen hilflosen Zustande befanden, so sprach aus allen Mienen die nervöse Unsicherheit, was uns denn eigentlich da vormusiziert werde?

(Eduard Hanslick on *Scheherazade,* 1897, in his collection of criticisms, *Am Ende des Jahrhunderts,* Berlin, 1899)

[Rimsky-Korsakov commands the extreme left of the young Russian School. The content of this story from the Arabian Nights has unfortunately escaped my memory, and I could not say with assurance just what Prince Kalender recounts, nor why there is a festival in Bagdad. Since most listeners often found themselves in the same helpless situation, their facial expressions bespoke the nervous uncertainty as to just what was played to them.]

-:-

If the fair and ingenious Scheherazade related her stories as confusedly and unmeaningly, not to say cacophonously, as the composer has related them musically, the sultan would have ordered her to be bowstrung or to have her head lopped off after the second or third night. . . That he would have permitted her to gabble away, Korsakov-wise, for two years, eight months and odd days, is wholly improbable. The music suggested a parvenu making an ostentatious display of his newly-acquired wealth by surrounding himself with gorgeously inharmonious furniture and wearing an excess of diamonds, in the belief that they will obliterate all indications of his innate vulgarity.

(Boston *Herald,* April 18, 1897)

-:-

The Rimsky-Korsakov suite, *Scheherazade,* was performed to the amazement of every concert-goer who had been brought up in the paths of Bach and righteousness; yet no one dare say that the mountain brought forth a mouse; it was rather a white elephant that emerged.

(Louis Elson, Boston *Daily Advertiser,* April 18, 1897)

-:-

Rimsky-Korsakov—what a name! It suggests fierce whiskers stained with vodka!

(*Musical Courier,* New York, October 27, 1897)

The *Antar* Symphony eclipsed both Wagner and Tchaikovsky in weird orchestration and unharmonic effects. . . The Russian composer Korsakov evidently has evolved a musical enigma which is too complex of solution now.

(Boston *Globe,* March 13, 1898)

-:-

The Russians have captured Boston! . . . The *Scheherazade* engagement began with a bombardment of full orchestra, under cover of which the woodwinds advanced on the right. The violins now made a brilliant sortie on the left flank of the main body. It was a magnificent charge; at one time the concertmaster was quite alone, but his cavalry soon rallied around him. A furious volley of kettledrums followed, while Gen. Gericke brought up the trombone reserves and the remaining brasses. At this the entire audience—including some very big guns—surrendered.

(Louis Elson, Boston *Daily Advertiser,* February 6, 1905)

-:-

Sadko is a kind of Russian Jonah who became the chief guest at a submarine *soirée musicale* given by the Muscovite Neptune. His playing upon his lyre (and Russian lyres are well known in diplomatic circles) caused the sea to become tempestuous and sank many ships. The companions of Sadko throw him overboard into the middle of the *Tannhäuser* Overture. He sinks at once in Wagner's sea of tone and begins his lute-playing quite à la Beckmesser, developing, however, into a Peer Gyntian vein.

(Louis Elson, Boston *Journal,* March 27, 1905)

RUGGLES Den *Sonnenläufer* von Carl Ruggles sollte man getrost in *Latrinenläufer* umtaufen. Dieser Titel kommt dem Charakter der Musik schon näher, die in einem von Arnold Schönberg unabhängigem Zwölftönesystem verfasst wurde; so verrät das Programm. Mag sein, mag nicht sein. Ich jedenfalls hatte nur die Vorstellung von Darmverrenkungen in atonaler Tristanekstase.

(Paul Schwers, *Allgemeine Musikzeitung*, Berlin, March 18, 1932)

[*Sun-Treader* by Carl Ruggles should have been surely renamed 'Latrine-Treader.' This title comes nearer to the character of the music, which was composed, so the program divulges, in a non-Schoenbergian 12-tone idiom. Might be, or might not be. I for one, had only the impression of bowel constrictions in an atonal Tristanesque ecstasy.]

-:-

A line from William Blake lets us into the secret intent of Mr. Ruggles: 'Great things are done when men and mountains meet.' We do not know just what mountains Mr. Ruggles has met. . . . It is possible that one episode referred to Potato Hill, but it was not a sweet potato as Mr. Ruggles saw it. This sturdy American is an uncompromising foe of all the foibles and follies of the old masters. . . . He goes his own way, sings his own shattered and acidulous melodies. . . . Krehbiel said of a certain composition: 'It may be music in a hundred years; it is not music now.' Perhaps that will be the splendid future of *Men and Mountains.*

(W. J. Henderson, New York *Sun,* March 20, 1936)

-:-

Carl Ruggles is home-taught, home-spun . . . a mixture of radical creed and American populism. . . . The populism has a brawling note in it. . . . Having begun with cyclopean concepts . . . lamely using the Schoenbergian paraphernalia, Ruggles descended to *Evocations,* chants for piano. This is true music of the Vermont drawing-room, sort of great-grandnieces of Field's nocturnes, but mildly acidized with atonal drops. . . . All of it of a cheerless gray strain—stark, but how small!

(Lazare Saminsky, *Living Music of the Americas,* New York, 1949)

SAINT-SAËNS The *Déluge* by Saint-Saëns bears utter vapidity, spiritual and intellectual poverty, and hopeless emptiness stamped upon its very forehead. In the *Déluge*, every possible noise, whistling, howling, sighing, rustling, roaring, clashing, banging, that can be drawn from a combination of instruments, by the aid of pure concords and atrocious dissonances, is made for the benefit of the dumfounded listeners.

(New York *Tribune*, December 15, 1879)

-:-

It is one's duty to hate with all possible fervor the empty and ugly in art; and I hate Saint-Saëns the composer with a hate that is perfect.

(J. F. Runciman, *Saturday Review*, London, December 12, 1896)

-:-

Saint-Saëns has, I suppose, written as much music as any composer ever did; he has certainly written more rubbish than any one I can think of. It is the worst, most rubbishy kind of rubbish.

(J. F. Runciman, *Saturday Review*, London, February 19, 1898)

-:-

In his *Danse Macabre*, Saint-Saëns has succeeded in producing effects of the most horrible, hideous and disgusting sort. Among the special instruments in the score was the xylophone, the effect of which inevitably suggested (as doubtless intended) the clattering of the bones of skeletons. Another, and scarcely less hideous device, was the tuning of the first string of the solo violin half a note lower than usual, and the reiteration of the imperfect fifth many times in succession. The piece is one of many signs of the intense and coarse realism that is entering into much of the musical composition (so-called) of the day. Manufacture would be the more proper term; and, in some cases, very clumsy manufacture.

(London *Daily News*, June 3, 1879)

-:-

Samson and Delilah, revived after a lapse of over twenty years, has come in for its full share of critical vituperation. . . . The most kindly reception has been one of resignation to the inevitable—as one accepts influenza, fog in November, or a tainted egg in the ration.

(*Musical Opinion*, London, January 1953)

SCHOENBERG Schönbergs sinfonische Dichtung *Pelleas und Melisande* ist nicht von Missklängen erfüllt, etwa in dem Sinne wie der *Don Quixote* von Strauss: es ist ein einziger, auf fünfzig Minuten verteilter, langgedehnter Missklang. Dies ist buchstäblich zu nehmen. Was sonst noch hinter diesen Kakophonien stecken mag, das zu untersuchen ist einfach nicht mehr möglich.

(Ludwig Karpath, *Signale,* Berlin, March 1, 1905)

[Schoenberg's symphonic poem *Pelleas and Melisande* is not just filled with wrong notes, in the sense of Strauss's *Don Quixote*: it is a fifty-minute-long protracted wrong note. This is to be taken literally. What else may hide behind these cacophonies is quite impossible to find out.]

-:-

Schönberg ist der extremsten einer; die Kakophonien sind hier zum Gesetz erhoben. . . Es gibt aber auch eine Aesthetik des Hässlichen.

(*Signale,* Berlin, May 29, 1907)

[Schoenberg is one of the extremists; here cacophony is elevated to a law. . . After all, there is an esthetics of the hideous.]

-:-

Noch wäre die Aufführung eines neuen Streichquartets von Arnold Schönberg zu erwähnen. Ich beschränke mich auf die Konstatierung, dass es zu einem heillosen Skandale kam. . . Mitten drinn in den einzelnen Sätzen wurde anhaltend und stürmisch gelacht und mitten drinn im letzten Satze schrie man aus Leibeskräften: 'Aufhören! Schluss! Wir lassen uns nicht narren!' Ich muss zu meinem Leidwesen konstatieren, dass ich mich zu ähnlichen Rufen hinreissen liess. Gewiss, ein Kritiker hat im Konzertsaale kein Missfallen zu äussern. Wenn ich aus meiner gewohnten Reserve trotzdem heraustrat, so will ich damit nur den Beweis liefern, dass ich physische Schmerzen ausstand, und wie ein arg Gepeinigter, trotz aller guten Absicht selbst das Schlimmste zu überwinden, nun doch aufschreien musste.

(Ludwig Karpath on Schoenberg's String Quartet No. 2, op. 10, *Signale,* Berlin, January 6, 1909)

[The performance of a new string quartet by Arnold Schoenberg must also be mentioned. I will confine myself to the statement that it resulted in an unholy scandal. Right in the middle of the movements there was persistent and uproarious laughter, and in the middle of the last movement people shouted at the top of their voices: 'Stop! Enough! We will not be treated like fools!' And I must confess to my sorrow that I, too, let myself be driven to similar outbursts. It is true that a critic should not express his disapproval in the concert-hall. If I nevertheless abandoned my customary reserve, I only proved by it that I suffered physical pain, and as one cruelly abused, despite all good intentions to endure even the worst, I still had to cry out.]

-:-

Arnold Schönberg ist heute der radikalste Moderne von Wien. . . Die drei *Klavierstücke*, opus 11, stellen sich als methodische Negation bisher geltender Musikelemente dar, Negation jeder Syntax, des Begriffes der Tonalität, des geltenden Tonsystems. Man vernimmt ein tönendes Nacheinander, Folgen und Klänge, die ohne Zusammengehörigkeit nicht zusammenfassbar sind. Schönberg tötet das tonale Empfinden; seine Klänge sind nicht mehr ableitbar. Debussy droht nur, Schönberg führt aus. Seine Folgen stellen sich als anarchistisches Herumschweifen im Chroma dar. Eines dieser Stücke endet zum Beispiel mit dem Klange Es, A, D, Gis! Schönbergs Tonreihen in seinen letzten Werken bleiben uns stumm, starr, leer, ausdrucklos. Sie sind das Resultat eines mit geistreicher Konsequenz verfolgten Irrtums.

(*Signale*, Berlin, February 9, 1910)

[Arnold Schoenberg is the most radical Vienna modernist of today. The Three Piano Pieces, op. 11, represent a methodical negation of all heretofore accepted musical rules, negation of syntax, of conception of tonality, of all valid tonal systems. One perceives a succession of tones and sounds which cannot be grasped in their continuity because they do not belong together. Schoenberg kills tonal perception; his sounds are no longer derived from one another. Debussy only threatens; Schoenberg carries out the threat. His musical progressions represent an anarchistic wandering in colors. One of these pieces actually ends with the combination E flat, A, D, and G sharp! The tonal rows in Schoenberg's latest works impress us as mute, numb, empty, expressionless. They are the result of error followed through with ingenious consistency.]

Das Konzert war von besonderem Interesse, weil es die *Drei Klavierstücke,* op. 11, von Arnold Schönberg brachte. . . Ich sehe hier die völlige Auflösung von alledem, was man bisher unter musikalischer Kunst verstand. Möglich, dass die Musik der Zukunft so aussehen wird–ich habe für ihre Schönheiten kein Verständnis. . . . Ob der Pianist die Stücke gut oder schlecht spielte, kann ich nicht beurteilen, weil der Hörer bei dieser Musik zwischen richtig und falsch nicht unterscheiden kann.

(Hugo Leichtentritt, *Signale,* Berlin, January 11, 1911)

[The concert was particularly interesting because of the Three Piano Pieces, op. 11, by Arnold Schoenberg. I see in them a complete dissolution of all that was heretofore regarded as musical art. It is possible that the music of the future will be like that, but I have no understanding of its beauty. Whether the pianist played the pieces well or badly, I cannot judge, because in this music the listener cannot distinguish between right and wrong.]

-:-

Gänzlich ablehnen muss ich die fünf Orchesterstücke vom Jahre 1909. . . Ein tragikomisches Schauspiel, zu dieser tollen Katzenmusik das Gesicht des dirigierenden Schönberg zu sehen, der mit bald verzücktem, bald verzweifeltem Ausdruck die Spieler anfeuerte. Schreckhafte Visionen erwecken diese Klänge, schauerliche Nachtgespenster drohen, und nichts, ach gar nichts von Freude und Licht, von dem, was das Leben lebenswert macht! Wie arm müssten unsere Nachkommen sein, wenn dieser freudlose, gramvolle Schönberg ihnen einst als der Inbegriff des Empfindens ihrer Zeit gelten sollte! Und dies sollte die Kunst der Zukunft sein????

(Hugo Leichtentritt, *Signale,* Berlin, February 7, 1912)

[I must reject completely the five orchestral pieces of 1909. It is a tragicomic spectacle to see Schoenberg conducting this crazy cat music, urging on the players with an entranced or despairing expression on his face. These sounds conjure up hideous visions; monstrous apparitions threaten–there is nothing of joy and light, nothing that makes life worth living! How miserable would our descendants be, if this joyless gloomy Schoenberg would ever become the mode of expression of their time! Is this destined to be the art of the future????]

If this is 'music of the future,' one can only say that Schoenberg is about a thousand years ahead of his time, for the ear, as well as the brain, cannot readily grasp the significance, if there is any, of such music.

(*Daily Mail*, London, September 1, 1912)

-:-

Five Orchestral Pieces by Arnold Schoenberg form an essay in dissonance. . . It was like a poem in Tibetan; not one single soul could possibly have understood it. . . The listener was like a dweller in Flatland straining his mind to understand the ways of that mysterious occupant of three dimensions, man. At the conclusion, half the audience hissed. That seems a too decisive judgment, for after all they may turn out to be wrong.

(London *Times*, September 4, 1912)

-:-

The music of Schoenberg's *Five Orchestral Pieces* resembled the wailings of a tortured soul, and suggested nothing so much as the disordered fancies of delirium or the fearsome, imaginary terrors of a highly nervous infant.

(London *Globe*, September 4, 1912)

-:-

Imagine the scene of the bleating of sheep in *Don Quixote*, the sacrificial procession in *Elektra*, and the scene of the opponents in *Heldenleben* all played together, and you will have Schoenberg's idea of orchestral color and harmony. As to theme or subject, it must be supposed that he would consider it an insult to be told that he has any traffic with such things. . . We must be content with the composer's own assertion that he has depicted his own experiences, for which he has our heartfelt sympathy.

(*Daily News*, London, September 4, 1912)

-:-

It is impossible to give an idea of the music of Schoenberg's *Five Orchestral Pieces*. The endless discords, the constant succession of unnatural sounds from the extreme notes of every instrument . . . baffle description. Herr Schoenberg, in short, is to Strauss at his wildest what Strauss is to Mozart. He does not even end his pieces with recognizable chords.

(*Manchester Guardian*, September 5, 1912)

According to Dr. Anton von Webern, Schoenberg's music 'contains the experience of his emotional life,' and that experience must have been of a strange, not to say unpleasant character. . . If music at all, it is music of the future, and we hope, of a distant one.

(*Daily Mail,* London, September 7, 1912)

-:-

Herr Schönberg ist musikalischer Spiritist. Wie wenigstens seine immer wütenden Anhänger versichern, schreibt er Musik künftiger Jahrtausende, das die Sonne nur mehr als rotglühendes Nachtlämpchen am Himmel hängen wird, unsere Ur-Ur-Enkel am Aequator Schlittschuh laufen und in einem grönlädischen Ball-Lokale nach Vierteltönen Walzen tanzen werden.

(*Signale,* Berlin, October 23, 1912)

[Herr Schoenberg is a musical spiritualist. At least, according to the assurances of his rabid adherents, he writes the music of the future millennia, when the sun will hang in the skies only as a glowing red night lamp, and our great-grandchildren will skate on the equator, and will dance in a Greenland dance hall to waltz music in quarter-tones.]

-:-

If an examination of Schoenberg's so-called treatise of harmony yields but a distorted notion of the subject, it at least affords a distinct impression of its author's personality. . . Anyone curious to gain an insight into the workings of the brain of this musical futurist, and courageous enough to wade through his wordy, incoherent, exclamation-bristling periods, may turn his thoughts on the possible subdivision of the scale into fifty-three tones or . . . ponder such oracles as: 'The order which we call artistic form is not an end in itself, but a makeshift.' It is not often that any author so obligingly furnishes the *reductio ad absurdum* of his own work as does the naive writer of this rambling grammar of cacophony.

(G. B. Weston, *Harvard Musical Review,* November 1912)

-:-

Arnold Schoenberg may be either crazy as a loon, or he may be a very clever trickster who is apparently determined to cause a sensation at any cost. His *Pierrot Lunaire* is the last word in cacophony and musical anarchy. Some day it may be regarded as of historical interest, because it represents the turning point, for the outraged muse surely can endure no more of this. Such noise must drive even the moonstruck Pierrot back to the realm of real music. . . A musical, or rather, unmusical ensemble, consisting of a piano, violin, viola, cello, piccolo, and clarinet . . . discoursed the most ear-splitting combinations of tones that ever desecrated the walls of a Berlin music hall. Schoenberg has thrown overboard all of the sheet anchors of the art of music. Melody he eschews in every form; tonality he knows not and such a word as harmony is not in his vocabulary. . . The remarkable part of this whole farce is that Schoenberg is taken seriously. A musically cultured audience sits through such an atrocity with hardly a protest. . . He even has adherents who rally round his standard and swear by his muse, declaring that this is music of the future. Otto Taubmann, the critic of the *Börsen-Courier,* expressed the feeling of all sane musicians when he wrote: 'If this is music of the future, then I pray my Creator not to let me live to hear it again.'

(Arthur M. Abell, *Musical Courier,* New York, November 6, 1912)

-:-

I fear and dislike the music of Arnold Schoenberg. . . Certainly, he is the hardest musical nut to crack of his generation, and the shell is very bitter in the mouth. His moon-stricken Pierrot chants—rather declaims—his woes and occasional joys to the music of the Viennese composer. . . The musicians were concealed behind the screens (dear old Mark Twain would have said, to escape the outraged audience), but, *ach Gott!* we heard them, we heard them only too clearly. It is the decomposition of the art, I thought, as I held myself in my seat. . . What did I hear? At first, the sound of delicate china shivering into a thousand luminous fragments. In the welter of tonalities that bruised each other as they passed and repassed, in the preliminary grip of enharmonies that almost made the ears bleed, the eyes water, the scalp to freeze, I could not get a central grip on myself. Schoenberg is the cruelest of all composers for he mingles with his music sharp daggers at white heat, with which he pares away tiny slices of his victim's flesh. Anon he twists the knife in the fresh wound and you receive another horrible thrill. . . There is no melodic or harmonic line, only a series of points, dots, dashes, or phrases that sob and scream, despair, explode, exalt, blaspheme. . . A man who could portray in tone sheer ugliness with such crystal clearness is to be reckoned with in these topsy-turvy times. . . Every composer has his aura; the aura of Arnold Schoenberg is, for me, the aura of original depravity, of subtle ugliness, of basest egoism, of hatred and contempt, of cruelty, and of the mystic grandiose. . . If such music-making is ever to become accepted, then I long for Death the Releaser.

(James Gibbons Huneker, New York *Times*, January 19, 1913)

-:-

Fünfzehn brave Musiker liessen uns Schönbergs *Kammersymphonie* hören. 'Schreckenskammersymphonie' wäre ein passenderer Name. . . . Es ist als wenn irgend ein böser Geist diesem Komponisten die Maxime eingeblasen hätte, die Zukunft der Musik beruhe in der Verleugnung jedes Tonalitätsbegriffs. . . Lautlos sassen die hundert Zuhörer da, als das halbstündige Dissonanzengewitter an ihnen vorübergerauscht war. Aber es gibt doch noch tapfere Menschen. Gleich zu Anfang war gedroht worden, dass die *Kammersymphonie* zweimal hintereinander gespielt werden würde, und richtig blieben die meisten sitzen! Oder war das am Ende doch keine Tapferkeit, war das bloss die Angst vor der Möglichkeit, die Zukunft möchte dieses kunsthandwerklich zusammengebraute Chaos für Kunst ansehen?

(August Spanuth, *Signale*, Berlin, May 14, 1913)

[Fifteen brave musicians presented to us Schoenberg's Chamber Symphony. 'Chamber-of-Horrors Symphony' would be a more fitting title. It is as though an evil spirit whispered to him that the future of music lies in the repudiation of every concept of tonality. . . A hundred listeners sat silent as this storm of dissonance roared past them. But there still are men of courage. Right at the beginning a threat was uttered that the Chamber Symphony would be played twice in succession, and yet the majority remained in their seats. Or was it not bravery, but simply fear that this skillfully concocted chaos might some day become the art of the future?]

-:-

Arnold Schoenberg has once more baffled the critics and public in Berlin, this time with the performance of his Chamber Symphony for fifteen solo instruments. In order to give the listeners an opportunity to become accustomed to and to find a meaning in the unintelligible mixture of sounds, the whole work was gone through twice, but its interest did not seem to be increased even by this stringent measure, and not a hand was raised to applaud. The audience sat perfectly silent as if stunned. One Berlin critic compared the harmonic structure of the work to a field of weeds and turnips mixed together, and the general opinion was that the composition was a most unaccountable jumbling together of abnormalities.

(*Musical Courier,* New York, May 28, 1913)

-:-

Arnold Schoenberg, the musical anarchist from Vienna, and his followers are claiming that his is the music of the future. His opponents do not dispute this claim. In fact, they concede its extreme probability, pointing out that the future embraces a certain locality with a climate of great torridity. The chief of this place is constantly looking for just such novelties as the music of the composer in question wherewith to amuse his guests.

(Cincinnati *Enquirer,* October 12, 1913)

-:-

This typewriter cannot find similes for the bestial racket. Most of Schoenberg's chords can be analyzed and shown to be based upon some sort of logic. For instance, a diminished fifth upon a perfect fourth is one of his milder and most useful invectives. How it sounds is a matter which may not be confided to this page on account of postal regulations. But these impertinences hurled into the ear pell-mell, and with a crash of thunderous percussions, rouse first of all a desire to laugh in ribald exasperation; next, one is annoyed at the brazen impudence of the man; lastly comes that mood which puts us all in the dentist's chair—a sort of 'oh—well, who wants to live anyway?' Schoenberg's *Five Pieces for Orchestra* sound like a pandemonium of cross-eyed devils playing a big score without transposing instruments and with careful disregard of each and every other devil.

(Eric De Lamarter, *Inter-Ocean,* Chicago, November 1, 1913)

-:-

If there is anything more utterly monstrous, more hideous and more artistically squalid than Schoenberg's *Five Orchestral Pieces,* it can only be some other composition by their creator or by one of his disciples. . . A cat walking down the keyboard of a piano could evolve a melody more lovely than any which came from the Viennese composer's consciousness. . . To the average listener, if the performers had played the music in a condition of helpless intoxication and had delivered themselves of anything that had come into their heads, the results of Schoenberg's inspiration would have sounded much the same.

(Felix Borowski, Chicago *Record Herald*, November 1, 1913)

-:-

To one critic, the music of Schoenberg's *Five Orchestral Pieces* suggested feeding-time at the zoo; also 'a farmyard in great activity while pigs are being ringed and geese strangled.' On another the identical section of the work produced the impression of 'a village fair with possibly a blind clarinetist playing at random.' The same listener heard sounds as of 'sawing steel' and the 'distant noise of an approaching train alternately with the musical sobs of a dynamo.'

(London *Daily Telegraph*, January 24, 1914)

-:-

Quite the queerest sensation of the year in a musical way was the first hearing of Schoenberg's 'cubist' quartet, op. 7, at the hands of the Flonzaleys. . . Kaleidoscopic Schoenberg starts where Strauss left off, with themes like Till Eulenspiegel's funeral. But it seems as if last year's famous picture of the Nude Falling Downstairs had furnished the corpse, for all is confusion worse confounded until the four instruments begin to festoon the bier with chromatic couplets, and then sing a chorale and ring a carillon with bell-like overtones of mutes, harmonics and plucked strings. Rigid fugue melts almost to a barcarolle, with whole-tone daisy chains. There is a suggested scherzo of the 'wind over the grave,' which dies to an old wives' croon of quaint falsettos and tremolos. Attention flags, for it needs long ears to wag both ways.

(New York *Sun*, January 27, 1914)

-:-

Schönberg's Kammersymphonie—Selbstmarterung eines Flagellanten, der sich mit der Knotenpeitsche geisselt, der sich selbst beschimpft! Wenn die zusammen geballten Hörner durch die Streicher aufwärts stiessen klang das wie 'Die Scheusal!' Ein grauenhaftes modernes Geisslerlied! Schönberg's unerbittliche Natur wurde klar: rücksichtlose Selbstzerfleischung und rücksichtloses Eingestehen: 'so bin ich!' Eine Art Katermusik, jaulend, jammernd, desparat. . . Schönberg ist unbeherrscht, schlägt sich vor aller Welt mit seinen Privatdämonen herum, ja in einer wahren Bekennerwut reisst er die Brust auf, zeigt seine Wundmale—und es ist erschütternd; doch, wenn man von Brahmsischer Keuschheit gesprochen hat, darf man wohl von Schönbergscher Unschamhaftigkeit sprechen.

(Ernst Decsey, *Signale*, Berlin, February 4, 1914)

[Schoenberg's Chamber Symphony—self-torture of a flagellant who whips himself with a cat-o'-nine-tails, while cursing himself! When a conglomeration of horns pushes upwards through the strings, it sounds like the words 'You, monster!' A hideous modern song of the scourge! Schoenberg's unappeasable nature is made clear: reckless self-mutilation, and a reckless admission: 'I am like that!' A sort of cat music, whining, wailing, desperate. Schoenberg is uncontrolled: he surrounds himself before the whole world with his private demons. He bares his breast in a fury of penitence, and shows his scars—and the spectacle is shocking. Yet, if people could talk about Brahms's chastity, one ought to be allowed to speak of Schoenberg's shamelessness.]

-:-

The behavior of the audience was highly creditable to Boston. There was smiling; there was giggling at times; there was applause. Nobody rose to remonstrate. Nothing was thrown at the orchestra. There was no perturbation of nature to show that Schoenberg's pieces were playing; the sun did not hasten its descent; there was no earthquake shock. It was as it should have been in Boston.

(Philip Hale, Boston *Herald*, December 19, 1914)

-:-

It has been said that it is difficult to score a noise well. In his *Five Orchestral Pieces*, Schoenberg has certainly succeeded in doing this. There were passages that suggested a bomb in a poultry-yard; cackles, shrieks, caterwauls; and then—crash!

(Louis Elson, Boston *Daily Advertiser*, December 19, 1914)

A polite and well-intentioned audience laughed outright as the first of Arnold Schoenberg's *Five Pieces for Orchestra* was played for the first time in Boston. . . The sonorities of the orchestra are so intense in pitch and quality that it is a physically taxing experience for the ear. The only pieces which conveyed any definite impression were the third, an impressionistic effect; and the fourth piece, which really communicates sensations of terror, or horror. The first piece appeared to ordinary ears, untuned to the intensities of Schoenberg, simply laughable, and so it was received. The last piece was also very terrible, physically hurtful. . . At present this music is so disagreeable that, whatever its merits, we cannot find the courage to wish to hear it again. At the best, it appears as the music of raw and tortured nerves.

(Olin Downes, Boston *Post*, December 19, 1914)

-:-

Schoenberg denies the stigma of futurism and contends that he writes 'naturally,' that his idiom is his individual expression, and that it is grossly misunderstood by many, chiefly by those obnoxious persons called critics. If a man insists that the emotions of his soul clamor for perfect expression only through a chord of consecutive minor seconds, none can presume to deny his sincerity. The normal, that is the usual, ear, however, might decide that his emotions are fit subjects for a vacuum cleaner. . . Dissonance is chronic. Each of the *Five Orchestral Pieces* ends with every man choosing his note as by lottery. This is economical music, for what is the need of rehearsal? It is a sorry bit if the wrong note will not sound better than the right one. . . Mr. Schoenberg has opened the book of his life to the pages of yesterday and tomorrow. While his dreams for the future are not reassuring, the sins of his past must weigh heavily upon him. So a Merry Christmas to Mr. Schoenberg, a merrier one than he enjoyed before writing this score. In due time may he find that region of fellowship where due appreciation of his gifts will be granted him. May he revel in the shrieks of hissing firebrands shot in welcome of new inmates. May his ears dilate with the groans of the lost souls of the damned. May curling, sizzling spirals of flame enfold and caress him. May the snarling, sardonic mockeries of grimacing imps soothe his harassed nerves.

(Boston *Globe*, December 19, 1914)

There was a time when the keys of church organs were so wide and so hard to work that the fists and elbows were used to press them down. Schoenberg's piano pieces, op. 11, sounded just as if they were played that way. For a minute or two that sort of thing is quite funny, though not as funny as a clown was when he plunged into an upright piano and set all the strings twanging at once. . . Schoenberg's compositions show a characteristic disregard of other people's happiness.

(New York *Post,* January 27, 1915)

-:-

Arnold Schoenberg is the musical Von Tirpitz of Germany. Having failed to capture a hostile world by his early campaign carried on in accordance with the international laws of music, he began to torpedo the eardrums of his enemies, as well as neutrals, with deadly dissonances. A specimen of the extreme Schoenberg was presented in his *Chamber Symphony;* and *Pelleas and Melisande,* which, however, is an earlier work, composed before he had fully entered on his policy of musical frightfulness. Nevertheless, even in *Pelleas* he boxes the ears of his hearers with some extremely rude and loud dissonances. He also introduces some bleating noises, which sound as if a sheep or calf were hidden under the stage. . . Its dearth of musical ideas is so appalling that one might suppose it was written in collaboration with Max Reger.

(New York *Evening Post,* November 20, 1915)

-:-

The leader of cacophonists . . . is Arnold Schoenberg. . . He learned a lesson from militant suffragettes. He was ignored till he began to smash the parlor furniture, throw bombs, and hitch together ten pianolas, all playing different tunes, whereupon everybody began to talk about him. In Schoenberg's later works, all the laws of construction, observed by the masters, from Bach to Wagner, are ignored, insulted, trampled upon. The statue of Venus, the Goddess of Beauty, is knocked from its pedestal and replaced by the stone image of the Goddess of Ugliness, with the hideous features of a Hottentot hag.

(Henry T. Finck, *Musical Progress,* New York, 1923)

-:-

Arnold Schoenberg is one of the most learned of Austrian professors, a musician of profound attainments. Unfortunately for his happiness, he also tried to be a creative artist. He wrote, among other things, a sextet, *Verklärte Nacht,* which contained some rather pretty things, buried in bombast and gasbags. As that did not make him famous with the masses, he tried to achieve notoriety by being 'real naughty,' defying musical grammar, placing a thumb against his nose with fingers spread out, and putting out his tongue. A specimen of this sort of tomfoolery was Schoenberg's melodrama *Pierrot Lunaire,* an unutterably silly thing . . . emitting strange noises which seldom have anything to do with music.

(Henry T. Finck, New York *Evening Post,* February 5, 1923)

-:-

Schoenberg's *Pierrot Lunaire* is a variedly rhythmical and dynamic succession of disagreeable noises. . . The impression upon the unattached music lover is simply null, or more or less wearisomely repugnant.

(Richard Aldrich, New York *Times,* February 5, 1923)

-:-

Schoenberg's *Pierrot Lunaire* is so new that enjoyment of it by persons who believe that music is an expression of beauty in art will have to wait until all such persons are dead or chaos be come again. . . It was a wearisome and futile experiment which some of the hearers were brave enough to smile at. . . Distinguished musicians who are striving to bring on the millennium in which cacophony shall reign were in last night's audience—among them Leopold Stokowski, Alfredo Casella, Georges Enesco, Darius Milhaud and Willem Mengelberg.

(H. E. Krehbiel, New York *Tribune,* February 5, 1923)

-:-

Suppose a thousand Schoenbergs say 'Evil, be thou my good!'—shall millions be asked to accept the dictum? The French Five and the American Six or the International Sixteen may go hang. . . Suppose a thousand painters or authors think that their duty to truth compels them to reproduce the image of excrement; shall the millions who do not enjoy the contemplation of such things say that excreta are proper subjects for the painter's and poet's art?

(H. E. Krehbiel, New York *Tribune,* February 11, 1923)

Arnold Schönbergs neuestes Werk, *Variationen für Orchester,* ist eine errechnete und erklügelte nur vom Intellekt diktierte musikalische Mathematik eines von einer verstiegenen Idee Besessenen. . . Ich kann ihn und sein Werk nicht ernst nehmen, dessen Logik zum Unsinn führen muss, weil die Prämissen seines Werkes falsch sind.

(Fritz Ohrmann, *Signale,* Berlin, December 12, 1928)

[Arnold Schoenberg's latest work, *Variations for Orchestra,* is calculated and excogitated musical mathematics dictated by intellect alone to one obsessed with a single eccentric idea. I cannot take seriously someone or his work when his logic leads perforce to an absurdity because the premises of such a work are false.]

-:-

In the Schoenberg *Variations* there is a very rancid odor of the midnight oil. This is machine-made music, the fruit of travail and long sleepless hours. . . But when it is all done, one feels that Schoenberg reached some such conclusion as 'a straight line tangent to a circle is perpendicular to the radius drawn to the point of contact.' Schoenberg's music is huge labor to demonstrate a simple enough theorem, namely, that if you employ the chromatic scale as fundamental, you can make some very weird harmonies.

(New York *Sun,* October 23, 1929)

-:-

The concert given by the Philadelphia Orchestra last night in Carnegie Hall was distinguished by mingled hisses and applause for the first New York performance of the extremely cacophonous *Variations for Orchestra,* op. 31, of Arnold Schoenberg. The music is so bloodless, such paper music. How we would have been thrilled by some good old red-blooded, rousing tune of Edgar Varèse! He, alas, is in Europe, and apparently nothing has erupted from his pen for some time. Schoenberg, after all, is a rather pale and wan substitute. If Mr. Varèse's music is strepitant and irresponsible, if he runs amuck in ways neither of reason nor righteousness, it at least makes loud and strange noises, while the music of Schoenberg . . . is tortuous, meager-hued music, anemic music. It is geometrical music, important only on paper; hideous, without vitality, and signifying nothing that matters. If it were uglier and more salient, it would be welcomed. . . Schoenberg places by his own theme and his own counterpoint a short subject of four notes built on Bach's great name. . . Is Schoenberg guilty of such megalomania that he really thinks he is a modern Bach and is thus slyly revealing himself and his cunning to a comprehending posterity?

(Olin Downes, New York *Times*, October 23, 1929)

-:-

Schoenberg is one of those who believe that the classic keys and their relations are of little use to musical progress and indeed detrimental to it. The action of *Die Glückliche Hand* is not complex. The wailing complaints of the man and the caterwauling of the chorus have neither musical nor dramatic value. They are simply tonal eccentricities, fruit of the deliberate attempt to destroy the fundamentals of musical art and substitute for them a new chaos, without form, and void.

(W. J. Henderson, New York *Sun*, April 23, 1930)

-:-

The name of Schoenberg is, as far as the British public is concerned, mud.

(*Musical Times*, London, May 1930)

-:-

Schönberg ist ein Fanatiker des Nihilismus, der Auflösung. . . Ob man es Zwölftonsystem nennt oder Atonalität oder noch anders ist belanglos gegenüber der Tatsache, dass hier in Klanggebilden geschrieben wird, die unseren Ohren nichts sagen, die aber ebenso vom Juden selbst abgelehnt werden.

(H. Gerigk, 'Eine Lanze für Schönberg,' *Die Musik*, November 1934)

[Schoenberg is a fanatic of nihilism and destruction. Whether one calls it twelve-tone system or atonality, is immaterial in the face of the fact that here something is expressed in musical formations that says nothing to our ears, something that is rejected even by the Jews themselves.]

-:-

The music [Arnold Schoenberg's *Suite for String Orchestra*] was . . . preceded by the miracle of Wagner's *Lohengrin* Prelude, and followed by the sensuous song and the throbbing humanity of Tchaikovsky's Fifth Symphony. In this environment the Schoenberg music was mercilessly revealed, a pale monument of lifeless theory . . . an empty and unbeautiful exhibition. A fatigued person might thus make a show of gymnastics. One! Two! Three! Four! Up go the arms and down go the legs, up go the legs and down go the arms. It is hollow; it is 'ersatz.' Ersatz music, music on and of paper.

(Olin Downes, New York *Times*, October 18, 1935)

-:-

The unmusicality of Schoenberg seems evident from the inner content of his art. In such music as the *Five Orchestral Pieces,* the heroic steed of Wagnerism cavorting amidst a Covent Garden conflagration has been grotesquely diminished to a gaunt and fleshless sea-horse poking furtively among atonal weeds.

(Harriet Cohen, *Music's Handmaid,* London, 1936)

-:-

A regular Friday audience, 90 percent feminine and 100 percent well-bred, sat stoically yesterday through thirty minutes of the most cacophonous world première ever heard here—the first performance anywhere of a new Violin Concerto by Arnold Schoenberg. . . . A handful of dowagers, however, gave up the fight and walked out, noses in the air. . . Yesterday's piece combines the best sound effects of a hen yard at feeding time, a brisk morning in Chinatown and practice hour at a busy music conservatory. The effect on the vast majority of hearers is that of a lecture on the fourth dimension delivered in Chinese.

(Edwin H. Schloss, Philadelphia *Record,* December 7, 1940)

-:-

Die Tendenz Schönbergs, alles bisher Dagewesene zu vereinen ist die altbewährte jüdische Taktik, die immer dann zur Anwendung gelangte, wenn es galt, die Kulturewerte der Wirtsvölker zu zerstören, um an deren Stelle die eigenen als allein gültige zu setzen.

(T. Stengel and H. Gerigk, *Lexicon der Juden in der Musik,* Berlin, 1941)

[Schoenberg's tendency to negate all that was before him is the old tested Jewish tactics which are always put into practice, at an opportune moment, to destroy the cultural values of the host peoples in order to set up their own as the only valid ones.]

What has happened to Schoenberg? In his *Ode to Napoleon* he all but scuttles the famous 12-tone system of composition. . . There are dark hints of sequential developments, and there are plain evidences of harmony! Is this work a confession, an armistice, or a revolution? The old, uncompromising Schoenberg was hard to take. But the new, indulgent Schoenberg is harder still.

(*Musical America*, December 10, 1944)

-:-

It is clear that each of these composers . . . has been badly bitten by the *Schön-bug*, with results that make one regret that the complaint is not made notifiable by law, just as an outbreak of foot-and-mouth disease or the appearance of the Colorado beetle on our shores requires a report to the authorities and isolation, so far as possible, of the infected area. . . Some of these pages resemble a kitchen fly-paper during the rush hour on a hot August afternoon.

(C. W. Orr, *The Music Review*, London, February 1948)

-:-

The Three Pieces, op. 11, are now more than forty years old; they are rarely performed, which is not surprising, since no pianist of the first rank would bother to learn, or desire to inflict on his audience, such unrelievedly ugly and unrewarding abstractions. . . Schoenberg states: 'I write what I feel in my heart.' If this is really so, we can only assume that from 1908 or so, Schoenberg has been suffering from some unclassifiable and peculiarly virulent form of cardiac disease.

(*Musical Opinion*, London, December 1949)

-:-

To the faithful, *Pierrot Lunaire* evidently stands as the summit of musical ecstasy, but to some of us its 612 bars of etiolated and emasculated shreds of sound represent the nadir of decadence. . . The Schoenberg idiom is unintelligible and, indeed, repellent to all save the master's disciples and the inevitable handful of humbugs. The Master of the King's Musick, Arnold Bax, hit the nail well and truly on the head when he wrote: 'Atonalism appears to be a cul-de-sac, cluttered up with morbid growths emanating from the brains rather than from the imagination of a few decadent Central European Jews.'

(*Musical Opinion*, London, December 1949)

The New York première of Arnold Schoenberg's cantata *A Survivor from Warsaw* was given last night. . . It is poor and empty music, even though it be couched in the most learned Schoenbergian formulas of craftsmanship. The orchestra makes bogey noises which have been heard many times before in Schoenberg's scores. These sounds are neither novel nor convincing. A melodramatic concomitant of this occasion was the theatrical device by which the members of the chorus, as the narrator described the scene, rose to their feet, first one by one, the ranks filling more and more rapidly, until they stood, coats discarded, in the white shirts of the condemned. We regret to say that the effect was hammy, and regret still more to say that in this respect it was not incongruous with the character of the composition.

(Olin Downes, New York *Times*, April 14, 1950)

-:-

The case of Arnold Schoenberg vs. the people (or vice versa, as the situation may be) is one of the most singular things in the history of music. For here is a composer—the only one with the possible exception of Charles Ives—who operates on the theory that if you know how to put a bunch of notes on a piece of score paper you are, presto, a composer. . . Forty-five years have passed since Schoenberg wrote his *Chamber Symphony*, and it will certainly be another forty-five before it is programmed by popular demand. It never touches any emotion save curiosity, never arouses any mood save speculation on how the conductor can conduct it and how the musicians can count the bars.

(Rudolph Elie, Boston *Herald*, November 11, 1950)

-:-

Camouflaged behind the grandiloquent phrases about progressiveness and innovation, Schoenberg and his disciples among atonal composers constitute in actual fact an arch-reactionary sect that has played a sinister role in the destruction of contemporary musical art in several countries of Western Europe and in America. Schoenberg's notorious 'emancipation of dissonance' is nothing more than rampant musical anarchy, a refutation of euphony and affirmation of cacophony. Having slaughtered living natural melos, having distorted the very foundation of harmony, the atonalists write anti-musical dissonant stuff based entirely on cacophonous combinations of sound. . . The stillborn theories of Schoenberg, calculated to destroy melody and harmony, can lead only to retrogression, not to progress in art. . . They serve as a convenient springboard for propaganda of anti-democratic cosmopolitanism supporting the principles of imperialist esthetics. We believe that it is not by accident that Arnold Schoenberg, with his decaying individualistic philosophy of a frightened bourgeois, has found a fertile soil for his propaganda of perverted pathological experimentalism in the United States where art is completely subordinated to the bestial laws of capitalist society.

(G. Schneerson, *Music in the Service of Reaction,* Moscow, 1950)

-:-

I instantly developed an ice-cold antipathy to Schoenberg and his whole musical system on the far-away day when I first came upon those three piano pieces, op. 11. . . I believe that there is little probability that the twelve-note scale will ever produce anything more than morbid or entirely cerebral growths. It might deal successfully with neuroses of various kinds, but I cannot imagine it associated with any healthy and happy concept such as young love or the coming of spring.

(Arnold Bax in the symposium of opinions in *Music and Letters,* London, October 1951)

-:-

I love a *Figaro,* a *Meistersinger,* a *Falstaff* for the wealth of human spirit that transfigures them. Behind the works of Schoenberg I see only an inhuman lunar landscape; and I cannot warm to it.

(Arthur Bliss in the symposium of opinions in *Music and Letters,* London, October 1951)

-:-

To something stuffy in Schoenberg's mind, I suppose—to some kind of hot-house estheticism, cut off from the active world and healthy air—is to be put down the flabbiness of effect he makes. But no vigorous sort of intention can be expressed when the very medium is as rotten as Schoenberg's scale.

(G. H. M. Lockhart in the symposium of opinions in *Music and Letters,* October 1951)

-:-

The best preparation for Schoenberg is his setting of the morbid and quite deranged French poem *Pierrot Lunaire,* in which verbal insanity is matched by musical madness with results that are depressing. The listener leaves a performance of this work doubting his own sanity. The first work on last night's program was the Quartet allegedly in D major. Of course, it was in no key. Rather it was in the system which Schoenberg invented and which he called atonalism. It was like the babbling of a deranged man. A trio, opus 45, key undesignated, there being none, resembled the sounds an infant might make on the keyboard of a piano.

(Glenn Dillard Gunn, Washington *Times-Herald,* February 8, 1952)

-:-

Schoenberg's *Der Tanz um das goldene Kalb* was repulsive. . . A xylophone, alas, is heard . . . I admired the way the singers stuck to their line of country, though I doubt if anybody could have told, most of the time, what notes they were chasing. I am afraid that this demonstration of Schoenberg on Orgies is not my cup of tea—or even the cup of cold poison that the composer's worshippers seem to long to administer to those of us who can't take very seriously some of the old man's sequential squeals.

(W. R. Anderson, *Musical Times,* London, May 1952)

-:-

There is no doubt that Schoenberg was a master of counterpoint and that the Quartet, op. 37, and Suite, op. 29, are—*on paper*—triumphs of twelve-tonal logic and precisely calculated mathematical organization. Mathematics, however, are not music, and to non-dodecaphonists the effect of such works on the ear is one of unintelligible ugliness and a labored self-conscious straining after effect that is inexpressibly tedious when it is not thoroughly repugnant in its pathological morbidity. . . The multitudinous freak effects and frenetic caperings defeat their own ends by becoming monotonous and afford little beyond a quasi-masochistic pleasure to the uninitiated.

(*Musical Opinion,* London, July 1952)

SCHUMANN Wir suchten vergeblich (in Schumanns *Allegro*, op. 8) nach einer ruhig entfalteten Melodie, nach einer Harmonie die nur einen Takt aushielte—überall nur verworrene Combinationen von Figuren, Dissonanzen, Passagen, kurz für uns eine Folter.

(L. Rellstab, *Iris*, Berlin, March 4, 1836)

[We looked in vain (in Schumann's *Allegro*, op. 8) for a steadily developing melody, for a harmony that would hold for even one bar —everywhere only bewildering combinations of figurations, dissonances, transitions, in brief, for us, a torture.]

-:-

Not long ago, this good town of Leipzig fulfilled 'the forms' of a capital, as far as music was concerned, having its conservatives, its liberals, and its radicals. Herr Schumann was the leader of the last party, being editor of the revolutionary periodical which set itself against the 'rights divine' of authority, rhythm, and melody, as understood by the old composers. His compositions, like those of M. Berlioz, were considered as too profoundly poetical for any, save the initiated, to comprehend. The prevalent mood of mind might indeed be inferred from certain works being graced, by way of title, with the name of Hoffmann's bandmaster, Kreisler. . . Not even the solid and intellectual playing of the composer's lady, Mlle. Clara Wieck, could make these rhapsodies intelligible.

(H. F. Chorley, *The Athenaeum*, London, October 19, 1844)

-:-

It is wonderful to remark how long a persevering seeker may wait, how far he may wander, before he is admitted to be capable of judging of the compositions of Dr. Schumann. Should he find quartets dull, monotonous, an idea stale and trifling, he will be referred to pianoforte music. Should this appear to him so licentious in its discords and suspensions that half-a-dozen false notes on the part of the player would be of small consequence, he will be requested to believe in some unheard *Lied*. . . Not to leave a single means untried, our composer does not scruple to introduce the triangle to set off a meager phrase in his Symphony in B flat. . . The mystagogue who has no real mysteries to promulgate, would presently lose his public, did he not keep curiosity entertained by exhibiting some of the charlatan's familiar tricks.

(H. F. Chorley, *The Athenaeum*, London, December 18, 1852)

-:-

Schumann baut jetzt Künstlichere, verwickeltere Perioden, verwischt die erkennbaren Abscheidungen derselben, wie die symmetrische Gliederung der Gedanken mehr und mehr, und bringt deshalb bei dem Hörer bisweilen das Gefühl hervor als befinde er sich in einem Irrgarten.

(J. C. Lobe, *Musikalische Briefe*, Berlin, 1852)

[Schumann builds nowadays more artificial, more intricate periods, obliterates their recognizable divisions such as the symmetric formation of phrases to a still greater degree, and therefore creates sometimes a feeling in the listener as if he is in a labyrinth.]

-:-

An affectation of originality, a superficial knowledge of the art, an absence of true expression, and an infelicitous disdain of form have characterized every work of Robert Schumann hitherto introduced in this country. His general style betrays the patchiness and want of fluency of a tyro; while the forced and unnatural turns of cadence and progression, declare neither more nor less than the convulsive efforts of one who has never properly studied his art, to hide the deficiencies of early education under a mist of pompous swagger.

(H. F. Chorley, *Musical World*, London, April 9, 1853)

-:-

In certain of Dr. Schumann's Variations for two pianofortes, the harmonies are so obtrusively crude that no number of wrong notes would be detected by the subtlest listener. Ours are days when taste must be carefully watched, and the works of Dr. Schumann (with some trifling exceptions) are too pretending to be endured.

(H. F. Chorley, *The Athenaeum*, London, May 10, 1856)

-:-

The chief novelty of the evening was Madame Schumann's performance of Dr. Schumann's Concerto in A minor, which was received with a warmth well merited by the Lady's playing. Because we cannot fancy the Concerto adopted by any performer in London, we will forbear to speak of the composition as a work.

(H. F. Chorley, *The Athenaeum,* London, May 17, 1856)

-:-

Madame Schumann seems determined to offer Dr. Schumann's music in all the fullness of its eccentricity to the public. What is more, Madame Schumann, resolute in her faith, will not allow us to forget that Dr. Schumann's attempts were put forward under pretext of a 'mission,' and in scorn of others who thought more modestly of their place in the world of art than himself. She was ill-advised when she ventured the remarks on one of its features, namely, Dr. Schumann's *Carnival Music.* We can find nothing of the carnival in these fourteen little pieces; which are as insignificant in scale as in a child's lesson, yet without the prettiness and the character which alone make such trifles pass. Uncouth, faded, and wanting in clearness, they seem to us. These *Davidsbündler* have made their noise. They have blotted their reams of newspapers—full of dismal jokes at others and fulsome mutual admiration. . . If these things are to be thrust on us, we must speak the plain truth, in protection of the modest and the half-instructed.

(H. F. Chorley, *The Athenaeum,* June 21, 1856)

-:-

We are quite sure that the subscribers would have preferred hearing Madame Goldschmidt (Jenny Lind) in anything rather than in Dr. Schumann's *Paradise and Peri,* which, besides its other peculiarities, is essentially unvocal from first to last. The principal solo voice parts are written as much in contempt of the resources and capabilities of voice as the most uncouth performances of Signor Verdi himself.

(H. F. Chorley, London *Times,* June 24, 1856)

-:-

Dr. Schumann is not possessed of that musical organization without which all the talent and ingenuity in the world avail nothing. . . He produces by some mysterious rule of his own; but nothing he does springs naturally from the heart. For years Schumann reigned a high authority on musical matters; but in an evil hour he fancied he could compose, and began, as he imagined, to exemplify his doctrines of taste by music of his own. Finding he could not follow in the path of the really great masters, he determined to strike out a new one for himself, which he affected accordingly in a totally opposite direction. . . Dr. Schumann was hailed as an apostle of a new school, and became the prophet of a certain clique. The new preacher, nevertheless, did not boast of many disciples; and Schumann was soon compelled to abdicate in favor of another apostle, who brought with him greater eloquence, subtlety, and daring, with an equal contempt for precedents. The old was deserted for the new; Schumann was dethroned, and Richard Wagner sat in his place. Such is a brief outline of Schumann's career. The asylum at Düsseldorf can tell the sequel.

(H. F. Chorley, *Musical World*, London, June 28, 1856)

-:-

Like other so-called innovators, Dr. Schumann is essentially as trivial in idea and as poor in resource as the most intolerable of the 'Philistines.'

(*The Athenaeum*, London, June 28, 1856)

-:-

La musique de Schumann manque de clarté. . . Le désordre et la confusion envahissent parfois jusqu'aux meilleures pages du musicien, comme hélas! ils one envahi plus tard le cerveau de l'homme.

(*Le Ménestrel*, Paris, February 15, 1863)

[The music of Schumann lacks clarity. . . The disorder and confusion at times invade even his best pages as—alas!—they invaded his brain.]

-:-

This symphony in C has what the French would call a 'faux air de Beethoven,' from beginning to end; and, perhaps, a more appropriate denomination for Schumann could hardly be found than that of a would-be-if-he-could Beethoven. Schumann went for his melody to a dried-up well. Schumann's faculty of invention was next door to null; and Schumann, though a laboriously studied, was, at the best, a half-formed musician.

(*Musical World*, London, June 4, 1864)

SCRIABIN The Russian Symphonic Society played Scriabin's Second Symphony. I think there was a gross error in the program: instead of 'symphony' they should have printed 'cacophony,' because in this alleged 'composition' there seems to be a complete absence of all consonance. For thirty or forty minutes silence is broken by a continuous series of discords piled up one on another without any sense whatsoever. I cannot understand why Liadov conducted such nonsense. I went to hear it just for amusement. Glazunov did not go, and Rimsky-Korsakov, whose opinion I asked, said that he fails to understand how anyone can devalue euphony to such an extent.

(Anton Arensky in a letter to Taneyev, dated January 17, 1902, published in a collection of Taneyev's correspondence, Moscow, 1951)

-:-

Scriabin's *Divine Poem* has more convolutions than the *Sinfonia Domestica* of Strauss and it is charged with more shrieking discords than anything that Vincent d'Indy ever conceived in his most abandoned moments. It was performed with deadly effect. When it was past, the audience called out Mr. Scriabin and took a good look at him.

(W. J. Henderson, New York *Sun*, March 16, 1907)

-:-

Scriabin's *Divine Poem* is the work of a neurotic, a Fourth of July celebration in which every member of the orchestra has signed a Declaration of Independence and makes just as much noise as he possibly can.

(*Musical America*, New York, March 23, 1907)

-:-

The nerves of the audience were worn and racked as nerves are seldom assailed even in these days. Scriabin's *Poème de l'Extase* was the cause. This composition was heralded as a foster child of theosophy. Certainly it conveyed a sense of eeriness and uncanny connotation. Most of the time, the violins were whimpering and wailing like lost souls, while strange undulating and formless melodies roved about in the woodwind. A solo violin spoke occasionally, growing more and more plaintive, and finally being swallowed in a chaos of acid harmonies with violins screaming in agony overhead. There were three such climaxes in the composition, all built upon a basis of cymbals, drums and inchoate blarings of the brass. It all seemed far more like several other things than ecstasy.

(W. J. Henderson, New York *Sun*, December 11, 1908)

-:-

The ultra-moderns all resemble each other. When one of these extreme gentlemen comes at you with a *Poem of Ecstasy*, you may be sure of one thing, he is going to use every known instrument. Stendhal says that the radical works of one generation become the classical works of the next, in which we pity the next generation. Some of this ecstasy was extremely bitter, while some of it reminded of the ecstasy of the too convivial gentleman who thought that the air was filled with green monkeys with crimson eyes and sparkling tails, a kind of ecstasy that is sold in Russia at two rubles a bottle.

(Louis Elson, Boston *Daily Advertiser*, October 22, 1910)

-:-

As a composer, as an artistic innovator, Alexander Scriabin is a failure of no little brilliance. . . Mr. Scriabin does not even have the outward and visible tokens of artistic genius. His face was clean, his hair was neatly cropped, his clothes were admirably fitted to his body. He did not, when he played, snort with tremendous emotions nor roll his eyes with passionate frenzy. His *pièce de résistance* was a sonata of his own composition. This creation was so portentously dull that all who heard it must have been convinced that Mr. Scriabin was a writer of most serious and sterling worth.

(Felix Borowski, Chicago *Record-Herald*, August 1, 1912)

-:-

If cacophonous discordance and noise which irritates the ear reflects the music of the antediluvian days, then Scriabin's *Prometheus* describes most successfully the chaos of those days . . . It may be true that the Russian composer is too far advanced for the present generation and that his doctrine and music will be accepted in years to come, but as the writer is not a reader of the future, the work is condemned for the present.

(*Musical Courier*, New York, March 10, 1915)

Scriabin may be laboring under the delusion which is common to all neurotic degenerates, whether men of genius or ordinary idiots, namely, that he has enlarged the boundaries of art by making it more comprehensive. He has not done so. He has taken a step backward.

(*Musical Courier*, New York, March 25, 1915)

-:-

Scriabin's *Prometheus* is the product of a once fine composer suffering from mental derangement, and Schoenberg's lucubrations are simply nothing at all. You cannot expect either a journalist or his public to see any difference between a lunatic and an idiot.

(Frederick Corder, 'On the Cult of Wrong Notes,' *Musical Quarterly*, July 1915)

-:-

Scriabin's *Prometheus* remains for us as incomprehensible, as inexpressive as at its first hearing. . . One becomes increasingly conscious that Scriabin's mind is working in an exalted mood, out of relation to facts, which is a polite way of saying what is often put more shortly. All the elaborate sanity of technique will not hide the fact that we are in the atmosphere of the revivalist meeting, where zealots speak with tongues and utter strange words divorced from their plain meaning. . . The question is whether this music is the outcome of a sane mind or of a deranged one, and that is beyond the range of purely musical criticism to decide, though it may be able to offer strong presumptive evidence.

(London *Times*, September 27, 1919)

-:-

As a kind of drug, no doubt Scriabin's music has a certain significance, but it is wholly superfluous. We already have cocaine, morphine, hashish, heroin, anhalonium, and innumerable similar productions, to say nothing of alcohol. Surely that is enough. On the other hand, we have only one music. Why must we degrade an art into a spiritual narcotic? Why is it more artistic to use eight horns and five trumpets than to use eight brandies and five double whiskies?

(Cecil Gray, *A Survey of Contemporary Music*, London, 1924)

SHOSTAKOVITCH Concert-goers who were aware of the character of the principal number on the program . . . may have expected to find bombing planes hovering over Carnegie Hall . . . the auditorium guarded by squads [of police] armed with tear-gas bombs, the balconies studded with machine guns. . . . But nothing of this was to be observed . . . [Police] seem not to have been informed of the fact that Red Propaganda of the most virulent kind was to be spread at the concert, that brazen incitements to mob violence were planned. . . Happily for the Established Order, this singular negligence of the authorities had no evil results. Although for something like half an hour, the atmosphere of Carnegie Hall resounded with Communistic preachments and revolutionary proclamations and the songs of Comrades and Workers and the reverberations of the Five-Year Plan . . . not a capitalistic hair was seen to rise upon its scalp, nor a white waistcoat burst with indignation. . . Mr. Dmitri Shostakovitch . . . had written the last section of his Proletarian or May Day Symphony as a choral finale, set to words which proclaimed the purpose of the singing Comrades to 'destroy by fire the olden time.'. . . But this choral part was dispensed with in performance. . . Mr. Shostakovitch in this Symphony has given us an admirably definite and whole-souled utterance of political and economic faith. But the work appears to have one slight defect: in impregnating his Symphony with political and economic doctrine, the composer unfortunately neglected to transmit to it any musical ideas. . . It is obvious that Mr. Shostakovitch's heart is full; but it is also obvious that his head is empty. One would be hard put to it to think of a recent score of like dimensions that is equally vacuous and sterile. Mr. Shostakovitch appears to have made a virtue of musical impotence. . . If this brainless and trivial music with its unrelieved indigence, its blatant banality, its naive portentousness, is the result of impregnating music with Marxian ideology, all one can say is that esthetic birth control in Russia is a lamentable failure.

(Lawrence Gilman, New York *Herald Tribune*, January 4, 1933)

-:-

Lady Macbeth of Mzensk is a bed-chamber opera. We see much of the coarse embrace of the two sinners, mumbling and fumbling about in bed with the side of the house removed so we shall miss nothing. For their first embraces the composer has written music which for realism and brutal animalism surpasses anything else in the world. Here indeed we can indulge in superlatives. Shostakovitch is without doubt the foremost composer of pornographic music in the history of the art. He has accomplished the feat of penning passages which, in their faithful portrayal of what is going on, become obscene. . . And to crown this achievement he has given to the trombone a jazz slur to express satiety, and this vulgar phrase, rendered tenfold more offensive by its unmistakable purpose, is brought back in the last scene to help us to understand how tired the lover is of his mistress. The whole scene is little better than a glorification of the sort of stuff that filthy pencils write on lavatory walls.

(W. J. Henderson, New York *Sun*, February 9, 1935)

-:-

Several theaters have presented the opera, *Lady Macbeth of the Mzensk District* by Shostakovitch. . . The listener is from the very first bewildered by a stream of deliberately discordant sounds. Fragments of melody, beginnings of a musical phrase appear on the surface, are submerged, then emerge again and disappear once more in the roar. . . On the stage, singing is replaced by screaming. If the composer happens to hit on a simple and understandable melody, he, as if frightened by such a calamity, flees into the jungle of musical confusion, at times reaching complete cacophony. . . . The music quacks, grunts, growls, strangles itself in order to represent the amatory scenes as naturalistically as possible. 'Love' is smeared all over the opera in the most vulgar manner. The merchant's bed occupies the central place on the stage. On it all 'problems' are solved. *Lady Macbeth* enjoys great success with the bourgeois audiences abroad. . . It tickles the perverted tastes of the bourgeois audiences with its fidgeting, screaming neurasthenic music.

(*Pravda,* Moscow, January 28, 1936)

-:-

Shostakovitch's Ninth Symphony induced this writer to flee the hall in a state of acute irritation. One was grateful to be spared the pomposities and crude programmatics of the Leningrad, the pseudoprofundities of the Sixth and Eighth Symphonies; but for these Shostakovitch has substituted only a farrago of circus tunes, gallop rhythms, and dated harmonic quirks whose smart cleverness resembles the tea-table talk of an ultra-precocious child.

(E. Chapman, *Tempo*, London, September 1946)

-:-

The fugue in the first movement of Shostakovitch's Fourth Symphony illustrates the practice of 'neo-classicisim.' The subject of the fugue is absolutely meaningless and aimless. Its wanderings can continue interminably. The appearance of the second voice does not contribute any new quality to the fugue. Meaninglessness is multiplied by meaninglessness, and instead of one unpleasantness, the listener experiences two unpleasantnesses. Having meandered in this way for two pages, Shostakovitch introduces a third voice. He is not in the least interested whether these voices can go together and what quantity of dissonances results from it—the more the better. . . But this is not all. With sadistic determination the composer releases the fourth formalistic serpent, and all four serpents, in monstrous entanglement, abuse the human ear and human nerves. From this torture great Bach himself must turn in his grave and wonder: 'Can it be that this shameless formalistic orgy has its sources in my music?'

(Marian Koval, *Sovietskaya Musica,* Moscow, May 1948)

-:-

The Shostakovitch Fifth Symphony is an uneven work. There are agreeable passages and also a deal of triviality, of vulgarity and bombast. . . . It can also be urged that the playing by America's major symphony orchestra of a work designed to celebrate the twentieth anniversary of Soviet Russia is giving aid and comfort to those who seek to destroy us.

(Warren Storey Smith, Boston *Post,* October 25, 1952)

-:-

The Fifth Symphony of Shostakovitch always has been singularly irritating to this chronicler. . . . Whenever I hear one of his marches my imagination fastens upon a picture of the parades in Red Square and the banners of Uncle Joe, and my irritation becomes powerful.

(Cyrus Durgin, Boston *Globe,* October 25, 1952)

SIBELIUS Sibelius's Fourth Symphony is a puzzler. In this work Sibelius seems to have left the ranks of his contemporaries and becomes a 'futurist.' The Symphony is neither fish, flesh nor fowl—nor good red herring. Even the part-writing shows crudities; in many places the music looks and sounds like the awkward efforts of amateur composers with little or no training. There are long rambling passages for the strings, with short, jerky fragments in the woodwinds. . . The composer tells us that the work is in A minor, and the last movement does end in that key, but the first movement has few signs of any tonality. The second movement begins in F major, but with a B natural instead of B flat. The third movement is even more incoherent than the first—it would take a Philadelphia lawyer to find any sense of form in it. It sounds like the improvisation of an unskillful organist. In the ninth bar of the last movement the second violins move from D sharp to E natural; the violas meanwhile go from the lower D sharp to E *sharp;* it sounds like a misprint. If this sort of thing continues, there will be no such thing as correcting mistakes in parts at a rehearsal—the composer will have to furnish an affidavit with every individual note. As the modern ear becomes accustomed to these things all standards will be swept away.

(W. M. Humiston, *Musical America,* New York, August 9, 1913)

-:-

Several persons applauded the Sibelius Symphony No. 4. Most of those in the large audience sat amused, smiling, wondering what to make of it. They had tasted cubist music at last. For the most part, this latest symphony from the pen of Finland's foremost composer is a tangle of the most dismal dissonances. It eclipses the saddest and sourest moments of Debussy.

(Boston *Journal,* October 25, 1913)

-:-

Sibelius is a Finnish composer who speaks with a loud, harsh voice through a full orchestra. He sees to it that every desk in the orchestra shall have something to do every minute even if it sometimes conflicts with what some other set of instruments are performing. His Fourth Symphony is a dismal failure.

(Boston *American,* October 25, 1913)

The score of the Sibelius Symphony No. 4 is almost the classical orchestra, but the classical ends there, for the treatment is of the twentieth, or perhaps the twenty-first century. There are sounds and lamentations in the air, that is, if there were any air, which there is not, for mere tune is left out of this miscalled symphony. There were dissonant and doleful mutterings, generally leading nowhere.

(Boston *Record*, October 25, 1913)

-:-

That the Fourth Symphony of Sibelius is in large degree experimental is evident. The composer has entered into the ultra-modern school of weird progressions and of restless rhythms. One finds the whole-tone progressions of Debussy (and of Siamese music) copiously employed. It is a composition which the earnest music-lover will 'first endure' and 'then pity,' but never embrace. We do not think that Sibelius has any business in the pasture of Schoenberg. The old-fashioned auditor who wants a tune will be decidedly disappointed, for instead of melody there is dissonance, gloomy mutterings. There are some of the most bitter harmonies and progressions that we have ever heard, a mixture of musical quassia and wormwood, which suggests that the composer is dissatisfied about something,—and, so, probably, are the general public. Many went into the corridor to get a little air, the first obtainable since the beginning of the program.

(Louis Elson, Boston *Daily Advertiser,* November 14, 1914)

-:-

Finlandia and *En Saga* are noisy and obvious effusions based on trivial themes. But . . . where the orchestral ingenuity of a Ravel most patently betrays a charlatan, Sibelius's skill is almost always presented with dignity.

(Edward Robinson, *The American Mercury,* New York, February 1932)

-:-

I found the Second Symphony of Sibelius vulgar, self-indulgent, and provincial beyond all description.

(Virgil Thomson, New York *Herald Tribune,* October 11, 1940)

STRAUSS Ich habe Damen und Wagner-Jünglinge von dem Strausschen *Don Juan* mit einer Begeisterung reden hören. . . . Andere fanden das Ding einfach abscheulich. . . Das ist kein Tongemälde, sondern ein Tumult von blendenden Farbenklecksen, ein stammelnder Tonrausch. Dass er, als Zögling der Berlioz-Liszt-Wagnerschen Schule den grössten Apparat für seine Tondichtung in Bewegung setzt, versteht sich von selbst. . . Die höchsten (bisher im Orchester ungebraüchlichen) Töne der Violine schneiden glasscharf in unser Ohr, ein Glockenspiel erhebt jeden Augenblick sein kindisches Geklingel. Fast möchten wir wünschen es würden bald noch recht viel solcher Tongemälde komponiert als non plus ultra einer falschen zügellosen Richtung. Eine Reaktion könnte dann nicht ausbleiben, die Rückkehr zu einer gesunden, zu einer musikalischen Musik.

(Eduard Hanslick, 1891)

[I have heard ladies and little Wagnerites speak of Strauss's *Don Juan* with enthusiasm. Others found the thing simply repellent. This is no tone picture, but a confusion of blinding color splashes, a stuttering tonal delirium. That he, as a disciple of the Berlioz-Liszt-Wagner school, has set in motion a huge orchestral apparatus for his tone poem, goes without saying. . . The highest (and heretofore inapplicable in the orchestra) violin notes cut as sharp as glass in our ears; a glockenspiel raises every moment its childish tinkle. We might almost wish that quite a lot more of such tone pictures were composed soon as a *non plus ultra* of a false unrestrained direction. Then a reaction will not fail to assure a return to a healthy musical music.]

-:-

Strauss uses music as the vehicle of expressing everything but music; for he has little invention, and his musical thoughts are of little worth. This symphonic poem is supposed to portray in music the recollections and regrets of a jaded voluptuary. Now, granting that music is capable of doing this, what do we find in this composition? There are recollections, not of Don Juan, but of Liszt and of Wagner. There are also regrets, but the regrets come from the hearers. Besides, Don Juan was more direct in his methods. His wooing was as sudden and as violent as his descent to the lower regions. According to Strauss, he was verbose, fond of turning corners, something of a metaphysician, and a good deal of a bore. When he made love, he beat upon a triangle, and when he was dyspeptic, he confided his woes to instruments that moaned in sympathy.

(Philip Hale, Boston *Post,* November 1, 1891; eleven years later, Hale wrote in the Boston *Journal* of November 2, 1902 of *Don Juan*: 'Why should anyone say this tone-poem is formless? Simply as a vain and impotent protest against a modern shape or form. . . A daring, brilliant composition; one that paints the hero as might a master's brush on canvas. How expressive the themes! How daring the treatment of them! What fascinating, irresistible insolence, glowing passion!')

-:-

From first to last, *Till Eulenspiegel* was musical obscenity of the most unique and remarkable description; in form a crazy-quilt, in orchestral color much the same. The editor of the program-book describes, or rather translates it as 'after an old rogue's tune by Richard Strauss.' Call it after an old roué's tune, and imagine this old roué on a spree and you hit the nail nearer on the head. It is a most inexplicable hodgepodge. Eulenspiegel's daily beverage was doubtless beer, and the music is unmistakably beerish. The tone-picture, with all its abnormal and hideously grotesque proportions, is that of a heavy, dull and witless Teuton. The orchestration of the work is sound and fury, signifying nothing, and the instruments are made to indulge in a shrieking, piercing, noisy breakdown most of the time.

(O. L. Capen, Boston *Journal,* February 22, 1896)

-:-

Till Eulenspiegel is a noisy, nerve-destroying, heavy piece of work, crude in color, confusing in design, and utterly unlovable.

(Boston *Gazette,* February 22, 1896)

-:-

Till Eulenspiegel casts into the deepest shade the wildest efforts of the wildest follower of the modern school. It is a blood-curdling nightmare.

(Boston *Herald,* February 23, 1896)

-:-

Eulenspiegel was a great hand at practical jokes—and Strauss thought he could imitate him by playing a practical joke upon the general public. Why should such things be given at a symphony concert? The orchestra would feel it infra dig to play Johann Strauss's waltzes; we wonder how they feel under the indignity of being made to play this monstrosity by Richard Strauss!

(Boston *Evening Transcript,* February 22, 1896)

-:-

Richard Strauss is the Maeterlinck of music; he has hitherto revelled in the more or less harmonious exploitation of the charnel house, the grave, and the gnawing worm. But in *Till Eulenspiegel* he set out to be humorous. Flutes chased one another all over the leger lines; oboes squeaked convulsively; clarinets coughed in their highest register; stopped cornets wailed in nasal tones; trombones bellowed; triangles and tambours rattled; and the timpani player lost his patience and several pounds of flesh in his desperate attempts to thump his three kettledrums as often and as hard as the score demanded. *Till Eulenspiegel* is a horrible example of what can be done with an orchestra by a determined and deadly decadent. There was a time when Brahms was regarded as the Browning of music. But even as the mystic symbolism of Maeterlinck has made Browning clubs appear to be a waste of time, so Richard Strauss has made the symphonies of Brahms sound like Volkslieder.

(New York *Times,* February 28, 1896)

-:-

In his stupidly unsuccessful attempt to produce a mirth-provoking setting to a very funny tale, Richard Strauss simply presents a grotesquely uninteresting tone-picture. The orchestration of *Till Eulenspiegel* is sound and fury, signifying nothing.

(New York *Recorder,* February 28, 1896)

-:-

I am bound to say that dreary though most musical humor is, Strauss's is the dreariest that has ever bored me. I contemptuously dismiss *Till Eulenspiegel* as a pretentious piece of smart shoddy.

(J. F. Runciman, *Saturday Review,* London, May 2, 1896)

-:-

Whatever its value as a philosophic treatise, Strauss's *Also Sprach Zarathustra* is a hopeless failure from the musical point of view.

While every kind of instrumental elaboration is exhibited, including an amorphous and remarkably hideous fugue, the actual material of the themes is of the poorest and least convincing order; and for many pages at a time, the possibilities of cacophony seem to be exhausted.

(London *Times,* March 8, 1897)

-:-

If the interpretation given by Strauss is in any way reliable, Zarathustra was possessed of pulmonic powers of a rhinoceros, and shouted his 'thus spake' through a megaphone of brobdingnagian proportions. . . The work is unhealthy; it suffers severely from basstubaculosis; and its utterances are too often basstubathetic. The score is at its worst in The Dance Song, a species of symbolic waltz, ushered in with unheard-of caterwauling and with a gruesomeness of execrably ugly dissonances . . . a realistic tone-picture of a sufferer from the worst pangs of sea-sickness.

(Boston *Herald,* October 31, 1897)

-:-

In *Thus Spake Zarathustra,* the genius of Strauss is merciless; it possesses huge lungs and stands close to one's ear. . . When a man is awakened by an entire city tumbling about his ears, the blowing up of a single building by nitroglycerine passes unnoticed. . . The composer plays the part of the howling dervish; he whirls madly about until he becomes hysterical, and then he bellows.

(Boston *Gazette,* October 31, 1897)

-:-

The chaos is entitled *Thus Spake Zarathustra,* but Zarathustra shouted and whispered, mumbled and roared, did everything but speak. . . Strauss introduces weird groans and strange pauses which are intended to make our flesh creep. . . At the end of the work there is a modulation from the key of B to the key of C, that is unique, for the Gordian knot is cut by the simple process of going there and going back again. If such modulations are possible, then the harmony books may as well be burnt at once.

(Louis Elson, Boston *Daily Advertiser,* November 1, 1897)

-:-

Nietzsche, though he lives in a lunatic asylum, is one of Germany's favorite philosophers, and his crazy rambling works have even been translated into English. . . Strauss, like Nietzsche, is impotent to create anything new, but as you cannot abuse people in music, he abuses the divine art itself. His mind seems to be an absolute desert as regards tangible musical thoughts; what he does invent is new cacophonies.

(New York *Evening Post,* December 12, 1897)

-:-

There is only one thing for a man like Strauss to do if he desires to escape oblivion, and that is to plunge into the grossest materialism in music and seek to puzzle or shock you, because he cannot touch your heart. . . The compositions of Richard Strauss do not even leave a clean taste in one's mouth. . . Strauss is a musical Maeterlinck, a tonal Ibsen.

(W. J. Henderson, New York *Times,* Supplement, December 26, 1897)

-:-

The music of Strauss is full of diabolically clever effects; it almost out-Berliozes the music of Berlioz. . . At the same time it is only doing Berlioz the barest justice to say that sometimes he rises to a dignity, a passion, a nobility of sentiment, of which there is not the faintest trace in the maunderings of Mr. Strauss. . . His is indeed the music of the future . . . when man has lost all his healthy instincts, his faculty of divine emotion, his sense of beauty, his brains, his common sense. . . If ever this kind of music becomes acceptable to the people at large, then may I not be here to see and hear.

(J. F. Runciman, London correspondence in the *Musical Record,* Boston, March 1, 1898)

-:-

If *Don Quixote* is no music, it may possibly be something else—a big, huge, monumental, colossal joke, a joke of such magnitude as only a master and a genius like Strauss is able to perpetrate. I can see him chuckling over his morning chocolate as he reads the learned essays upon the unesthetic noises made by the herd of bleating muttons.

(*Musical Courier,* New York, December 28, 1898)

-:-

Don Quixote is described as a series of variations. . . Strauss left harmony and melody a long way behind when he gives us the horrible bleating of sheep in the second variation with an effect that is positively earsplitting. . . It is questionable if such music is not a century in advance of today. A hundred years from now there will be greater knowledge and appreciation of the tremendous crashes which occur in the music which Strauss writes.

(*Musical Courier*, New York, January 18, 1899)

-:-

Richard Strauss's latest orchestral work, his alleged symphony, *Ein Heldenleben* . . . is revolutionary in every sense of the word. . . The composer indulges in a self-glorification of the most barefaced kind. . . The Hero's antagonists are described by him with the utmost scorn as a lot of pigmies and snarling, yelping, bowwowing nincompoops. . . The composer's now progressing impotency, however, is most plainly perceivable in the chapter devoted to his wife. She is represented by a solo violin, which is not a bad insinuation, as much as to say that she plays first fiddle in his life, but what she has to say is so unimportant and so artificial that the lady should object to such musical characterization. . . But the climax of everything that is ugly, cacophonous, blatant and erratic, the most perverse music I ever heard in all my life, is reached in the chapter 'The Hero's Battlefield.' The man who wrote this outrageously hideous noise, no longer deserving of the word music, is either a lunatic, or he is rapidly approaching idiocy.

(Otto Floersheim, *Musical Courier*, New York, April 19, 1899)

-:-

One might have read in the daily papers of Berlin the following item of town news: 'A deplorable and sudden murderous attack. Last evening, the Royal Opera House orchestra, by the command of the composer, Richard Strauss, committed an assault upon a most unsuspecting and completely innocent audience. Only a few of the large and fashionable audience were able to escape. Some resigned themselves to their fate without a murmur, and apparently died peacefully, while others suffered the most excruciating agony before they finally succumbed.' In *Ein Heldenleben*, Strauss has tried to characterize his position in the musical world. There are six movements. It is impossible to analyze them separately; suffice it to say that for every second of really beautiful music, there are minutes which often seem hours of the most unheard-of discord, which some people call 'clever counterpoint.' But what is the use of counterpoint when, if played, one imagines that four different orchestras are playing at the same time four different tunes in four different keys and measures? A veritable nightmare!

(Arthur Bird, *Musical Record*, Boston, May 1, 1899)

-:-

Till Eulenspiegel by Richard Strauss was a revelation of the possibilities of the modern school. . . . Whether such fearful complexity is necessary for such a result in art may yet be doubted; the great steam hammer can crack an eggshell, but it is not employed in cracking eggshells. . . . The score is adorned with everything from contra-bassoon to a watchman's rattle. Steam whistles and dynamite cartridges still remain to be used by the composer who desires to push further on. . . . The musical dictionary of the future will certainly give the following definitions: RHYTHM—Four or five different subdivisions of the measure which must be employed simultaneously. KEY—Any succession of tones; but the succession which is indicated by the signature must be avoided, especially at the close. TUNE—The beginning of a melody; this ought to be sparingly employed and should never be brought to a conclusion.

(Louis Elson, Boston *Daily Advertiser*, November 26, 1899)

-:-

Die instrumentale Armee, welche Richard Strauss zu diesem philosophischen Feldzug aufgeboten hat, steht auf einem bisher ungeahnten Kriegsfuss. Bei der modernen Tendenz, sich an Musik nicht zu erfreuen, sondern den Kopf zu zerbrechen, dürften Richard Strauss' nächste Symphonien 'frei nach Nietzsche' heissen: Götzendämmerung, Menschliches Allzumenschliches, und Wie man mit dem Hammer philosophiert.

(Eduard Hanslick, *Am Ende des Jahrhunderts*, Berlin, 1899)

[The instrumental army which Richard Strauss summons to this philosophic campaign, stands on a heretofore unimagined war footing. The modern tendency being not to enjoy music, but to break one's head over it, the next symphonies of Richard Strauss ought to be named The Twilight of the Idols, Human All-Too Human, and How to Philosophize with a Hammer.]

Composers seem to be afraid to write tunes now. They appear to think that if they write unmelodic fragments someone will proclaim them new Wagners. Or perhaps they hope to be mistaken for Brahmses. . . You may have heard *Till Eulenspiegel* of Richard Strauss. No gentleman would have written that thing. It is positively scurrilous. There are places for such music, but surely not before miscellaneous assemblages of ladies and gentlemen.

(W. J. Henderson, *Musical Record*, Boston, January 1, 1900)

-:-

I saw the score of *Don Quixote*. What a shameless [epithet deleted] this Richard Strauss is!

(From Rimsky-Korsakov's letter to Taneyev, dated Brussels, March 15, 1900, published in a symposium on Taneyev in Moscow, 1925; the deletion of the obscene epithet is made by the Russian editor in the printed text)

-:-

The Strauss symphonic poem, *Also Sprach Zarathustra,* makes a cruel demand on the patience of the listener. Most of it is ugly, and consequently at variance with the well-founded principle that claims for high art a devotion to the beautiful. It is hardly wise to pass an adverse judgment on the music of the end of the century of extremists, for as time passes, it may turn out that this work is overflowing with charm that the future will make clear. One becomes accustomed to everything through prolonged acquaintance with it—even misery. All that the opponent of this latter-day music is safe in saying is that he does not like it.

(Boston *Herald,* March 18, 1900)

-:-

How insipid are all the last efforts of a Richard Strauss! I am at war with this devilish modern 'bend or break' polyphony; this beating-about-the-bush music; this experimenting with the chromatic scale; this Zarathustra culture; this conglomeration of sounds which under the name of music is scarcely more than a hideous brawl. We have here a certain circle of superhuman beings; some are weary musicians, but many more flatulent amateurs, who fancy that the more intricate the harmony, the more complicated the counterpoint, the louder the orchestra is, the sublimer the music. If the *Twelfth Rhapsody, Blue Danube,* and the third *Leonore*

Overture were played at the same time, and the program named Richard Strauss as the author of this cacophonic poem, there are idiots who would exclaim—'What a genius! What a master of polyphonic form! Heavenly!! Perfectly seraphic!!!'

(Arthur Bird, *Musical Courier*, New York, December 19, 1900)

-:-

We cannot consider *Ein Heldenleben* an advance over the preceding works of Strauss; we cannot rid ourselves of the idea that the attempt to play in two different keys at the same time is as disastrous as the attempt of two railroad trains to pass each other on the same track. After the Strauss work, the orchestra rinsed our ears with Beethoven's Second Symphony.

(Louis Elson, Boston *Daily Advertiser*, December 8, 1901)

-:-

At the end of the forty minutes exacted by the performance of Richard Strauss's latest tone poem (*Ein Heldenleben*), one is inclined to pull himself together and be thankful to the friend who will assure him of his continued sanity. . . Boston always has on hand and in reserve a fad or a cult of the incomprehensible.

(Boston *Herald*, December 8, 1901)

-:-

Strauss may be characterized in four words: little talent, much impudence. His method is to overwhelm the listener at once. That is why he makes his violins scream, his flutes hiss, his trumpets blare, his cymbals crash. A free for all, everybody for himself, resulting in a terrible cacophony and noise, in which one is lost. So it goes on for about four or five minutes. Then there is a sharp contrast and a lull with something resembling decent music. This music is of the most ordinary sort, but after the preceding it sounds like paradise. But even into these trivial episodes, Strauss constantly throws various wrong notes, perhaps to cover up this triviality. After that the wild cacophony is resumed, like a real bedlam. Then there is another lull, and a forced original ending, as flabbergasting as the beginning. This is not music, this is a mockery of music. Yet, Strauss has his admirers. How can this be explained? One can understand the desire of some composers to attain fame cheaply with the aid of an insolent, wild, and ludicrous cacophony, but the attitude of the listeners who tolerate it without realizing that they are being mocked at, is incomprehensible. It would be interesting to make this experiment: put blank music sheets before the conductor and the players. Let the musicians play anything they wish and let the conductor conduct anything he wishes, giving cues, and indicating the time, the tempo, and the intensity of sound at random. Perhaps the result would be even more remarkable in its genius than Strauss himself!

(From a letter by César Cui, dated December 5, 1904, after hearing a performance of *Sinfonia Domestica*)

-:-

Dr. Strauss's counterpoint may be compared generally to a motor car charging through the traffic in Cheapside at noon.

(*Referee*, London, February 27, 1905)

-:-

Ein Heldenleben was twice set before the Philharmonic audiences some years ago. Since then it has not been heard; but it would not be patiently heard by a large part of the Philharmonic's audiences under any circumstances. In no other work has Strauss so deliberately affronted the ear with long-continued din and discord or has so consciously used ugliness in music to represent conceptions of ugliness. In no other has he, or perhaps any other musician, gone further beyond the limits of beauty and euphony, or so tortured the instruments of the orchestra into utterance abnormal to them, or indulged in so much extravagance of every sort.

(Richard Aldrich, New York *Times*, November 11, 1905)

-:-

The chromatics in *Salome* begin with the second note of the score. At times we find the bass in a flat key and the other harmonies in sharps (not in enharmonic unity either), so that the Scriptural precept—'Let not thy right hand know what thy left hand doeth' —is given a new meaning. . . As regards tonality, it has gone so far that it is utterly unnecessary for Strauss to give any key signature to his music, although he still follows the old custom in this. It is impossible to know whether one is playing true or false, and any misprints could not be detected by any known musical rule. The libretto is a compound of lust, stifling perfumes and blood, and cannot be read by any woman or fully understood by any one but a physician. . . Meanwhile Wagner's Music of the Future has become the music of the past, and he is much too simple for the modern neurotic. The new fiat is—*In the sweat of thy brow shalt thou hear thy Music!*—and the perspiration of the auditor is not much less than that of the conductor and the musicians.

(Louis Elson, Boston *Daily Advertiser,* February 10, 1906)

-:-

I am a man of middle life who has devoted upwards of twenty years to the practice of a profession that necessitates a daily intimacy with degenerates. I say after deliberation that *Salome* is a detailed and explicit exposition of the most horrible, disgusting, revolting and unmentionable features of degeneracy that I have ever heard, read of, or imagined.

(From a physician's letter, New York *Times,* January 21, 1907)

-:-

A reviewer . . . should be an embodied conscience stung into righteous fury by the moral stench with which *Salome* fills the nostrils of humanity, but, though it makes him retch, he should be sufficiently judicial in his temperament calmly to look at the drama in all its aspects and determine whether or not as a whole it is an instructive note on the life and culture of the times and whether or not this exudation from the diseased and polluted will and imagination of the authors marks a real advance in artistic expression. . . There is a vast deal of ugly music in *Salome*—music that offends the ear and rasps the nerves like fiddlestrings played on by a coarse file. . . There is not a whiff of fresh and healthy air blowing through *Salome* except that which exhales from the cistern. . . The orchestra shrieked its final horror and left the listeners staring at each other with smarting eyeballs and wrecked nerves.

(H. E. Krehbiel, New York *Tribune,* January 23, 1907)

-:-

Strauss has a mania for writing ugly music: a modern harpy, he cannot touch anything without besmearing it with dissonance. What more natural then that he should cast about for a subject which imperatively demands hideous din to correspond with and justify his concatenated discords? And what more natural than that the noisome Salome should seem an ideal companion for his noisy music? The presentation of such a story is ethically a crime; Richard Strauss's music is esthetically criminal or at least extremely coarse and ill-mannered. His music often suggests a man who comes to a social reception unkempt, with hands unwashed, cigar in mouth, hat on, and who sits down and puts his feet on the table. No boor ever violated all the laws of etiquette as Strauss violates all the laws of musical composition. There is one consolation. Thanks to the prevailing dissonance, nobody knows—or cares—whether the singers sing the right notes—that is, the notes assigned to them—or not. Who can fail to see the stupendous originality of Richard Strauss? What composer before him has been so clever as to be able to write music in which it makes no difference whether or not you sing or play correctly?

(W. J. Henderson, New York *Sun*, January 23, 1907)

-:-

Richard Strauss has never regarded art as a lofty, ennobling thing. When he set out to compose his first opera, he frankly sought for an unclean topic and found it in *Feuersnot*. That there is a certain lewd humor in this story cannot be denied, but it is not seemly for men and women to talk to one another about the plot. . . It is pretty safe to say that when Richard Strauss turned to look for a second opera book, he desired one which would be even more radical than *Feuersnot*. In the drama of Oscar Wilde, *Salome*, he found it. . . . Strauss has done more for Wilde than Wilde for Strauss, but they were perfectly mated: two souls with but one nasty thought; two pens that drool as one. . . Doubtless Mr. Strauss saturates himself in the spirit of Bach and Beethoven and bows before the statue of Wagner when he sits down to compose. But his contracts are models of financial skill. A master technician of orchestral combinations, he knows also how to orchestrate a bank account. Creator of carnal visions in three-four time, he is also a dreamer of dollars, florins, reichsmarks, francs. Everywhere he sees them. Everywhere he gets them. He may have heard a high and holy call to study the conscience of Salome. . . Perhaps Art sat upon her chaste throne and beckoned to him to do this but there was money in it. . . If this be art, then let the music of the future find her mission in sewer, pesthouse and brothel.

(W. J. Henderson, New York *Sun*, February 3, 1907)

The author's passion for notoriety is no doubt responsible in great measure for his choice of Oscar Wilde's *Salome* as the subject of an opera. . . Music itself cannot be prostituted to base uses, though various qualities incidental to music may be turned to the purposes of pornography. There is plenty of passion in the work, and there is no doubt that on the average hearer it produces a sense of nausea.

(J. A. Fuller Maitland in Grove's *Dictionary of Music and Musicians*, volume IV, 1908)

-:-

Modern Opera

Hark! from the pit and fearsome sound
That makes your blood run cold.
Symphonic cyclones rush around—
And the worst is yet untold.

No—they unchain those dogs of war,
The wild sarrusophones,
A double-bass E-flat to roar
Whilst crunching dead men's bones.

The muted tuba's dismal groan
Uprising from the gloom
And answered by the heckelphone,
Suggests the crack of doom.

Oh, mama! is this the earthquake zone?
What ho, there! stand from under!
Or is that the tonitruone
Just imitating thunder?

Nay, fear not, little one, because
Of this sublime rough-house;
'Tis modern opera by the laws
Of Master Richard Strauss.

(New York *World, circa* January 1909)

-:-

Salome was written by the most immoral man in England. The theme of the opera cannot be discussed in a mixed audience. There is music which degrades. New York is not puritanical or provincial. It is more like Paris. The directors of the Metropolitan Opera House have never been accused of being straightlaced or prudish. They are the foremost men of the city, financially and socially. Yet, they felt that they must withdraw that degrading, loathsome opera, *Salome.*

(From a sermon by Rev. Dr. William T. McElveen at the Shawmut Congregational Church in Boston, reported in the Boston *Herald,* February 25, 1909)

-:-

Elektra has known for some time that her papa was killed by mamma and her mamma's gentleman friend. . . She screams and then gets down and digs up out of the dirt the axe her papa was killed with. . . Her mother is afraid of her. Elektra keeps on howling. . . . The orchestra breaks into strange and unearthly noises. . . Muted trumpets, woodwind in the lowest register and strings leaping in intervals of ninths and sevenths mingle in a medley of sounds which gives the idea of a snarling, frightened animal. In the great scene in which Elektra accuses her mother of murdering her father, the music ends with a long shrill whistle like that of a locomotive entering a tunnel. Elsewhere the music reproduces sounds of smashing glass and china, the bursting of bottles, the clashing of shovels and tongs, the groaning and creaking of rusty hinges and stubborn doors, avalanches in the mountains, the crying of babies, the squealing of rats, the grunting of pigs, the bellowing of cattle, the howling of cats and the roaring of wild beasts. . . I didn't pick out a tune that I should imagine would be later on included in 'Gems from the Opera for the Parlor Organ.'

(New York dispatch in the Boston *Herald,* January 31, 1910)

-:-

In *Elektra* of Strauss, jarring discords, the desperate battle of dissonances in one key against dissonances in another, settle themselves down into total delineation of shrieks and groans, of tortures physical in the clear definition and audible in their gross realism. Can you conceive of the inward scream of a conscience in the flames of the inferno being translated into the polyphonic utterances of instruments writhing in a counterpoint no longer required to be the composition of two or more melodies which shall harmonize with one another but of melodies which shall spit and scratch and claw at each other, like enraged panthers? Snarling of stopped trumpets, barking of trombones, moaning of bassoons and squealing of violins are but elementary factors in the musical system of Richard Strauss.

(W. J. Henderson, New York *Sun*, February 2, 1910)

-:-

Elektra

The bass fiddles groan and the large trombone
Gives a bellowing yowl of pain,
While the deep bassoon grunts a sordid tune
And the flutes make wind and rain.

The flageolet squeaks and the piccolo shrieks
And the bass drum bumps to the fray,
While the long saxophone with a hideous groan
Joins in the cacophonous lay.

It's a deep blood lust and we're taught we must
Gulp it down and pronounce it grand,
And forget the lore when Trovatore
Was sweet to understand.

Ah, these dear old airs, it now appears,
Were never to be classed as Art;
We must shake with fear through a great nightmare
And awake with a terrible start.

O, the nameless dance and the hideous trance
That the audience wallows in,
And the strange, strange noise and the murderous joys
And the fun of a farflung Sin!

No more, no more; it was fun galore
While we plunged through the rotting weeds,
But the time has come to be going home
To the fine old musical creeds.

(An unidentified New York newspaper, February 1910)

-:-

In *Elektra* Strauss lets loose an orchestral riot that suggests a murder scene in a Chinese theater. He has a constitutional aversion to what sounds beautiful. . . If the reader who has not heard *Elektra* desires to witness something that looks as its orchestral score sounds, let him, next summer, poke a stick into an ant hill and watch the black insects darting, angry and bewildered, biting and clawing, in a thousand directions at once. It's amusing for ten minutes, but not for two hours.

(H. T. Finck, New York *Post,* February 2, 1910)

-:-

It is not every family which has double fugues for breakfast, but this Strauss family is a peculiar one. If *Sinfonia Domestica* were a true autobiographical sketch, we fancy that the wife would be portrayed on trombones and tubas while the husband would be pictured on the second violin.

(Louis Elson, Boston *Daily Advertiser,* January 12, 1917)

-:-

Der Rosenkavalier, Ariadne auf Naxos, Joseph's Legend and the *Alpine Symphony* are makeshift, slack, slovenly. . . . Strauss's music is singularly flat and hollow and dun, joyless and soggy. . . . It is as the victim of a psychic deterioration that one is forced to regard this unfortunate man. . . . The thing that one sees happening to so many people, the dulling and coarsening of the sensibilities, the decay of mental energies, seems to have happened to him, too. . . . Many people have thought a love of money the cause of Strauss's decay. . . . It is probable that Strauss's desire for incessant gain is a sort of perversion, a mania that has gotten control over him because his energies are inwardly prevented from taking their logical course and creating works of art. . . . He is indeed the false dawn of modern music.

(Paul Rosenfeld, *The Dial,* New York, February 1920)

-:-

What could be more natural, more understandable, than that this artistic Don Juan, this intellectual Faust, satiated with the exotic charms of Salome, and nauseated by the hate-drunken ravings of Elektra, should at the last turn back to the little country maid—his Mozart?. . [But] the divinely innocent and virginal Mozartean muse cannot be wooed and won like an Elektra or a Salome; all we find in *Der Rosenkavalier* is a worn-out, dissipated demimondaine, with powdered face, rouged lips, false hair, and a hideous leer.

(Cecil Gray, *A Survey of Contemporary Music,* London, 1924)

STRAVINSKY M. Stravinsky, peut-il s'imaginer qu'une mélodie parce qu'elle sera doublée pendant cinquante mesures à la seconde supérieure ou inférieure ou aux deux à la fois, va gagner une intensité et une éloquence décisive? Il faut le penser puisque les nouveautés que renferment la partition du *Sacre du Printemps* sont ordinairement de cet ordre.

(H. Quittard, *Figaro,* Paris, May 31, 1913)

[Does Mr. Stravinsky imagine that a melody will gain intensity and decisive eloquence because it is doubled during fifty measures with a second above, a second below, or both? One must think so because the innovations embodied in the score of *Le Sacre du Printemps* are mostly in this category.]

-:-

Le Sacre du Printemps a pour caractère essentiel d'être la musique la plus dissonante et la plus discordante que l'on ait encore écrite. . . . Jamais le système et le culte de la fausse note n'ont été pratiqués avec tant d'industrie, de zèle et d'acharnement. De la première mesure de l'oeuvre à la dernière, quelle que soit la note que l'on attende, ce n'est jamais celle-là qui vient, mais c'est la note d'à côté, c'est la note qui ne devrait pas venir; quel que soit l'accord précédent, c'est un autre accord que l'on entend; et cet accord et cette note sont faits tout exprès pour donner l'impression de fausseté aiguë et presque atroce. Lorsque deux thèmes se superposent, bien loin que l'auteur ait pris des thèmes qui aillent ensemble; il les a tout au contraire choisis de telle sorte que leur superposition produise les frottements, les grincements les plus agaçants qui se puissent imaginer.

(Pierre Lalo, *Le Temps,* Paris, June 3, 1913)

[The most essential characteristic of *Le Sacre du Printemps* is that it is the most dissonant and the most discordant composition yet written. Never was the system and the cult of the wrong note practiced with so much industry, zeal and fury. From the first measure to the last, whatever note one expects, it is never the one that comes, but one on the side, which should not come; whatever is suggested by a preceding chord, it is another chord that is heard; and this chord and this note are used deliberately to produce the impression of acute and almost cruel discord. When two themes are superposed, far be it from the composer's mind to use themes that fit together; quite to the contrary, he chooses such themes that their superposition should produce the most irritating friction and gnashing that can be imagined.]

-:-

The music of *Le Sacre du Printemps* baffles verbal description. To say that much of it is hideous as sound is a mild description. There is certainly an impelling rhythm traceable. Practically it has no relation to music at all as most of us understand the word.

(*Musical Times*, London, August 1, 1913)

-:-

On se souvient du spectacle scandaleux que fut ce *Sacre du Printemps*—bien plutôt un *Massacre du Printemps.* Jamais ne se vit un tel défi aux oreilles humaines. . . Ce n'est pas que le *Rossignol* soit tout à fait aussi outrageant que le *Sacre du Printemps.* . . À part quelques coassements de grenouilles intempestifs et le mugissement d'une génisse . . . cela se tient à peu près. . . Tout change dès le deuxième acte et nous entrons dans la nouvelle manière de M. Stravinsky. Et c'est alors une cacophonie insupportable, une accumulation d'accords bizarres qui se succèdent sans rythme ni vraisemblance; c'est comme une gageure qu'on peut tout faire avaler au public bonasse ou aux snobs de nos salles de spectacles.

(H. Moreno, *Le Ménestrel*, Paris, June 6, 1914)

[One recalls the scandalous spectacle of this *Sacre du Printemps*, or rather a *Massacre du Printemps.* Never before had such a challenge been made to human ears. One cannot say that *The Nightingale* is quite as outrageous as *Le Sacre du Printemps.* Apart from some croaking of frogs out of season, and the mooing of a young cow, the music holds together more or less. But all is changed beginning with the second act, and we enter the new manner of Mr. Stravinsky. It is then that we hear intolerable cacophony, an accumulation of strange harmonies that succeed each other without rhythm or sense; this music sounds like a wager that one could make the simple-minded public and the snobs of our concert halls swallow anything at all.]

-:-

In his *Fireworks,* Stravinsky hurls a whole orchestra at the head of the public, and calls it music. . . What some of the brass dissonances meant, we could not imagine, unless the man who lit the pieces had burned his fingers and made a few resultant remarks.

(Louis Elson, Boston *Daily Advertiser,* December 12, 1914)

-:-

The Flonzaley Quartet regaled a large and eagerly expectant audience with a few morsels of 'advanced' musical fare in the shape of three little pieces concocted by Igor Stravinsky. . . The first provides a capital imitation of a bagpipe, which reiterates a scrap of melody. . . . Then something abruptly goes wrong with the bagpipe and the thing stops. . . Some doleful and very uncomfortable sounds introduce the circus clown; then some light skipping ones; then sadness again and some queer feline squeaks. It was all so excruciatingly naive and childish that the audience laughed immoderately.

(Herbert F. Peyser, *Musical America,* December 4, 1915)

-:-

I'm not competent to discuss *Le Sacre du Printemps* as I have heard it only on the piano. But assuming . . . that Stravinsky is mechanism become music. . . I don't want it. . . . I'm bored with imitations of noises . . . and their monotonous cacophony. Of course, it sounds like cacophony because I'm not used to it, and it probably sounds all alike for the same reason that Chinamen all look alike to me: I'm not well acquainted.

(Deems Taylor, *The Dial,* New York, September 1920)

-:-

The audience expressed directly and flatly its dislike of Stravinsky's *Concertino*. . . The fiddles had spoken bitterly: futility. They had spoken angrily: boredom. . . The Stravinsky music is a drab, rasping tired shuffle and breakdown. It is like a locomotive which has fallen off the track, making its wheels revolve in air. Rhythms prolong themselves out of sheer inertia; pound on, wearily. A lyric coda of a few measures, a sort of momentary illumination of a darkened landscape, breaks off into silence.

(Paul Rosenfeld, *The Dial,* New York, February 1921)

-:-

Stravinsky's *Symphony for Wind Instruments* written in memory of Debussy . . . was greeted with cheers, hisses, and laughter. I had no idea Stravinsky disliked Debussy so much as this. If my own memories of a friend were as painful as Stravinsky's of Debussy seem to be, I would try to forget him.

(Ernest Newman, *Musical Times*, London, July 1921)

-:-

The Paleozoic Crawl, turned into tone with all the resources of the modern orchestra, clamored for attention at the Philadelphia Orchestra concert when Igor Stravinsky's *Rite of Spring* was given its first airing on this side of the vast Atlantic. It was the primitive run riot, almost formless and without definite tonality, save for insistently beating rhythms that made the tom-tom melodies of the gentle Congo tribes seem super-sophisticated in comparison. . . Without description or program, the work might have suggested a New Year's Eve rally of moonshine addicts and the simple pastimes of early youth and maidens, circumspectly attired in a fig leaf apiece.

(Philadelphia *North American*, March 4, 1922)

-:-

Aside from the excuse that it may offer as an example of the distressingly dissonant extremes to which some of the latter-day composers are going, listening to the *Rite of Spring* might be regarded as more of an affliction than a privilege.

(Philadelphia *Evening Bulletin*, March 4, 1922)

-:-

Unless you can feel the primitive urge . . . the *Rite of Spring* will merely seem one more horrible jargon from the start to finish, sheer discord with no right to a place on the same program with true music.

(Philadelphia *Public Ledger*, March 4, 1922)

-:-

Petrushka offers an incomprehensible phantasmagoria of tone with only an occasional meaning in and of itself. There were moments of obvious amusement when one instrument or another did funny things. But whether those who laughed dilated with exactly the proper emotion may be doubted.

(Richard Aldrich, New York *Times*, February 5, 1923)

Some naughtiness, some sins and some crimes against music were perpetrated yesterday. The most venial was the performance of Stravinsky's music to *Petrushka.* We are not writing in disparagement of the composition, but of the use to which it is put. . . Time and again it excited frank and unrestrained laughter. The antics of a buffoon would have done the same thing, but we doubt if Mr. Coates, the conductor, would have thought them proper as a feature in a symphonic concert. . . His act in playing burlesque music left us puzzled in mind concerning his artistic sincerity and seriousness. . . . It is but a disjointed series of funny sounds, squeaks and squawks, imitations of wheezy hand organ and hurdy-gurdy, grunting snatches of tune from a bassoon, clatterings of a xylophone and whirring noises. If we must have music of this kind in the concert-room let us by all means also have moving pictures to explain it.

(H. E. Krehbiel, New York *Tribune,* February 5, 1923, under the heading: SYMPHONY PRESENTS CONCERT MARRED RY BURLESQUE—PETRUSHKA, PLAYED WITHOUT CHOREOGRAPHIC SETTING, INTRODUCES BUFFOONERY INTO PLEASING PROGRAM)

-:-

All the signs indicate a strong reaction against the nightmare of noise and eccentricity that was one of the legacies of the war. . . What has become of the works that made up the program of the Stravinsky concert which created such a stir a few years ago? Practically the whole lot are already on the shelf, and they will remain there until a few jaded neurotics once more feel a desire to eat ashes and fill their belly with the east wind.

(*Musical Times,* London, October 1923)

-:-

This outline of Stravinsky's *Rite of Spring,* a tone picture of spring-fever in a zoo, is suggested as a means for helping the uninitiated to understand and enjoy this epoch-making work.

I. The Rebellion and Escape.

Introduction: Harbingers of rebellion; consultation of the beasts.

1. Slaying of the keepers. Escape of the animals.
2. The mad flight of the crowd. Sudden silence.
3. March of the militia. Shooting, shouting and general uproar, increasing to a final abrupt climax.

II. The return of half-starved beasts. Subdued trumpeting, braying, roaring, chattering, howling, growling, etc. Terror of the populace. Bear's choice of a victim. The dance of death. Noisy approach of a bombing plane. Bursting of a large bomb that finishes everyone and everything suddenly.

1. Many different keys are used here in consideration of the scientific fact that no two animals vocalize in the same key.
2. By a frequent change of tempo, the composer ingeniously suggests the different gaits of the various animals.
3. This gives the audience a moment's respite. It is suggested that this time be spent in repeating the formula 'Bar by bar, measure by measure, discord by discord, my ears are growing stronger and stronger.'

(Boston *Herald*, January 27, 1924)

-:-

Such music as *Le Sacre du Printemps* is physical. . . Whether the calmer heights of spiritual glory are accessible to the new methods of composition, remains to be seen. They are not likely to be scaled by Stravinsky who is a stark realist, a cave man of music.

(W. J. Henderson, New York *Sun*, February 1, 1924)

-:-

The Rite of Spring

Who wrote this fiendish *Rite of Spring*,
What right had he to write the thing,
Against our helpless ears to fling
Its crash, clash, cling, clang, bing, bang, bing?

And then to call it *Rite of Spring*,
The season when on joyous wing
The birds melodious carols sing
And harmony's in everything!

He who could write the *Rite of Spring*,
If I be right, by right should swing!

(Boston *Herald*, February 9, 1924)

-:-

It is as if Stravinsky had discovered in certain rhythmic units [in *Le Sacre du Printemps*] a latent energy, just as it has been claimed that the day is near when the scientists will discover and release enough energy now contained in every atom to blow a battleship from its harbor to a mountain top. . . . But there is that in this music which repulses as well as attracts. It is an orgy, and an explosion of force, but very brutal and perhaps perverse. It is easy to believe it the expression of one who is fundamentally a barbarian and a primitive, tinctured with, and educated in, the utmost sophistications and satieties of a worn-out civilization.

(Olin Downes, New York *Times,* March 16, 1924)

-:-

The music of *Les Noces* flouts Western civilization. Western civilization will probably return the compliment, for our musical functions provide no frame to fit the work. . . But the music is a first-class curiosity, one of the documents of our hapless age. And Stravinsky has a fist—a will—a way with him.

(*Musical Times,* London, August 1926)

-:-

Stravinsky, the big chief of the modernists, the head and fount of those first performances which have inundated our concert halls since the thump-thump of the sexy violins of *Le Sacre* first outraged our best families . . . dispatched manifestos from Paris to the effect that *Oedipus Rex* was the largest of all his works. . . He swaddles the text in the borrowed overcoats of men who cut their musical garments to the shape of their emotions. Oedipus sings his tortured soul in the accents of Bach. but only in the accents. The chorus shouts *Gloria* like the peasants in the coronation scene of *Boris Godunov*. . . Every once so often, Stravinsky reverts to the veteran rhythmic thump-thump of *Le Sacre,* but at the finish one is only conscious of a presumptuous drive with nothing of any consequence to back it up.

(Samuel Chotzinoff, New York *Telegram,* March 9, 1928)

-:-

The *History of a Soldier* is tenth-rate Stravinsky. It is probably the nearest that any composer of consequence has ever come to achieving almost complete infantilism in a score that is presumably intended to be taken with some degree of seriousness. Regarded as a sort of musical comic strip, it is abysmally inferior, in wit, comedic power, and salience of characterization, to Mr. Herriman's

'Krazy Kat,' for instance. If one chooses to regard the score as an etude in the use of limited instrumental means, it is beyond question ingenious and resourceful. But the technical mastery displayed was hardly worth the effort, so poverty-stricken and tedious is the issue.

(Lawrence Gilman, New York *Herald Tribune*, March 26, 1928)

-:-

[*History of a Soldier*] is a degenerate and eviscerated product of the composer who once wrote the score for *Petrushka*. . . The music feels as if Stravinsky had written it without enthusiasm, certainly without faith and without pity.

(Olin Downes, New York *Times*, March 26, 1928)

-:-

Stravinsky . . . is entirely unable to formulate a musical idea of his own. As a member of a savage orchestra he might perhaps be allowed to play a recurrent rhythm upon a drum—as the only evidence of real form in his work is that kind of primitive repetition which birds and babies also do very well.

(Rutland Boughton, *Musical Times*, London, June 1929)

-:-

The Violin Concerto impresses me as possibly the most willful, insincere and meretricious score that the creator of *Petrushka* and *Le Sacre* has promulgated in years. . . I do not object so much to the gargoyle features of its wanton ugliness as to the patent calculation and the obvious futility of this ugliness. It may be that closer acquaintance with this music may modify the feeling of ignoble artifice, vacuity and cynical sophistication which it diffuses. . . For one hearer, at any rate, the Concerto stands in the vanguard of Stravinsky's most regrettable aberrations.

(Herbert F. Peyser, New York *Times*, November 15, 1931)

-:-

It is probable that much, if not most, of Stravinsky's music will enjoy brief existence. . . Already the tremendous impact of *Le Sacre du Printemps* has disappeared, and what seemed at the first hearing to be the inner glow of inspirational fire is now only a smoldering ember.

(W. J. Henderson, New York *Sun*, January 16, 1937)

Stravinsky is the father of the rebarbarization in music. He has transformed music into a collection of qualified noises. He has reduced melody to the primitive, inarticulate refrain of a Zulu, and has converted the orchestra into a gigantic rattle, the toy and mouthpiece of the new savage.

(Lazare Saminsky, *Music of Our Day*, New York, 1939)

-:-

Stravinsky's *Oedipus Rex* is not even musical Esperanto, but a cipher, a code for the initiated. . . In this sense, a parallel to *Oedipus Rex* is not only Stravinsky's *Symphony of the Psalms* with its sanctimonious Christian mysticism, but also his fraudulent *Circus Polka,* composed in the midst of war and dedicated to a young elephant in a New York circus. All this is modernistic bigotry which covers up a panic fear of stormy forces dynamiting capitalist reality, the terror of the inescapable downfall of a social structure of which modernism is a product, bound with it in life and death.

(V. Gorodinsky, *Music of Spiritual Poverty,* Moscow, 1950)

-:-

Stravinsky's Cantata for mezzo-soprano, tenor, women's choir and five instruments, based on Tudor verses, is a mercilessly dull, wholly unleavened essay in boredom . . . a triumph of musical vacuity over the literary vigor of its text. . . The most invigorating sound I heard was a restive neighbor winding his watch.

(Mildred Norton, *Daily News,* Los Angeles, November 12, 1952)

-:-

The whole score [of *The Rake's Progress*] is in very short fragments, in a dozen different styles, which . . . remind of many different works which other composers were thoughtless enough to write before Mr. Stravinsky made his appearance. . . Stravinsky's looking backward . . . results in music which is 'ersatz,' artificial, unreal and actually unexpressive! . . . The opera remains a study in still-life.

(Olin Downes, New York *Times,* February 15 and 22, 1953)

TCHAIKOVSKY Dr. von Bülow's concert was distinguished especially by the production of a new grand concerto by the Russian composer Tchaikovsky. This elaborate work is, in general, as difficult for popular apprehension as the name of the composer... There are long stretches of what seems, on the first hearing at least, formless void, sprinkled only with tinklings of the piano and snatchy obbligatos from all the various wind and string instruments in turn.

(Boston *Evening Transcript*, October 25, 1875)

-:-

Tchaikovsky is unmistakably a disciple of the 'new school,' and his work is strongly tinged with the wildness and quaintness of the music of the North. Taken as a whole, his Piano Concerto appeared interesting chiefly as a novelty. It would not soon supplant the massive production of Beethoven, or even the fiery compositions of Liszt, Raff, and Rubinstein.

(Boston *Journal*, October 25, 1875)

-:-

This extremely difficult, strange, wild, ultra-modern Russian Concerto is the composition of Peter Tchaikovsky, a young professor at the Conservatory of Moscow. . . We had the wild Cossack fire and impetus without stint, extremely brilliant and exciting, but could we ever learn to love such music?

(*Dwight's Journal of Music*, Boston, November 13, 1875)

-:-

Tchaikovsky's First Piano Concerto, like the first pancake, is a flop.

(Nicolai Soloviev, *Novoye Vremya*, St. Petersburg, November 13, 1875)

-:-

Tschaikowsky zeigt sich von der Epidemie der Zukunftsmusik ergriffen, von jener Epidemie, welche sich wasserscheu von der Logik abwendet, im Dusel schwelgt und ein über das andere Mal in Dissonanzenkrämpfe verfällt. Von ursprünglicher Erfindung ist bei diesen Leuten, die höchstens pathologisch interessant sind, blutwenig wahrzunehmen.

(*Wiener Fremdenblatt*, November 28, 1876)

[Tchaikovsky appears to be a victim of the epidemic of the Music of the Future, that in its hydrophobia, scorns logic, wallows in torpor, and time and again, collapses in dissonant convulsions. Of basic inspiration in these people, who present interest at most as pathological cases, there is very little indeed.]

-:-

Wie das ganze junge Russland, so ist Tschaikowsky natürlich Zukunftsmusiker . . . Auch in Tschaikowskys Ouvertüre zu Romeo und Juliet qualmt dieser kalte glänzende Rauch, tost dieser erhitzte Lärm. . . Für eine Illustration der Veroneser Familienfehde klingt das Allegro doch etwas zu russisch; man hört förmlich die Knutenhiebe in wuchtigen, an keinen Takt sich bindenden Schlägen niederfallen. In Petersburg sagt man wahrscheinlich poetischer: 'So pocht das Schicksal an die grosse Trommel.' Acht besänftigende Takte . . . sagen uns unzweideutig dass wir vor der Liebescene stehen. . . Aber dieses aus dem Wechsel zweier dissonierender Akkorde bestehende Motiv erinnert ungefähr an das Kratzen eines scharfen Messers auf einem Glasteller. Wie eine kalte Schlangenhaut läuft uns dieses Liebesglück über den Rücken.

(Eduard Hanslick, *Neue Freie Presse,* Vienna, November 30, 1876)

[Like all young Russia, Tchaikovsky is naturally a 'musician of the future.' In his overture *Romeo and Juliet,* steams cold glistening smoke, rages heated noise. . . As an illustration of a Verona family feud, the *Allegro* sounds decidedly too Russian; one actually hears the blows of the knout falling in heavy strokes unconnected with any bar division. In St. Petersburg they probably say it more poetically: 'Thus pounds Fate on the bass drum.' Eight softening bars tell us unambiguously that we approach a love scene. But this motive built on the alternation of two dissonant chords sounds rather like scratching a glass plate with a sharp knife. Like a cold snakeskin runs this love bliss down the spine.]

-:-

Francesca da Rimini von Tschaikowsy ist ein musikalisches Monstrum . . . eine Ohrenschinderei.

(Richard Würst, *Berliner Fremdenblatt,* September 17, 1878)

[Tchaikovsky's *Francesca da Rimini* is a musical monster . . . earflaying horror.]

The Finale of the Fourth Symphony of Tchaikovsky pained me by its vulgarity. . . Nothing can redeem the lack of nobleness, the barbarous side by which, according to ethnographs and diplomats, even the most polished Russian at times betrays himself.

(*Musical Review*, New York, February 26, 1880)

-:-

Der russische Componist Tschaikowsky ist sicherlich kein gewöhnliches Talent, wohl aber ein farciertes, geniesüchtiges, wahl- und geschmacklos producierendes. . . So auch sein neuestes, langes und anspruchsvolles Violin Concert. Eine Weile bewegt es sich massvoll musikalisch und nicht ohne Geist, bald aber gewinnt die Rohheit Oberhand, und behauptet sie bis ans Ende des ersten Satzes. Da wird nicht mehr Violine gespielt, sondern Violine gezaust, gerissen, gebläut. . . Das Adagio . . . ist wieder auf besten Wege, uns zu versöhnen, zu gewinnen. Aber es bricht schnell ab, um einem Finale Platz zu machen, das uns in die brutale, traurige Lustigkeit eines russischen Kirchweihfestes versetzt. Wir sehen lauter wüste gemeine Gesichter, hören rohe Flüche und riechen den Fusel. Friedrich Vischer behauptete einmal bei Besprechung lasciver Schildereien, es gebe Bilder die man stinken sieht. Tschaikowskys Violine Concert bringt uns zum erstenmal auf die schauerliche Idee ob es nicht auch Musikstücke geben könne die man stinken hört.

(Eduard Hanslick, *Neue Freie Presse*, Vienna, December 5, 1881)

[The Russian composer Tchaikovsky is surely not an ordinary talent, but rather an inflated one, with a genius-obsession without discrimination or taste. Such is also his latest, long and pretentious Violin Concerto. For a while it moves soberly, musically, and not without spirit. But soon vulgarity gains upper hand, and asserts itself to the end of the first movement. The violin is no longer played; it is pulled, torn, drubbed. The *Adagio* is again on its best behavior, to pacify and to win us. But it soon breaks off to make way for a finale that transfers us to a brutal and wretched jollity of a Russian holiday. We see plainly the savage vulgar faces, we hear curses, we smell vodka. Friedrich Vischer once observed, speaking of obscene pictures, that they stink to the eye. Tchaikovsky's Violin Concerto gives us for the first time the hideous notion that there can be music that stinks to the ear.]

Tschaikowskys Violin Konzert ist eine Anhäufung von Missklängen, verworrenen Steigerungen und aufgeputzten Trivialitäten, bedeckt mit der Nationalfahne des barbarischesten russischen Nihilismus.

(Theodore Helm, *Wiener Signale,* December 5, 1881)

[Tchaikovsky's Violin Concerto is an accumulation of discords, confused climaxes and dressed-up trivialities, covered by the national flag of the most barbarous sort of Russian nihilism.]

-:-

As for Tchaikovsky's *Slavic March,* one feels that the composer must have made a bet, for all that his professional reputation was worth, that he would write the most absolutely hideous thing that had ever been put on paper, and won it, too. Verily, the passion for the fantastic and horrible has brought composition to a pretty pass nowadays. . . . True, he may have wished to give a musical sketch of the sort of country his Slavs were marching through, but even this was no excuse for his writing a piece of music so frightful that, to call it a tone-picture of Pandemonium, would have been thought, twenty years ago, an unkind aspersion on the devil.

(Boston *Evening Transcript,* February 26, 1883)

-:-

There are people who constantly complain about their fate, and tell with especial fervor all about their maladies. In his music, Mr. Tchaikovsky also complains about his fate and talks about his maladies. The Overture to his opera *Eugene Onegin* begins with a whimper. . . . The whimpers continue in the form of a duet. . . . Lensky's aria in the duel scene is pitiful diatonic whining. . . . The duel itself produces a comical impression because of the ridiculous position of the opponents. . . . As an opera, *Eugene Onegin* is stillborn and absolutely incompetent.

(César Cui, *Nedelya,* St. Petersburg, November 5, 1884)

-:-

The Tchaikovsky Fifth Symphony was in part a disappointment. One vainly sought for coherency and homogeneousness. . . The second movement showed the eccentric Russian at his best, but the Valse was a farce, a piece of musical padding, commonplace to a degree, while in the last movement, the composer's Calmuck blood got the better of him, and slaughter, dire and bloody, swept across the storm-driven score.

(*Musical Courier*, New York, March 13, 1889)

-:-

The Fourth Tchaikovsky Symphony proved to be one of the most thoroughly Russian, i.e., semi-barbaric, compositions ever heard in this city. The keynote of the whole work is struck by the Rienzian blare of brass, which opens it, and which recurs at intervals. There is an extraordinary variety in the orchestral colors, some of which are decidedly too loud for a symphony. If Tchaikovsky had called his Symphony 'A Sleigh Ride Through Siberia' no one would have found this title inappropriate.

(New York *Post*, February 1, 1890)

-:-

Of the Fifth Tchaikovsky Symphony one hardly knows what to say. It is less untamed in spirit than the composer's B-flat minor Concerto, less recklessly harsh in its polyphonic writing, less indicative of the composer's disposition to swear a theme's way through a stone wall. In the Finale we have all the untamed fury of the Cossack, whetting itself for deeds of atrocity, against all the sterility of the Russian steppes. The furious peroration sounds like nothing so much as a horde of demons struggling in a torrent of brandy, the music growing drunker and drunker. Pandemonium, delirium tremens, raving, and above all, noise worse confounded!

(Boston *Evening Transcript*, October 24, 1892)

-:-

The Tchaikovsky Fifth Symphony is to the Reinecke Overture as a strong and rebellious liquor to sterilized milk. The Finale is riotous beyond endurance. Instead of applying local color with a brush, Tchaikovsky emptied the paint pot with a jerk. There are conservatives in the audience who are accustomed to protest against the barbaric muse of Russia. Perhaps if these honest people were to listen to orchestral works by Balakirev, Rimsky-Korsakov, Glazunov, Moussorgsky, and other radical Russians, they might then regard Tchaikovsky as a moderate man, or as a Russian Reinecke.

(Boston *Herald*, October 24, 1892)

Tchaikovsky's Violin Concerto is a very uneven work. The Finale is nothing less than music run mad, a frenzy of notes of incomprehensible savagery.

(Boston *Herald,* January 14, 1893)

-:-

The Pathétique Symphony of Tchaikovsky was the heavy number of the bill. It is difficult to be sentimental on the bass drum. But through all the clash and riot of brass and percussive instruments, there are high ideals. Had Tchaikovsky lived longer, he might have become the equal of Rubinstein as a melodist and formalist.

(Brooklyn *Daily Eagle,* February 29, 1896)

-:-

Eine Sonderbarkeit ist das Scherzo [*Allegro con grazia*], welches durchaus im Fünfvierteltakt geht. Diese unangenehme Taktart . . . beunruhigt Hörer und Spieler. Für das Tschaikowskysche Scherzo scheint obendrein dieser Störenfried ganz überflüssig, denn ohne den mindesten Nachteil lässt sich das Stück leicht in den Sechsachteltakt einrichten.

(Eduard Hanslick, *Fünf Jahre Musik,* Berlin, 1896)

[The oddity (of Tchaikovsky's Sixth Symphony) is the Scherzo (*Allegro con grazia*) which goes throughout in five-four time. This disagreeable meter upsets both listener and player. In Tchaikovsky's Scherzo, this discomfort is quite unnecessary: the movement can without the least inconvenience be arranged in six-eight time.]

-:-

Now followed a sweet little slumber song entitled the *1812 Overture* by Tchaikovsky. On a second hearing, or rather a second deafening . . . the coda was as loud as the explosion of a powder-mill. Although not a barcarolle, the roar of the serf was plainly audible in its dynamite explosions. The fight between the Marseillaise and the Russian hymn came to an end in one round, the former being knocked out completely. . . . Altogether one can best sum up this remarkable musical earthquake by saying that it is sound and fury signifying—*something.*

(Louis Elson, Boston Daily *Advertiser,* April 27, 1896)

Selbst wenn wir uns von den Traditionen unserer Meister lossagen, eine Grenze muss doch inne gehalten werden, soll der Begriff *Sinfonie* überhaupt noch einen Sinn haben. Tschaikowsky setzt an die Stelle des musikalischen Gedankens die Phrase, oft der bedenklichsten Art; noch schlimmer sind seine melodischen Gebilde. . . Höchst unangenehm macht sich auch das hartnäckige Festhalten derselben rhythmischen Figuren geltend, die den Komponisten wie Zwangsvorstellungen durch ganze Sätze verfolgen. Denselben halbasiatischen Geschmack zeigt die Instrumentierung, die neben verdriesslicher Klangenthaltung unmittelbar die grellsten und buntesten Farben setzt.

(*Berliner Tageblatt* on Tchaikovsky's Fourth Symphony, quoted in the *Musical Courier,* December 1, 1897)

[Even if we are to reject the traditions of our masters, a limit should be established if the word Symphony is to have a meaning. . . Tchaikovsky substitutes phrases, of the most dubious sort, for musical ideas; still worse are his melodic configurations. . . Most disagreeable is the obstinate adherence to the same rhythmic figures, which pursue the composer like an obsession, through all the movements. The same semi-Asiatic taste is shown in the orchestration, which immediately after an annoying deficiency in sonority, employs the shrillest and gaudiest colors.]

-:-

Tschaikowskys Vierte Sinfonie, bunt instrumentierter Schnickschnack dessen Inhalt sich in der klassischen Form wunderlich genug ausnimmt. . . Die Schnurrpfeifereien des russischen Komponisten irritierten meine Stimmung. . . Blech-Unfug und Missbrauch der Paukenfelle trieben mich hinweg.

(*Kleines Journal,* Berlin, quoted in the *Musical Courier,* December 1, 1897)

[Tchaikovsky's Fourth Symphony, tittle-tattle in motley orchestration the content of which looks rather strange in classical form. . . The Russian composer's twaddle perturbed my mood. The confusion in brass and the abuse of the kettledrums drove me away.]

-:-

The Pathétique Symphony threads all the foul ditches and sewers of human despair; it is as unclean as music well can be. One might call the first movement Zola's *Confession de Claude* set to music! That unspeakable second theme may tell of what Heine called 'Die verschwundene, süsse, blöde Jugendeselei': the impotent senile remembrance of calf love. But of what a calf love! That of Hogarth's lazy apprentice. Indisputably there is power in it: who but Tchaikovsky could have made the vulgar, obscene phrase powerful? The second movement, with its strabismal rhythm, is hardly less ignoble; the third, sheer billingsgate. In the finale, bleary-eyed paresis meets us face to face; and that solemn closing epitaph of the trombones might begin with: 'Here continues to rot . . .'

(W. F. Apthorp, Boston *Evening Transcript,* October 31, 1898)

-:-

Tschaikowskys Klaviertrio in A-moll ist in Wien zum ersten Male gespielt worden; aus den Mienen der Zuhörer sprach beinahe der Wunsch es möchte auch das letzte Mal gewesen sein. . . Es gehört zu der Klasse der Selbstmörder unter den Kompositionen, zu jenen, welche durch unbarmherzige Länge sich selbst umbringen.

(Eduard Hanslick, *Am Ende des Jahrhunderts,* Berlin, 1899)

[Tchaikovsky's Piano Trio in A minor was played in Vienna for the first time; the faces of the listeners almost expressed the wish that it should be also the last time. . . It belongs to the category of suicidal compositions, which kill themselves by their merciless length.]

-:-

Tchaikovsky's Piano Concerto is broken, incoherent, and in at least a dozen instances the entry of the piano is an impertinent intrusion permitted by the composer because the pianist had to be given something to do. Here is Tchaikovsky, a most 'advanced' musician, caring nothing for the rules and forms that served his musical forebears; and he wrote a concerto in his earlier days, and instead of withdrawing it altogether in later life, he revised it! The themes are without exception orchestral themes; not one has been thought in the piano idiom. They are simply faked, by means of scales and arpeggios, to suit the piano.

(J. F. Runciman, *Saturday Review,* London, June 17, 1899)

VARÈSE Was der junge Komponist Edgard Varèse in seiner Orchestertondichtung *Bourgogne* zu reden hatte, war Blech in des Wortes musiktechnischer Bedeutung, ja es war mehr: infernalischer Lärm, eine Katzenmusik.

(Bruno Schrader, *Zeit am Montag,* Berlin, December 19, 1910)

[What the young composer Edgard Varèse had to offer in his orchestral tone-poem *Bourgogne* was, as a matter of musical terminology, brass; but there was more than just that: infernal noise, cat music.]

-:-

It remained for Edgard Varèse (to whom all honor) to shatter the calm of a Sabbath night, to cause peaceful lovers of music to scream out their agony, to arouse angry emotions and tempt men to retire to the back of the theater and perform tympanal concertos on each others' faces. This is a big triumph.

(W. J. Henderson, New York *Herald,* March 5, 1923)

-:-

An Octandre is a flower having eight stamens. Mr. Varèse's *Octandre* was no flower; it was a peach. It cannot be described. It ought not to be. Such music must be heard to be appreciated. It shrieked, it grunted, it chortled, it mewed, it barked—and it turned all the eight instruments into contortionists. It was not in any key, not even in no key. It was just a ribald outbreak of noise. Some people laughed because they could find no other outlet for their feelings. The thing was not even funny.

(W. J. Henderson, New York *Herald,* January 14, 1924)

-:-

Varèse's *Hyperprism* reminded us of election night, a menagerie or two and a catastrophe in a boiler factory.

(Olin Downes, New York *Times,* December 17, 1924)

-:-

Goats are not raised in this town, as they once were, and not even Mr. Varèse can forcibly annex any from a New York audience. No words can describe this extraordinary production, not even the strange word *Hyperprism.* But Bully Bottom in his proudest moments could not have given such imitations of the roaring of the lion, the shrieking of the wind, the pattering of hailstones and the swearing of the distracted menagerie. No cat smaller than a Bengal tiger would have ventured into such company. If Mr. Varèse honestly believes this sort of thing is music, then he is a deluded and impotent follower of that eminent Viennese juggler who makes his trickery almost plausible. The lover of art can only declare his faith that the time will come when all these decompositions will be swept violently down a steep place into the sea.

(W. J. Henderson, New York *Sun,* December 17, 1924)

-:-

Mr. Varèse has not told us what was at the back of his mind when writing his *Hyperprism*. . . But if the crude expression be permissible, I should say that what was at the back of Mr. Varèse's mind was an alarm of fire at the Zoo, with the beasts and birds all making appropriate noises—the lion roaring, the hyena howling, the monkeys chattering, the parrots squealing, with the curses of the distracted attendants cutting through them all. The work has, of course, not the slightest connection with music.

(Ernest Newman, New York *Evening Post,* December 17, 1924)

-:-

And there was Edgard Varèse's latest mystery entitled *Intégrales*. If it be music to blow one piercing tone from the piccolo and a squeal from an E-flat clarinet for five minutes while other wind instruments in other keys make sounds like an injured dog's cry of pain or a cat's yell of midnight rage, and sundry instruments of percussion crash and bang apparently just for the sake of crashing and banging, then this is the real thing.

(W. J. Henderson, New York *Sun,* March 2, 1925)

-:-

The grand finale was Edgard Varèse's *Intégrales*. It sounded a good deal like a combination of early morning in the Mott Haven freight yards, feeding time at the zoo and a Sixth Avenue trolley rounding a curve, with an intoxicated woodpecker thrown in for good measure.

(Ernest Newman, New York *Evening Post,* March 2, 1925)

-:-

Amériques seemed to depict the progress of a terrible fire in one of our larger zoos. The animals sensed the conflagration before their keepers, and set up awful howls and emitted cavernous groans. Suddenly the siren is heard in the distance. It grows louder and more piercing. The engines arrive. For twenty minutes the howling of the animals and the shrieks of the siren reach to the skies. There the piece ends without any resolution. One will never know what happened. Was the fire put out? Was the menagerie rescued? Mr. Varèse, like a true artist, doesn't commit himself.

(Samuel Chotzinoff, New York *World*, April 14, 1926)

-:-

One concludes that Mr. Varèse, the distinguished classicist, must be a particularly trying person to live with at a time when he is preoccupied with certain moods and certain thoughts. We should indeed fear to meet him on a dark night if he is liable frequently to emotional states of the sort articulated in his music. . . The score [*Arcana*] is long and infinitely wearying in its revelations of the unspeakably hideous.

(Edward Cushing, Brooklyn *Daily Eagle*, April 13, 1927)

-:-

Varèse's *Arcana* plunged the listener into morasses of sound which seemingly had little relation to music. . . There was no mercy in its disharmony, no pity in its successions of screaming, clashing, plangorous discords. . . A series of gunpowder explosions might similarly overawe the ear . . . but their musical quality would be open to question.

(Oscar Thompson, *Musical America*, April 23, 1927)

-:-

Zwei Stunden lang hieb Nicolas Slonimsky auf die Philharmoniker ein, die schliesslich aus ihrer üblen Laune gar kein Hehl mehr machten. . . Eindreiviertel Stunden ertrug das Publicum den Lärm. Beim Kakophonen Durcheinander *Arcana* von Varèse verlor es die Geduld. Der Skandal ging los. Es war begreiflich. Kein Ohr hält diese Musik auf die Dauer aus. Sie hat mit Musik nichts zu tun. Sie chokiert nicht und amusiert nicht. Sie ist einfach sinnlos.

(Heinrich Strobel, *Börsen-Courier*, Berlin, March 1, 1932)

[For two hours Nicolas Slonimsky bore down on the Philharmonic musicians until they finally made no secret of their ugly disposition.

For an hour and three quarters the public submitted to the noise. But after the cacophonous tumult of *Arcana* by Varèse, they lost patience. The pandemonium broke loose. It was understandable. Nobody's ears can stand this music for any length of time. It has nothing to do with music. It does not shock and it does not amuse. It is simply senseless.]

-:-

Kühnste Phantasie vermag sich nicht auszudenken, was Edgard Varèse met den Tönen alles gemacht hat. . . Die letzten Erinnerungen an Musik hat man sich aus dem Gehirne zu reissen, irgendwelche Vorstellung an Linie, Thema oder ähnliches zu verbannen. Denn Straussens *Elektra* und der ganze Stravinsky sind Choräle gegenüber diesem, *Arcana* betitelten Stück. Brüllende, stöhnende Klangsetzen, eine irrsinnig durcheinandertobende Menagerie, Schlachtenlärm, Schreie von Verwundeten oder eine Menschenmasse, die man zu grauenvollstem Verenden in einen brodelnden Vulkankrater wirft—irgend so etwas muss man sich mit Notwendigkeit vorstellen. Es ist das Tollste, was man je in Berlin während des letzten Jahrzehntes gehört hat—eine Ausgeburt tönenden Wahnsinns, die vielen Hörern rein physiologisch schon so unerträglich wurde, dass sie die Flucht ergriffen.

(F. Brust, *Germania,* Berlin, March 16, 1932)

[The boldest imagination cannot conjure up what Edgard Varèse has done with notes. The last vestige of music must be torn out from one's brain, and any conception of line, themes, or anything like that must be banished. Strauss's *Elektra* and all of Stravinsky are chorales compared to this piece, named *Arcana.* Roaring, groaning tonal assaults, an insanely raging zoo, noise of battle, cries of the wounded, or a mass of men thrown into the crater of an erupting volcano in a hideous slaughter—one must necessarily imagine something like that. This is the maddest thing that has been heard in Berlin during the last decade, an abortion of sounding madness which was purely physiologically so unendurable to many of the listeners, that they fled.]

-:-

Zum Schluss gab es eine end- und sinnlose Klangferkelei von Edgard Varèse. *Arcana* ist dieses Tönescheusal betitelt, das ohne geistige Disziplin und künstlerische Vorstellung die Hörer mit Skorpionenpeitschen traktiert und friedsame Konzertbesucher zu Hyänen werden lässt. Grosser Arnold Schönberg, du bist mit deinen berühmten fünf Orchesterstücken glänzend rehabilitiert! Das sind Aeusserungen neuzeitlicher Klassik gegenüber diesem barbarischen Wahnwitz.

(Paul Schwers, *Allgemeine Musikzeitung,* Berlin, March 18, 1932)

[In conclusion, there was presented an endless and senseless tonal piggery by Edgard Varèse. This tonal monster is entitled *Arcana;* devoid of spiritual discipline and artistic imagination, it belabors the listeners with horsewhips and transforms peaceable concertgoers into hyenas. Great Arnold Schoenberg, you are with your famous Five Orchestral Pieces brilliantly vindicated! They are utterances of modern classicism beside this barbarous insanity.]

-:-

Ionization by Varèse, a symphony of noises which represents the wondrous actions of ions within the atom, recalls school days in the chemical laboratory where hydrogen sulfide was produced to the merriment of students and the horror of teachers. Anvils clanged, maracas jittered, drums thumped, sirens wailed, and there was hell to pay. Director Slonimsky performed the almost impossible feat of keeping one section of the orchestra in one rhythm with his left hand and another section in a different time with his right, and if you think that's easy, try patting your head with your left hand and rubbing your stomach with your right.

(Havana *Evening Telegram,* May 3, 1933)

-:-

After hearing Varèse's *Ionization,* I am anxious that you should examine my composition scored for two stoves and a kitchen sink. I've named it *Concussion Symphony,* descriptive of the disintegration of an Irish potato under the influence of a powerful atomizer.

A postcard, signed Iona Lotta Bunk, received by Nicolas Slonimsky after his performance of Varèse's *Ionization* at the Hollywood Bowl, July 16, 1933)

VERDI Le système musical de Verdi, vous le connaissez: il n'a pas encore existé de compositeur italien plus incapable de produire ce qui s'appelle vulgairement une mélodie.
(*Gazette Musicale de Paris,* August 1, 1847)

[You know Verdi's musical system: there has not yet been an Italian composer more incapable of producing what is commonly called a melody.]

-:-

It would be difficult to fancy a worse opera than *Attila* even from Verdi. The force of noise can hardly go further, unless we are to resort to the device of Sarti's cannon fired to time his Russian *Te Deum* on the taking of Ochakov, or imitate the anvil chorus which Spontini introduced in one of his operas. It is something to have touched the limits of the outrageous style—but this we think we have now done; unless the more recent *Alzira* and *Macbeth* by Verdi contain double parts for the ophicleides. May we never hear its likes again.
(*The Athenaeum,* London, March 18, 1848)

-:-

The music of the opera *Macbeth* is Verdiesque. Screaming unisons everywhere, and all the melodies of that peculiar style the parallel whereof is rope-dancing; first a swing and flourish, hanging on by the hands, then a somerset, and then another swing to an erect position of the rope . . . The unfortunate man is incapable of real melody—his airs are such as a man born deaf would compose by calculation of the distances of musical notes and the intervals between them.
(George Templeton Strong's Diary, April 28, 1850)

-:-

Rigoletto est le moins fort des ouvrages de Verdi. . . La mélodie y manque. . . Cet opéra n'a guère chance de se maintenir au répertoire.
(*Gazette Musicale de Paris,* May 22, 1853)

[*Rigoletto* is the weakest work of Verdi. It lacks melody. This opera has hardly any chance to be kept in the repertoire.]

When Verdi has an opera to compose, he waits patiently until the midnight bell has tolled. He then enters his study, in which there is a piano placed between a big drum and cymbals, and seating himself at the piano, he first bangs the drum on the right hand, then crashes the cymbals on the left hand, then thumps the piano in the middle, and while the air is reverberating with the mingled sounds he commences the first chorus. This is the way Verdi composes. Can anybody have a doubt on the subject?

(*Dwight's Journal of Music*, Boston, June 1853)

-:-

Time increases our conviction that in England and France the operas of Signor Verdi only pass because there is nothing else, and that the first more elegant and gracious Italian composer who arrives can sweep them away to the limbo of forgotten frenzies.

(H. F. Chorley, *The Athenaeum*, London, May 5, 1855)

-:-

Il Trovatore is written in contempt of all rules . . . no temporary success can atone for the want of refinement, the coarseness of style, the habitual contempt for pure forms, which are as apparent as in any of the previous attempts of the composer . . . they render it impossible to hope for any newly awakened desire on the part of Signor Verdi to become essentially an artist. Verdi should communicate with Richard Wagner—the other red republican of music, who wants to revolutionize the art after a fashion of his own. . . The firm of Wagner and Verdi would then be able to export their musical wares to all parts of the earth.

(*Musical World*, London, May 19, 1855)

-:-

Verdi was intended by nature for a composer, but I am afraid the genius given him—like girls kissing each other—is decided waste of the raw material.

(*Dwight's Journal of Music*, Boston, July 14, 1855)

-:-

The favorite opera of the season has been *La Traviata*. The highest society in England has thronged the opera house night after night to see a very young and innocent-looking lady impersonate the heroine of an infamous French novel, who varies her prostitution by a frantic passion. . . Verdi's music, which generally descends below his subjects, can in this case claim the ambiguous merit of being quite worthy of the subject. . . We should have thought the production of *La Traviata* an outrage on the ladies of the aristocracy who support the theater, if they had not by crowding their boxes every night shown that they did not notice the underlying vice of the opera.

(London *Spectator,* quoted in the London *Times,* August 4, 1856)

-:-

M. Verdi est un musicien de décadence. Il en a tous les défauts, la violence du style, le décousu des idées, la crudité des couleurs, l'impropriété du langage.

(P. Scudo, *Revue des Deux Mondes,* Paris, December 15, 1856)

[M. Verdi is a musician of decadence. He has all its defects, the violence of the style, the incoherence of ideas, the crudity of colors, the impropriety of language.]

-:-

The contest that Verdi's *I Due Foscari* provokes between vocalization and instrumentation can only be compared to the fight of the ironclads in Charleston harbor. Both sides blazed away with remarkable spirit; but if the crown for noise and perserverance must be awarded anywhere, let it be given to the gentleman who bangs the drum.

(*Albion,* New York, April 1863)

-:-

Ernani est de la musique épicée, irritant les palais délicats et fatigant même les estomacs robustes. Disons franchement que l'orchestration est d'une pauvreté et d'une rudesse impossibles, que ces accents ne sont que des cris, et qu'enfin ces unissons continuels du soprano et du ténor ont une acuité énervante fort peu harmonieuse et d'une valeur négative.

(*Le Ménestrel,* Paris, December 20, 1863)

[*Ernani* is spiced music, irritating for delicate palates and affecting even strong stomachs. Let us say frankly that the orchestration is of impossible poverty and crudity, that the accents are nothing but shouts, and that these continuous unisons of soprano and tenor possess an enervating shrillness, inharmonious, and of inferior quality.]

-:-

There is lately come to town an Italian gentleman, to whose brassy screeds and tinkling cymbalics it is expected that all habitués of the opera must listen, to the utter exclusion and oblivion of the old musical worthies who delighted the world with their immortal works . . . before the Father of Evil had invented Signor Giuseppe Verdi.

(G. A. Sala, *Thrice Round the Block*, London, 1863)

-:-

These coarse and brutal Verdi commonplaces, raucous and clamorous choruses, these screaming unisons, these iron-clad, hard melodies, in which we have the most original and individual part of Verdi—how happy one is to forget it!

(A New York paper, February 21, 1874)

-:-

When Verdi sees a strong dramatic situation, he rushes straight into the thick of it like a mad bull.

(Boston *Evening Transcript*, March 27, 1882)

-:-

One has a humorous or a pitying reaction toward the 1900 horseless carriage. We have exactly the same picture in melodies composed by a Verdi or a Bellini: the mechanical efficiency is so low that it makes us smile if not laugh. The same melodies stimulate entirely different reactions among octogenarians surviving in our epoch of 400 miles per hour.

(*The Schillinger System of Composition*, New York, 1946)

WAGNER Ich glaube nicht dass von Wagner ein Stück seiner Komposition ihn überlebt.

(From a letter by Moritz Hauptmann, dated February 3, 1849, published in *Briefe von Moritz Hauptmann an Franz Hauser,* Leipzig, 1871)

[I do not believe that a single composition of Wagner will survive him.]

-:-

Cette séance a fini par une ouverture de M. Wagner, compositeur allemand. Son oeuvre ne nous a paru que l'accompagnement très bruyant d'une mélodie absente. Après tout, il n'y a point de loi que défende l'écrire lorsqu'on n'a point d'idée. L'œuvre de M. Wagner est donc parfaitement légale.

(*National,* Paris, November 30, 1850)

[This concert ended with an overture (to the opera *Tannhäuser*) by R. Wagner, a German composer. His work seemed to us nothing but a very noisy accompaniment to an absent melody. After all, there is no law prohibiting to write when one has no ideas whatsoever. The work of Monsieur Wagner is therefore perfectly legal.]

-:-

Dr. Schumann is as clear as Truth and as charming as Graces themselves, if he be measured against the opera-composer who has been set up by Young Germany, at the composer's own instigation, as the coming man of the stage:—I mean, of course, Herr Wagner. . . . The discoveries and innovations made by his betters he employs in the uncouth fashion of a schoolboy; writing audaciously in proportion as his real knowledge is limited. . . There is comfort however, in thinking that beyond Herr Wagner in his peculiar manner it is hardly possible to go. This saturnal of licentious discord must have here reached its climax. It is true, the 'conventionalisms' of the orchestra have still to be destroyed—only, were this done, since all pretext of music would cease, the thing produced would no longer be within the domain of Art, but would rather come under the care of a society for the suppression of nuisances.

(H. F. Chorley, *The Athenaeum,* London, December 18, 1852)

-:-

Lohengrin of Wagner was produced in Leipzig after much trouble and expense. The music is very much in the same style as the

Tannhäuser, only a little more so. In *that* opera it *is* possible to find several detached melodies. But in the *Lohengrin,* Wagner fully developed all his new ideas. The opera takes over four hours for representation, and during all that time not a scrap of melody can be heard with the exception of some ten bars at the beginning of the third act. *Lohengrin* has been given a few times since, and I scarcely think it will be able to keep the stage for any length of time.

(E. A. Kelley, in a correspondence from Leipzig, April 2, 1854, published in a London paper)

-:-

The almost impossible *Tannhäuser* Overture of Herr Richard Wagner introduced for the first time to an English audience . . . is a weak parody of the worst compositions, not of M. Berlioz, but of his imitators. So much fuss about nothing, such a pompous and empty commonplace, has seldom been heard.

(J. W. Davison, London *Times,* May 3, 1854)

-:-

After all the talk about Herr Richard Wagner's Overture to *Tannhäuser,* we certainly were led to expect something better than we heard. It is enormously difficult to play. . . With regard to the music, it is such queer stuff that criticism would be thrown away upon it. We never listened to an overture at once so loud and so empty.

(*Musical World,* London, May 6, 1854)

-:-

The overture to *Tannhäuser* is a piece of vapid rhodomontade and, as Herr Wagner paints him, the 'minstrel of love' is, after all, but a clamorous and empty personage. If the general ear of 'the future' is destined to be affected with such music as this, it is to be hoped that charitable posterity will institute some extra hospitals for the deaf wherever Herr Wagner and his compositions are allowed to penetrate.

(J. W. Davison, London *Times,* December 11, 1854)

-:-

Looking at Herr Wagner's songs, we are obliged to own our conviction that these compositions are remarkable only for the absence of everything that has been deemed beautiful in music, added to the presence of some of the most intolerable offenses to which either the ear or the principles of harmony need ever be subjected. . . Unmeaning and absurd as is the voice part of these songs, their harmonic structure is still more reprehensible. It reminds us of nothing but the extemporizing of some man who, ignorant of music, has discovered a number of chords on the pianoforte, and straightway proceeds to string them together, wholly insensible to their want of mutual relation. . . Anything more rambling, incoherent, and unmasterly than all this cannot be conceived. . . And we are really to accept this wild senseless dabbling about among chords, without form, without idea, invention, expression, as music! . . . The more we see and hear of Richard Wagner, the more are we convinced that music is not his special birthright, is not for him an articulate language. . . Either Richard Wagner is a desperate charlatan endowed with worldly skill and vigorous purpose enough to persuade a gaping crowd that the nauseous compound he manufactures has some previous inner virtue; or else he is a self-deceived enthusiast . . . too utterly destitute of any perception of musical beauty to recognize the worthlessness of his credentials.

(Henry Smart in the London *Sunday Times,* quoted in *Musical World,* May 12, 1855)

-:-

Destitute of melody, extremely bad in harmony, utterly incoherent in form and inexpressive of any intelligible ideas whatever, we must set down the *Tannhäuser Overture* as a most contemptible performance. If it be a foreshadowing of the music of the future, Polyhymnia is doomed to sing in Purgatory of the direst kind, for none but a terribly tormented soul could send forth such shocking sounds.

(W. H. Glover, *Morning Post,* London, May 15, 1855)

-:-

Of the Overture to *Tannhäuser* we have already spoken, and the execution last night gave us no cause to modify our first impression. A more inflated display of extravagance and noise has rarely been submitted to an audience; and it was a pity to hear so magnificent an orchestra engaged in almost fruitless attempts at accomplishing things which, even if readily practicable, would lead to nothing.

(J. W. Davison, London *Times,* May 16, 1855)

Another slice from that cake of harmony to which the posterior world is destined was tasted in anticipation. This was *Tannhäuser*. . . . The effect was stunning, windy, and preposterous. The audience was evidently perplexed and (the 'elect' excepted) postponed their verdict to 'the future.'

(*Musical World*, London, May 19, 1855)

-:-

The Overture to *Tannhäuser* is one of the most curious pieces of patchwork ever passed off by self-delusion for a complete and significant creation. . . When it is stripped and sifted, Herr Wagner's creation may be likened, not to any real figure, with its bone and muscle, but to a compound of one shapely feature with several tasteless fragments, smeared over with cement, but so flimsily that the paucity of good material is proved by the most superficial examination.

(H. F. Chorley, *The Athenaeum*, London, May 19, 1855)

-:-

The Overture to *Tannhäuser* does not improve on closer acquaintance. So much incessant noise, so uninterrupted and singular an exhibition of pure cacophony, was never heard before. And all this is intended to describe the delights and fascinations which lured the unwary to the secret abode of the Goddess of beauty. . . We sincerely hope that no execution, however superb, will ever make such senseless discord pass, in England, for a manifestation of art and genius.

(J. W. Davison, London *Times*, June 12, 1855)

The contrast between the Macfarren Overture and the *Tannhäuser* Overture marks well two very opposite styles of taste in modern music—the one being intelligible and animating to all listeners; the other, unintelligible and uninteresting except to educated admirers who labor to explain its beauties to the uninitiated.

(*Literary Gazette*, London, June 16, 1855)

-:-

Look at *Lohengrin*. . . It is poison—rank poison. All we can make out is an incoherent mass of rubbish, with no more real pretension to be called music than the jangling and clashing of gongs and other uneuphonious instruments with which the Chinamen, on the brow of a hill, fondly thought to scare away our English 'blue-jackets.'

(*Musical World,* London, June 30, 1855)

-:-

Being a Communist, Herr Wagner is desirous of forcing the arts into fellowship with his political and social principles. He affirms that national melody is unhealthy and unreal, being simply the narrow-souled emanation from oppressed peoples. . . The symmetry of form . . . ignored, or else abandoned; the consistency of keys and their relations . . . overthrown, contemned, demolished; the charm of rhythmic measure . . . destroyed; the true basis of harmony, and the indispensable government of modulation, cast away, for a reckless, wild, extravagant and demagogic cacophony, the symbol of profligate libertinage! Are we then to have music in no definite key whatever? . . This man, this Wagner, this author of *Tannhäuser,* of *Lohengrin,* and so many other hideous things—and above all, the overture to *Der Fliegende Holländer,* the most hideous and detestable of the whole—this preacher of the 'Future,' was born to feed spiders with flies, not to make happy the heart of man with beautiful melody and harmony. . . Who are the men that go about as his apostles? Men like Liszt—madmen, enemies of music to the knife, who, not born for music, and conscious of their impotence, revenge themselves by endeavoring to annihilate it. . . These musicians of young Germany are maggots, that quicken from corruption. They have no bone, nor flesh, nor blood, nor marrow. The end of their being is to prey on the ailing trunk, until it becomes putrid and rotten.

(*Musical World,* London, June 30, 1855)

-:-

Tannhäuser is not merely polyphonous, but polycacophonous.

(*Musical World,* London, October 13, 1855)

-:-

Wagner est le Marat de la musique dont Berlioz est le Robespierre.

(A. Gasperini, *Le Siècle,* Paris, 1858)

[Wagner is the Marat of music, and Berlioz is its Robespierre.]

On a commencé par l'ouverture du *Vaisseau-Fantôme*. . . Je ne sais s'il me manque un sixième sens qui est nécessaire à ce qu'il parait pour comprendre et apprécier cette nouvelle musique, mais j'avoue qu'une roulée de coups de poing qu'on m'eût donnée sur la tête, ne m'eût point causé une sensation plus désagréable. C'est une série d'accords stridents, de sifflements aigus, de grincements de cuivres enragés, sans aucune trêve, aucun repos pour l'oreille. Si l'auteur a voulu peindre une tempête, il en a au moins rendu l'effet le plus pénible: cela donne le mal de mer.

(P.-A. Fiorentino, *Constitutionnel*, Paris, January 30, 1860)

[They began with the overture to the *Flying Dutchman*. . . I do not know whether I possess a sixth sense which seems necessary to understand and appreciate this new music, but I confess that violent fist blows on my head would not have caused a more disagreeable sensation. This is a series of strident chords, high-pitched hisses, screechings of infuriated brasses, without any respite or rest for the ear. If the composer wished to depict a storm, he at least produced its most painful effect, for it makes one seasick.]

-:-

L'Ouverture du *Vaisseau-Fantôme,* c'est le chaos peignant le chaos d'où il ne surgit que quelques bouffées d'accords exhalés par les trompettes dont l'auteur fait grand abus.

(P. Scudo, *Revue des Deux Mondes,* Paris, 1860)

[The Overture to *The Flying Dutchman* is a chaos depicting chaos, from which nothing emerges but a few puffs of chords emitted by the trumpets greatly abused by the composer.]

-:-

Tannhäuser a passé, et la musique de l'avenir n'était déjà plus. Imaginez un dieu indien à sept bras et trois têtes intronisé dans un temple grec; c'est l'emblème de l'opéra hétéroclite de M. Wagner. Sa partition n'est qu'un chaos musical. Les sons se heurtent, s'agglomèrent, s'entassent, se confondent, comme d'immenses nuages dans un ciel blafard. . . Tantôt c'est une obscurité opaque et pesante; . . . tantôt c'est un vacarme discordant qui ne parvient qu'à simuler les plus grossiers fracas des tempêtes physiques. . . 'Si je comprends ce que je mange, je te chasse,' disait un gourmet à son cuisinier. En deux mots, voilà la musique de M. Wagner. Elle impose, pour révéler ses secrets, des tortures d'esprit que l'algèbre seule a droit d'infliger. L'inintelligible est son idéal. C'est l'art mystique mourant orgueilleusement d'inanition au milieu du vide.

(Paul de Saint-Victor, *La Presse,* Paris, March 1861)

[*Tannhäuser* has passed by, and the music of the future was no more. Imagine a Hindu god with seven arms and three heads enthroned in a Greek temple; this is the emblem of the incongruous opera of Monsieur Wagner. . . His score is nothing but musical chaos. The sounds collide, accumulate, pile up, and mix like huge clouds in a pale sky. . . At times it is an opaque and oppressive darkness; then it is a discordant uproar which succeeds only in imitating the overwhelming loudness of physical tempests. . . 'If I understand what I eat, I will fire you,' said a glutton to his cook. In a few words, here is Wagner's music. In order to reveal its secrets, it imposes mental tortures that only algebra has a right to inflict. The unintelligible is its ideal. It is a mystic art proudly dying of inanition in a vacuum.]

-:-

Wagner est évidemment fou.

(Berlioz in a letter dated March 5, 1861)

[Wagner is evidently mad.]

-:-

Le public a été énervé, surexcité par une orchestration stridente, insatiable d'effets et de dissonances, par le paroxisme de la chanterelle, et surtout par une intempérance de récitatifs qui porte à la torpeur la plus prolongée et de la façon la plus dangereuse pour la santé des auditeurs. 'J'y ai survécu,' s'écriait un robuste feuilletoniste, au sortir de la dernière répétition générale; combien de dilettantes intrépides n'ont pu en dire autant à la première représentation!

(J.-L. Heugel, *Le Ménestrel,* March 17, 1861, after the Paris première of *Tannhäuser*)

[The public was enervated and over-excited by a strident orchestration insatiable of effects and dissonances, by the paroxism of high violins, and particularly by the intemperance of recitatives which induces a prolonged torpor in a manner most dangerous for the health of the listeners. 'I survived it!' exclaimed a robust columnist, as he left the dress rehearsal; but how many intrepid dilettantes could not tell as much after the first performance!]

-:-

The music of *Tannhäuser* is tumultuous, deafening, infernal. Here are exasperated trebles, enraged cymbals, chapeaux chinois in delirium. It produces the same effect upon you, and gives you the same pain, as if a hundred needles should enter your ear at once. The most courteous auditors, who wished to preserve a decent demeanor, suffered without stirring; others twisted about in their seats and changed sides like St. Laurent upon his gridiron.

(P.-A. Fiorentino quoted in Boston *Musical Times,* April 20, 1861)

-:-

L'auteur du *Vaisseau-fantôme,* de *Tannhäuser*, de *Tristan et Isolde* et de *Lohengrin,* ouvre-t-il comme il l'espère, une voie nouvelle à la composition? Non, assurément, et il faudrait désespérer de l'avenir de la musique, si l'on voyait se propager la musique de l'avenir.

(Oscar Comettant, *Almanach Musical,* Paris, 1861)

[The author of *The Flying Dutchman,* of *Tannhäuser,* of *Tristan and Isolde* and of *Lohengrin,* does he open, as he hopes, a new path to composition? Surely not, for we should despair of the future of music if the Music of the Future would become popular.]

-:-

Un dernier ennui, mais colossal, a été *Tannhäuser.* Il me semble que je pourrais écrire demain quelque chose de semblable en m'inspirant de mon chat marchant sur le clavier d'un piano.

(Prosper Mérimée in *Lettres à une Inconnue,* Paris, 1861)

[The latest annoyance, but colossal, was *Tannhäuser*. I believe that I could write tomorrow something similar, inspired by my cat walking down the keyboard of the piano.]

-:-

La seconde partie du programme a commencé par un prélude et l'introduction d'un opéra de M. Wagner qui s'intitule *Tristan et*

Isolde. Sur ce texte le compositeur a certainement dépassé tout ce qu'on peut imaginer en fait de confusion, de désordre et d'impuissance. On dirait d'une gageure contre le sens commun et les plus simples exigences de l'oreille. Si je n'avais pas entendu trois fois ce monstrueux entassement de sons discordants, je ne le croirais pas possible.

(P. Scudo, *L'Année Musicale,* Paris, 1861)

[The second part of the program began with a prelude and introduction of an opera by Monsieur Wagner, entitled *Tristan and Isolde.* On this text, the composer certainly has surpassed anything that one can imagine in confusion, disorder and impotence. One might say it was a challenge to common sense and the most elementary requirements of the ear. Had I not heard this monstrous piling of discordant sounds three times, I would not believe it possible.]

-:-

Ein musikalisches Scheusal, eine aus Abgeschmacktheit und Brutalität zu gleichen Theilen gemischte Mixtur ist die Ouverture zum *Fliegenden Holländer.*

(*Deutsche Musikzeitung,* Vienna, 1861)

[The Overture to the *Flying Dutchman* is a musical horror, a mixture concocted of bad taste and brutality in equal doses.]

-:-

Quand M. Wagner a des idées, ce qui est rare, il est loin d'être original; quand il n'en a pas, il est unique et impossible.

(P. Scudo, *L'Année Musicale,* Paris, 1862)

[When Monsieur Wagner has ideas, which is rare, he is far from being original; when he has none, he is unique and impossible.]

-:-

Wagner is a man devoid of all talent. His melodies, where they are found at all, are in worse taste than Verdi and Flotow and more sour than the stalest Mendelssohn. All this is covered up with a thick layer of rot. His orchestra is decorative, but coarse. The violins squeal throughout on the highest notes and throw the listener into a state of extreme nervousness. I left without waiting for the concert to end, and I assure you that had I stayed longer, both I and my wife would have a fit of hysterics. What nerves must Wagner himself possess?]

(Letter from César Cui to Rimsky-Korsakov, dated March 9, 1863)

-:-

Wagner, c'est Berlioz moins la mélodie. Sa partition du *Tannhäuser* ressemble à un livre qui serait écrit sans points ni virgules; on ne sait à quel endroit réspirer. L'auditeur étouffe.

(D.-F.-E. Auber on Wagner, quoted in *Le Ménestrel*, September 27, 1863)

[Wagner is Berlioz minus the melody. The score of *Tannhäuser* resembles a book written without periods or commas; one doesn't know when to take breath. The listener suffocates.]

-:-

Seither besitzen wir nun auch Richard Wagners *Tristan, Nibelungenring,* und seine Lehre von der 'unendlichen Melodie,' d.h. die zum Princip erhobene Formlosigkeit, die systematisierte Nichtmusik, das auf 5 Notenlinien verschriebene melodische Nervenfieber.

(Eduard Hanslick in the third edition of his *Vom Musikalisch-Schönen,* 1865; in the fourth edition, the following is added: 'der gesungene und gegeigte Opiumrausch für dessen Kultus ja in Bayreuth ein eigener Tempel eröffnet worden ist'—'opium reverie, sung and fiddled, for whose cult a special temple has been opened in Bayreuth.')

[We now have Richard Wagner's *Tristan, The Ring of the Nibelungs,* and his doctrine of 'endless melody,' i.e., formlessness elevated to a principle, a systematized non-music, a melodic nerve fever written out on the five lines of the staff.]

-:-

Then came Wagner's Introduction to the opera *Lohengrin.* I heard its opening movement at the rehearsal of a fortnight ago, supposed it was Hector Berlioz's *Carnival* Overture, and inferred that Hector Berlioz was experimenting on a new mechanical method. I did Hector B. injustice. This Introduction was as bad as anything he ever wrote and vastly less entertaining. Wagner writes like an 'intoxified' pig, Berlioz like a tipsy chimpanzee.

(George Templeton Strong's Diary, December 15, 1866)

Votre M. Wagner est sans pitié; quant il tient son clou, il vous l'enfonce lentement dans la tête à grands coups de marteau.

(From a conversation in the audience after the Paris première of *Tannhäuser,* as reported by P.-A. Fiorentino in his book, *Comédies et Comédiens,* Paris, 1867)

[Your Wagner is without pity; he drives the nail slowly into your head with swinging hammer blows.]

-:-

Wagner's Introduction to *Lohengrin* may be defined as two squeakinesses with a brassiness between them. It seems uncommon nonsense, with an occasional gleam of smartness, like the talk of a clever man who is just losing his wits.

(George Templeton Strong's Diary, March 7, 1868)

-:-

The Prelude to *Tristan and Isolde* reminds me of the old Italian painting of a martyr whose intestines are slowly unwound from his body on a reel.

(Eduard Hanslick, June 1868)

-:-

After *Lohengrin,* I had a splitting headache, and all through the night I dreamed about a goose.

(Letter from Mily Balakirev to Vladimir Stasov, dated St. Petersburg, November 3, 1868)

-:-

Herr Wagner, a noisy and empty pretender, with a host of satellites, such as Brahms, Raff, Bruch, Liszt (perhaps the very worst composer that ever existed), could no more achieve an oratorio like Pierson's *Jerusalem* than they could write a tragedy like *Hamlet.*

(From a letter to the Editor of the *Musical Standard,* London, December 1868)

-:-

Rienzi fait l'effet d'une macédoine de Verdi et de Meyerbeer pilée dans un mortier et entrée ensuite en fermentation.

(P. Veron, *Charivari,* Paris, April 8, 1869)

[*Rienzi* tastes like a mixture of Verdi and Meyerbeer pounded in a mortar until it begins to ferment.]

Ce diable de Wagner a mis l'explosion de la place de la Sorbonne en musique. S'il avait assisté à la curieuse soirée d'hier, il eût compris que ce public si facile à contenter, si amoureux des belles choses, ne se laissera jamais imposer la soi-disant musique de l'avenir, avec ses effets de casseroles et de porcelaine fêlée.

(Albert Wolff, *Figaro*, Paris, April 8, 1869)

[This devilish Wagner has set the explosion on Place de la Sorbonne to music. Had he been present last night at this curious performance, he would have understood that our public, so easy to please, so enamored of beautiful things, will never allow itself to be imposed upon by this so-called music of the future, with its effects of frying pans and broken china.]

-:-

In dem *Feuerzauber* umflutet uns ein Meer von fremdartigen Klängen. In das fieberhafte Tremolieren der Geigen tönt das Rauschen und Pizzikieren dreier Harfen, brüllen Posaunen und Ophikleïden, klirren die hellen Rufe gestimmter Glöckchen. Fast unausgesetzt schlagen eigentümliche blendende Orchester-Effecte an das betroffen lauschende Ohr des Hörers. In dem Raffinement ungewöhnlicher Klangmischungen wie in der Wucht des materiellen Lärms scheint uns Wagner an dem Punkt angelangt wo er nicht mehr weiter kann.

(Eduard Hanslick, 1869)

[In *Magic Fire*, a sea of strange sounds engulfs us. Above the feverish tremolos of the violins, are heard the rustling and the plucking of three harps; the trombones and ophicleides roar, and there clink the ringing calls of pitched bells. Almost incessantly the odd and dazzling orchestral effects strike the listening ear. In the artifice of strange sound mixtures, as in the impact of material noise, it seems to us that Wagner has reached the point beyond which he cannot possibly go.]

-:-

Wagner est un fou, un fou d'orgueil. Sa musique de l'avenir est une monstruosité. Improlifique par nature comme tous les monstres, Wagner est impuissant à se reproduire, à se multiplier.

(H. Prévost, *Etude sur Richard Wagner*, Paris, 1869)

[Wagner is a madman, a madman from pride. His music of the future is a monstrosity. Sterile by nature like all monsters, Wagner is impotent to reproduce himself, to proliferate.]

-:-

Die 'unendliche Melodie' ist die herrschende, d.h. die musikalisch unterwühlende Macht, in den *Meistersingern* wie im *Tristan.* Ein kleines Motiv beginnt, es wird ehe es zur eigentlichen Melodie, zum Thema sich gestaltet, gleichsam umgebogen, geknickt, durch fortwährendes Modulieren und enharmonisches Rücken, höher oder tiefer gestellt, durch Rosalien fortgesetzt, dann angestückelt und wieder verkürzt, bald von diesem, bald von jenem Instrument wiederholt oder nachgebildet. Mit ängstlicher Vermeidung jeder abschliessenden Cadenz fliesst diese knochenlose Ton-Molluske sich immer wieder aus sich selbst erneuernd, ins Unabsehbare fort.

(Eduard Hanslick, 1870)

[The 'endless melody' is the dominating, i.e., musically undermining power in the *Meistersinger* as in *Tristan.* A little motive begins, but before it develops into a real melody, or a theme, it is forthwith bent over, broken up, raised and lowered through incessant modulations and enharmonic shifts, followed through by sequences, then patched up and contracted again, repeated or imitated by this or that instrument. With scrupulous avoidance of all closing cadences. this boneless tonal mollusk, self-restoring, swims ever on into the immeasurable.]

-:-

Diesem Abschnitt Beispiele aus *Tristan* hinzufügen, schlage ich den Klavierauszug auf, um nochmals zu suchen. Aber suchen? Nein! Auf jeder Seite finden sie sich dutzendweise. . . Was dazu gesungen wird, ist natürlich für diese Harmonie ganz gleichgültig. Das ist höhere Katzenmusik. . . Sie kann entstehen wenn ein schlechter Klavierspieler statt der Obertasten die unteren greift oder umgekehrt.

(Heinrich Dorn, *Aus Meinem Leben,* Berlin, 1870)

[To illustrate this by examples from *Tristan,* I open the piano score, in order to look them up again. But why should I? No! There are dozens of these examples on every page. . . What is sung to these harmonies is naturally quite immaterial. This is advanced cat music. It can be produced by a poor piano player who hits black keys instead of white keys, or vice versa.]

-:-

Das tollste Attentat auf Kunst, Geschmack, Musik und Poesie, welches je dagewesen, ist die Keilerei in den *Meistersingern*.
(Ferdinand Hiller, 1870)

[The debauchery of the *Meistersinger* is the maddest assault ever made upon art, taste, music and poetry.]

-:-

Eine grauenvollere Katzenmusik könnte nicht erzielt werden, als Wagner in seinen *Meistersingern* erreicht und wenn sämtliche Leiermänner Berlins in den Renzschen Zircus gesperrt würden, und jeder eine andere Walze drehte.
(Heinrich Dorn, *Montagszeitung*, Berlin, 1870)

[A more horrendous Katzenjammer than Wagner achieves in his *Meistersinger* could not be accomplished even if all the organ grinders of Berlin were locked up in Renz's Circus, each grinding out a different tune.]

-:-

Wagners Unglück ist dass er sich nicht nur für den Dalai Lama selbst hält, sondern auch für Dalai Lamas Oberpriester in einer Person, und daher jedes seiner Exkremente für den Ausfluss seiner göttlichen Eingebung.
(Heinrich Dorn, *Aus Meinem Leben*, Berlin, 1870)

[Wagner's misfortune is that he not only takes himself for a Dalai Lama, but also for Dalai Lama's chief priest in one person, and therefore regards each of his excrements as an emanation of divine inspiration.]

-:-

Wir können die barbarische Rohheit dieses neuesten Wagner-Ausbruchs nicht anders bezeichnen, als eine Insulte gegen die erhabene Majestät des Deutschen Kaisers.

(Heinrich Dorn, *Montagszeitung*, Berlin, April 1871)

[We cannot describe the barbarous brutality of this latest Wagnerian outburst (the *Kaiser March*) as anything else but an insult against the exalted Majesty of the German Emperor.]

-:-

In *Lohengrin*, we wander through such a dreary waste of harmonic and occasionally dis-harmonic chords and combinations . . . through such a barren desert of tones in the high and middle registers, rambling and disconnected to all mortal senses—how the unfortunate singers ever make it possible to memorize their parts is an unfathomable mystery—that the thirsty, fainting ear drinks up every little rill of melody with an eagerness which makes it absolutely impossible to judge of its intrinsic worth, and we are much inclined to mistake a pool for an ocean, and a blade of grass for a tree. . . I believe that with Wagner's death 'the music of the future' will at once become a thing of the past, and ere long perish entirely, as many another system, containing no elements of life, no germs of immortal existence, passed away with its founder.

(Letter to the Editor, *Dwight's Journal of Music,* June 3, 1871)

-:-

Rienzi, dieses Opernmonstrum! Der musikalische Werth der Partitur ist gleich Null. . . Dass sich ein so geistloses Product noch auf der Bühne zu erhalten vermag, ist ein trauriges Zeichen der Geschmacksverirrung der Gegenwart.

(*Echo,* Berlin, 1871, No. 22)

[*Rienzi,* this operatic monster! The musical value of the score is precisely zero. . . That such a worthless product has reached the stage is a sad sign of the perversion of taste of the present times.]

-:-

Das wüste Wagnersche Korybantengetöse, dieses Blech-, Schilder- und Kesselgerumpel, dieses Chinesen- oder Karaibengeklapper mit Hölzern und Ohrenscalpirmessern . . . die herzlose Dürre, die Verödung aller Melodien, alles Tonzaubers, aller Musik . . . dieser in der Zerstörung alles Tongeistes schwelgende, als Orchester tobende

Satanismus, dieses teuflische Lustjauchzen . . . eine scandalsüchtige Revolvermusik mit Peternapoleonischer Ohrfeigenorchesterbegleitung. Daher denn auch die geheime Sympathie, die sie zum Schosskind schwachsinniger Fürsten, zur Spielpuppe der Camarilla, der mit Reptilschleim überzogenen Hofschranzen und blasiert hysterischen Hofschranzinnen macht, die solcher Elektrisierung durch massenhafte Instrumentalwirkungen bedürfen, um ihre reizerschöpften Froschschenkel in gewaltsame Zuckungen zu versetzen . . . Teufelslärmmusik dieses eisenstirnigen, mit Blech und Holz ausgefütterten, von Mephistopheles mit den mephitisch giftigsten Höllendünsten einer zerstörerisch tollen Selbstsucht, als Beelsebubs Hofkomponisten und Generaldirektor der Höllenmusik, aufgeblasenen Wagner!

(J. L. Klein, *Geschichte des Dramas,* Leipzig, 1871, vol. VIII, pp. 738-739)

[The wild Wagnerian corybantic orgy, this din of brasses, tin pans and kettles, this Chinese or Caribbean clatter with wood sticks and ear-cutting scalping knives. . . Heartless sterility, obliteration of all melody, all tonal charm, all music. . . This revelling in the destruction of all tonal essence, raging satanic fury in the orchestra, this demoniacal, lewd caterwauling, scandal-mongering, gun-toting music, with an orchestral accompaniment slapping you in the face. . . Hence, the secret fascination that makes it the darling of feeble-minded royalty, the plaything of the camarilla, of the court flunkeys covered with reptilian slime, and of the blasé hysterical female court parasites who need this galvanic stimulation by massive instrumental treatment to throw their pleasure-weary frog-legs into violent convulsion . . . the diabolical din of this pig-headed man, stuffed with brass and sawdust, inflated, in an insanely destructive self-aggrandizement, by Mephistopheles' mephitic and most venomous hellish miasma, into Beelzebub's Court Composer and General Director of Hell's Music—Wagner!]

-:-

Richard Wagner ist ein eigenthümliches Phänomen seiner Zeit; das Spiegelbild, welches wir von ihm entwarfen, passt auf die ganze Richtung, welche seinen Namen trägt. Auch sie zeigt die Symptome der geistigen Zerrissenheit und psychischen Entartung, welche wir bei ihrem Meister finden.

(Dr. Th. Puschmann, *Richard Wagner, eine psychiatrische Studie*, Berlin, 1873)

[Richard Wagner is a peculiar phenomenon of his time; the mirror image which we have sketched of him projects itself on the entire school which bears his name. It, too, betrays the symptoms of spiritual confusion and psychic degeneration which we find in its master.]

-:-

Ein wüstes Chaos von Tönen ist das Vorspiel zum *Tristan.* Es war, als sei eine Bombe in ein grosses musikalisches Werk gefahren und habe alle Noten über- und untereinander geworfen.

(J. Stettenheim, *Tribüne*, Berlin, February 6, 1873)

[The Prelude to *Tristan* is a wild chaos of tones. It was as if a bomb had fallen into a large music factory and had thrown all the notes into confusion.]

-:-

Wagner's *Faust* overture comes round upon us like a very heavy nightmare every year or two now for some fifteen years; we should have been rid of the vampire long ago. As a piece of music, it is uncouth, extravagant, and dreary and unlovely. As a conception of Faust, it is coarse and materialistic. The discontent which it expresses seems to be nothing mental, spiritual, suggestive of a deep soul's experience; but rather the result of some internal physical disturbance—a subject for a country doctor rather than for a Goethe or a great musician. For the life of us, we can discern no Faust in all that rumbling, groaning, heaving, yearning, the chaotic weltering mass of tones. The Overture called up the image, not of Faust, but rather of the monster Polyphemus, with his one eye put out, rolling upon the ground, groaning and gnashing his teeth, and bellowing curses after sly Ulysses and his comrades.

(*Dwight's Journal of Music,* May 30, 1874)

-:-

The *Faust* Overture exhibited the defects of Wagner's style in an exaggerated degree. . . It is beside the question to plead that the music accurately illustrates Faust's mental condition, and that its incoherence must therefore be excused. It may possibly do for the illustration of lunacy or chaos, or fifty other unpleasant things; but it is deficient in almost all the qualities which belong to really good music.

(*Sporting News*, London, October 17, 1874)

-:-

The introduction and finale to Wagner's *Tristan and Isolde* are the very extremes of the modern extravagance and willfulness in the spasmodic strife to be original in music. In its expression, its reiterated, restless, fruitless yearning and monotonous chromatic wail, we find it simply dreary and unprofitable.

(*Dwight's Journal of Music*, Boston, January 9, 1875)

-:-

In Wagner we find a prodigality of progressions which leaves no impress. There is the most inordinate use of chromatic chords, and meaningless employ of that 'refuge for the destitute,' the chord of the three minor thirds, which with Wagner means restlessness, indecision, and ceaseless turmoil. His music exhibits such a confusion of keys that tonality may be said to be non-existent. *Lohengrin* illustrates an illegitimate disregard of tonal relationship. Wagner's system is atomic. The atoms have no correspondency, but are engaged in one everlasting conflict. This antagonism of Wagner, this fight between song and the secondary chords which he commonly employs, is the true cause of his non-popularity.

(H. J. Gauntlett, *Concordia*, London, 1875)

-:-

Cette musique ne peut que remuer les sens les plus bas. La musique de Wagner réveille le cochon plutôt que l'ange. Je dis pire, elle assourdit les deux. C'est de la musique d'eunuque affolé.

(*Figaro*, Paris, July 26, 1876)

[This music can arouse only the basest instincts. Wagner's music awakens the swine rather than the angel. Worse, it deadens both. It is the music of a demented eunuch.]

With the last chords of the *Twilight of the Gods,* I had a feeling of liberation from captivity. It may be that the Nibelungs' Ring is a very great work, but there never has been anything more tedious and more dragged-out than this rigmarole. The agglomeration of the most intricate and contrived harmonies, colorlessness of all that is sung on the stage, interminably long dialogues—all this fatigues the nerves to the utmost degree. So, what is the aim of Wagner's reform? In the past, music was supposed to delight people, and now we are tormented and exhausted by it.

(From Tchaikovsky's letter to his brother Modest, dated Vienna, August 20, 1876)

-:-

Lest any of the 'crowd of music-lovers . . .' should be induced to visit Bayreuth for the third representation of Herr Wagner's *Ring des Nibelungen,* I beg your assistance to warn them against the most colossal musical swindle that even Germany has ever produced. . . The memory of the three days of excruciating mental pain at Bayreuth 'licks creation.'

(From a letter to the Editor, *Musical World,* London, September 2, 1876)

-:-

The term Music of the Future, which Wagner gives to his later productions, is utterly ridiculous. What does he know about the future, either in music or in anything else? Moreover, that name may not be acceptable to the future generations—to *our* children, whose ears perhaps object to be fed solely with spasmodic vocal phrases, composed of diminished and augmented fifths, sevenths, etc. Enough already has been done in the present century to lead the public away from the laws of nature. It may be original to have interminable successions of discords which don't resolve, but it is a matter of taste whether such proceedings are an improvement on the pleasurable sensations of man. Vinegar, mustard, and cayenne-pepper are necessary condiments in the culinary art, but I question whether even the Wagnerites would care to make their dinner of these articles only. When sound taste begins to fail, eccentricity will take its place. Let the young student beware of its malignant influence.

(From a letter to the Editor, *Musical World,* London, September 16, 1876)

Bei Wagners Musik bekimmt aan jeder musikalisch gesonde Mensch aan ferchterliches *Lamentum Katzarum,* deutsch *Katzenjammer.*

(Isaak Moses Hersch, *Herr Richard Wagner, der musikalische Struwelpeter,* Berlin, 1876)

[Listening to Wagner's music, every musically healthy person gets a terrible *Lamentum Katzarum,* that is, *Katzenjammer.*]

-:-

Siegfried war scheusslich. Von zusammengehörigen Melodien keine Spur. . . Wäre eine Katze krepiert und sogar Felsen wären vor Angst vor diesen scheusslichen Misstönen zu Eierspeisen geworden. . . Mir haben die Ohren gesummt von diesen Missgestalten von Akkorden, wenn man sie überhaupt noch so nennen kann. . . Der Anfang des dritten Aktes ist ein Lärm zum Ohrenzerreissen. . . Die ganze Scheisse kannst Du in 100 Takten ausdrücken, denn immer das Gleiche und immer gleich langweilig.

(Richard Strauss in a letter to Ludwig Thuille, written in 1879)

[*Siegfried* was abominable. Not a trace of coherent melodies. It would kill a cat and would turn rocks into scrambled eggs from fear of these hideous discords. My ears buzzed from these abortions of chords, if one can still call them such. The opening of the third act made enough noise to split the ears. The whole crap could be reduced to 100 measures, for it is always the same thing, and always equally tedious.]

(Many years later, in a letter to Roland Tenschert, reproduced in *Das Musik Leben* of March 1950, Strauss pleaded: 'Können künftig die albernen Lausbubenurteile nicht wegbleiben, die ich als Pennäler gegenüber Freund Thuille verübt habe? . . . Ich glaube doch, durch meine letzten sieben Parsifals in Bayreuth mir für alle Zeiten Absolution für diese blöden Jugendsünden erdirigiert zu haben'—'I wonder whether these silly tomfooleries of a callow schoolboy of which I delivered myself to friend Thuille could not be swept aside in the future? I still believe that the seven performances of *Parsifal* which I lately conducted in Bayreuth have earned me perpetual absolution for these idiotic youthful transgressions.')

-:-

In Berlin wuchert üppig die ohrenquälende Musik von Wagner. . . Bastard von Ton und Wort.

(Silvester Frey, *Mehr Licht,* Berlin, May 3, 1879)

[In Berlin, the ear-splitting music of Wagner—bastard combination of tones and words—is luxuriantly rampant.]

-:-

Wagner ist der leibhaftige Antichrist der Kunst.

(Max Kalbeck, *Wiener Allgemeine Zeitung*, April 28, 1880)

[Wagner is the Antichrist incarnate of art.]

-:-

After ten o'clock they began upon that terrible Wagner music, and for nearly an hour they kept at it with intense effort, till many of the audience, finding Wagner worse than caviar, and as indigestible as lobster salad, left in a gradually increasing stream. If we are permitted to express a plain opinion about Wagner, it is music with a stomach ache. It has knots and cramps and spasms, increasing in violence suddenly and subsiding as quickly, but never quite coming to a state of internal rest. The contortions are simply awful and exhibit all the symptoms of musical colic verging on cholera morbus. There are gnashings of teeth, groanings that cannot be uttered, bellowings as of the bulls of Bashan. It may be the music of the future, but it will be heard in the realms of Pluto.

(Cincinnati *Commercial*, May 18, 1880)

-:-

Wagner—nemico della melodia, ricercatore dello strano, corruttore dell'arte, eccentrico per natura.

(G. P. Zuliani, *Il Lohengrin di Riccardo Wagner*, Rome, 1880)

[Wagner—enemy of melody, seeker after the unorthodox, corrupter of art, eccentric by nature.]

-:-

La partition des *Maîtres Chanteurs*, longue et obscure, épaisse et touffue jusqu'a l'excès, fertile en combinaisons orchestrales d'un caractere presque inaccessible à la masse du public, offrant à chaque instant des partis-pris d'extravagance et comme des rébus absolument indéchiffrables, provoque chez l'auditeur le plus déterminé une lassitude cruelle et une souffrance véritable.

(Arthur Pougin in the Supplement to *Biographie Universelle des Musiciens*, Paris, 1880)

[The score of *Meistersinger*, long and obscure, thick and padded to excess, fertile in orchestral combinations of a character almost inaccessible to the majority of the public, offering at every instant deliberate extravaganzas and something like absolutely indecipherable puzzles, provokes in the most determined listener a cruel lassitude and real suffering.]

-:-

I cannot admit that *Siegfried* is a great work, unless tediousness is greatness. Not from the first strain of the opening overture to the last crash of sound as the play ends, is there a solitary melody. The story is simply a chaotic mass of triviality and filth. Where it is not silly, it is dirty. . . Any half-hour of it, from first to last, would make you blush, if you had a face on you as hard as a bronze statue, and a moral nature as tough as a section of New York pie-crust.

(*Sunday Herald,* London, May 30, 1882)

-:-

Herr Wagner's avoidance of full closes and the immense predominance of dissonance over consonance put a strain on the nerves which becomes often painful, and cannot be endured for the length of time exacted by the composer without causing utter prostration. If I say that the proportion of dissonance to consonance in the *Ring* is as nine to one, I do not think that I exaggerate.

(Friedrich Niecks, *Monthly Musical Record,* London, June 1, 1882)

-:-

Of all the bête, clumsy, blundering, boggling, baboon-blooded stuff I ever saw on a human stage, that thing last night (*Meistersinger*) beat—as far as the story and acting went; and of all the affected, sapless, soulless, beginningless, endless, topless, bottomless, topsyturviest, tongs- and boniest doggerel of sounds I ever endured the deadliness of, that eternity of nothing was the deadliest—as far as the sound went.

(Letter by John Ruskin to Mrs. Burne-Jones, dated June 30, 1882)

-:-

Ueberhaupt tritt die Dissonanz so massenhaft im *Parsifal* hervor, dass man Wagner füglich zum Doktor der Kakophonie ernennen könnte.

(W. Lübke, *Gegenwart*, Berlin, November 11, 1882)

[In *Parsifal*, dissonance is brought out on such a large scale that Wagner could fittingly be named Doctor of Cacophony.]

-:-

Während in manchen der Nibelungen-Motive der Schimmer eines fest umrissenen melodischen Gedankens herausleuchtete, machen die Parsifal-Motive, wenn man sie auf dem Klaviere durchnimmt, den Eindruck des Klavierstimmens mit Hindernissen, willkürlich aneinandergereihten Noten, bei denen sich absolut nichts denken lässt.

(A. de Mensi, quoted by W. Tappert in *Für und Wider, Eine Blumenlese aus den Berichten über die Aufführungen des Bühnenweihfestspieles Parsifal*, Berlin, 1882)

[Whereas in some of the Nibelung motives, there shone a gleam of a clearly outlined melodic thought, the *Parsifal* motives produce the impression, when played over on the piano, of piano tuning with obstacles, notes arbitrarily strung together, which suggest no thought whatsoever.]

-:-

—Have you ever heard Wagner's music?
—I think so, once.
—When?
—When the lightning struck a sheet iron dealer's store.

(*Musical Herald*, Boston, 1884)

-:-

M. Wagner a de beaux moments, mais de mauvais quart-d'heures.

(Rossini, quoted in the epigraph to *Wagnerism, a Protest*, by Major H. W. L. Hime, London, 1884)

[Wagner has good moments, but bad quarter-hours.]

-:-

There is not a single concord in the Prelude to *Tristan*. . . The drums, the triangles, the cymbals, the tamtams, the eighteen anvils in the *Rhinegold* certainly justify a passing fear that music threatens to end as it began—in noise.

(Major H. W. L. Hime, *Wagnerism, a Protest,* London, 1884)

-:-

Directions for Composing a Wagner Overture

A sharp where you'd expect a natural;
A natural where you'd expect a sharp;
No rule observe but the exceptional,
And then (first happy thought!) bring in a Harp!

No bar a sequence to the bar behind;
No bar a prelude to the next that comes;
Which follows which, you really needn't mind;—
But (second happy thought!) bring in your Drums!

For harmonies, let wildest discords pass;
Let key be blent with key in hideous hash;
Then (for last happy thought!) bring in your Brass!
And clang, clash, clatter, clatter, clang, and clash.

(A poem published in an unidentified American newspaper in 1884, and signed 'A Sufferer')

-:-

Après les amours sensuelles jusqu'au *delirium tremens* de *Tristan et Yseult,* gorgés de drogues aphrodisiaques, voici la *Walkyrie,* qui nous offre le tableau répugnant des amours incestueuses, compliquées d'adultère du frère et de la sœur jumeaux.

(O. Comettant, *Siècle,* Paris, March 8, 1886)

[After the sensuous amours to the point of a *delirium tremens* of *Tristan,* gorged with aphrodisiac drugs, comes the *Valkyrie* which offers us a repugnant spectacle of incestuous love, complicated by the adultery of a twin brother and sister.]

-:-

Ich habe aufmerksam zugehört, war aber herzlich froh, als endlich die musikalische Tortur vorüber war, und ich danke noch heute meinem Schöpfer, dass ich noch am alten Musikglauben festhalten kann und noch kein Anhänger der modernen Ketzerlehre geworden bin. Seit gestern Abend ist auch hier die moderne Orthographie eingeführt und man schreibt nicht mehr *Götterdämmerung*, sondern *Goddamnerung*.

(*Newyorker Staatszeitung*, May 23, 1888)

[I listened attentively, but was really glad when at last this musical torture was over. I am grateful even now to my Creator that I can still remain faithful to the old musical creed, and have not become an adherent to the modern heresy. Since last night, modern spelling was introduced here, too, and they no longer write *Götterdämmerung*, but *Goddamnerung*.]

-:-

Ist Wagner überhaupt ein Mensch? Ist er nicht eher eine Krankheit? Er macht Alles krank, woran er rührt—er hat die Musik krank gemacht. Ich stelle diesen Gesichtspunkt voran: Wagners Kunst ist krank. Die Probleme, die er auf die Bühne bringt—lauter Hysteriker-Probleme—das Convulsivische seines Affekts, seine überreizte Sensibilität, sein Geschmack, der nach immer schärfen Würzen verlangte, seine Instabilität, die er zu Principien verkleidete, nicht am wenigsten die Wahl seiner Helden und Heldinnen, diese als physiologische Typen betrachtet (eine Kranken-Galerie!), alles zusammen stellt ein Krankheitsbild dar, das keinen Zweifel lässt. *Wagner est une névrose*. . . Unsere Aerzte und Physiologen haben in Wagner ihren interessantesten Fall, zum Mindesten einen sehr vollständigen. Gerade, weil nichts moderner ist als diese Gesammterkrankung, diese Spätheit und Ueberreiztheit der nervösen Machinerie, ist Wagner der moderne Künstler *par excellence*, der Cagliostro der Modernität. In seiner Kunst ist auf die verführerischeste Art gemischt, was heute alle Welt am nötigsten hat—die drei grossen Stimulantia der Erschöpften, das Brutale, das Künstliche und das Unschuldige (Idiotische). Wagner ist ein grosser Verderb für die Musik. Er hat in ihr Mittel erraten, müde Nerven zu reizen—er hat die Musik damit krank gemacht.

(Friedrich Nietzsche, *Der Fall Wagner*, 1888)

[Is Wagner a human being at all? Is he not rather a disease? He contaminates everything he touches—he has made music sick. I postulate this viewpoint: Wagner's art is diseased. The problems which he brings to the stage—all of them, problems of hysterics—the convulsiveness of his emotion, his overwrought sensibility, his taste that always demands sharper spices, his instability, and, not the least, the choice of his heroes and heroines, considered as physiological types (a clinical exhibit), all this presents a picture of disease that leaves no doubt. *Wagner est une névrose*. . . Our physicians and physiologists have in Wagner the most interesting, or at least, the most complete case. And just because there is nothing more modern than this collective illness, this sluggishness and oversensitivity of the nervous machinery, Wagner is a modern artist *par excellence,* the Cagliostro of modernity. In his art, he mixes in the most tempting manner all that the world today needs most, the three great stimulants of the exhausted, the brutal, the artificial, and the innocent (idiotic). Wagner is a great corrupter of music. He has discovered in it a means to charm tired nerves—he has thereby made music sick.]

-:-

Wagner's *Faust* Overture begins with a snoring from a bass tuba in the agony of a nightmare, and there is in the whole work not one salient musical idea.

(*Home Journal,* Boston, November 1, 1890)

-:-

Die moderne Musik ist überhaupt keine Musik mehr. Die heutigen Komponisten sind keine geborenen Musiker mehr; sie sind meist nur angelernte Dilettanten. . . Durch die Wagner-Musik wird die Nervosität unserer Tage nur noch gesteigert; ihre äusseren Effecte in Verbindung mit ihrer inneren Formlosigkeit wirken auf das Nervensystem zerrütend und ermattend. Man könnte die neuere Musik nicht mit Unrecht eine anarchistische nennen. . . Richard Wagner hat das Kainszeichen auf das gegenwärtige Musikleben gedrückt.

(W. Hoffmann, *Richard Wagner-Taumel, Ein Mahnruf gegen den Verfall der Künste,* Leipzig, 1894)

[Modern music is no longer music. Contemporary composers are no longer born musicians; they are mostly only trained dilettantes. The nervousness of our times is only increased by Wagnerian music; its outward effects in connection with its inner formlessness perturb and exhaust the nervous system. One might not without justice call the newer music anarchistic. Richard Wagner has stamped the sign of Cain on contemporary musical life.]

-:-

I have been ardently reading the score of *Siegfried.* As always, after a long interval, Wagner's music repelled me. I am outraged by his various aural aberrations which surpass the limit of the harmonically feasible. Cacophony and nonsense are scattered in *Siegfried* all over the score. What terrible harm Wagner did by interspersing his pages of genius with harmonic and modulatory outrages to which both young and old are gradually becoming accustomed and which have procreated d'Indy and Richard Strauss!

(From a letter written by Rimsky-Korsakov in 1901)

-:-

I like Wagner's music better than anybody's. It is so loud that one can talk the whole time without people hearing what one says.

(Oscar Wilde, *The Picture of Dorian Gray*)

-:-

Wagner begins by praising the last period of Beethoven, and combines this music with the mystical theory of Schopenhauer, which is just as silly as Beethoven's music, and then, in accordance with his theory, he writes his own music, in connection with a still falser system of uniting all the arts. And after Wagner come still newer imitators, departing still further from art—Brahms, Richard Strauss and others.

(Leo Tolstoy, *What is Art?*, 1896)

-:-

If Hitler likes Wagner's music, it is all the more reason why every non-Nazi should shun and loathe it. . . . If we realized that what we are giving up is the music of Klingsor who for one hundred years has numbed our senses with his witchcraft and who allowed to grow up round us a garden of gorgeous flowers that at last have revealed themselves as poisonous and death-dealing: then we should retaliate, then we should ban and burn every scrap of Wagner's music and writings, and every book written about the amazing wizard, beginning with the books of the Anglo-Wagnerian Ernest Newman. What a small price to pay if it could help to fight and finally extinguish the Wagner-fanned fire of Nazism.

(Carl Engel, *Musical Quarterly*, New York, April 1941)

WEBERN If Anton von Webern had chosen merely to write whole-toned· [sic] scales and altered seventeenths, nobody would have minded. But he chose to write them with an instrumentation which can only be described in terms of the barnyard. Before ten measures of that slow, groaning, wheezing music of *Six Orchestral Pieces* had been played, there were grins. Then somebody giggled. The next moment a good quarter of the hall was in open hearty laughter. . . Inimical hisses spread to the high-priced seats and war began. It is probable that Mr. Von Webern wrote many strange directions in that score. Certain it is that in the second piece the flutist 'barbershopped' his way down the scale. The plaintive little meow, like that of a cat with catarrh, was too much, and the audience started off again. From that time on the pieces were played mostly amid laughter.

(Dispatch from Vienna, Boston *Evening Transcript*, April 17, 1913)

-:-

Webern's Five Pieces for Orchestra required of the listener the utmost concentration of attention. Inevitably these faint rustlings, these tiny squeaks and titterings called to mind the activities of insects.

(Warren Storey Smith, Boston *Post*, November 20, 1926)

-:-

The Five Pieces for Orchestra by Webern are . . . dabs of pale colors expressive of the inaudible . . . Webern was as a man condemned to hard labor and working out [his] punishment.

(Philip Hale, Boston *Herald*, November 20, 1926)

-:-

Webern's *Five Pieces* were as clearly significant and symptomatic as a toothache. . . Men of our generation . . . aim, in such extreme cases as that of Webern, at a pursuit of the infinitesimal, which may strike the unsympathetic as a tonal glorification of the amoeba. . . There is undeniably a touch of the protozoic . . . scarcely perceptible tonal wraiths, mere wisps and shreds of sound, fugitive astral vapors . . . though once or twice there are briefly vehement outbursts, as of a gnat enraged. . . The Lilliputian Fourth Piece is typical of the set. It opens with an atonal solo for the mandolin;

the trumpet speaks as briefly and atonally; the trombone drops a tearful minor ninth (the amoeba weeps) . . .

(Lawrence Gilman, New York *Herald Tribune,* November 29, 1926)

-:-

Symphony for Chamber Orchestra of Schoenberg's pupil, Anton von Webern, is one of those whispering, clucking, picking little pieces which Webern composes when he whittles away at small and futile ideas, until he has achieved the perfect fruition of futility and written precisely nothing. 'The Ultimate Significance of Nothing'—this would be the proper title of this piece. The audience laughed it out of court, and this laughter could not be restrained, as Webern's little orchestra suggested nothing so much as a cat, that, arching its back, glared and bristled its fur, and moaned or growled or spat. . . . The yells of laughter that came from all over the hall . . . nearly drowned the sounds of Webern's whimpering orchestra. This music . . . bore on the program the proud device: 'world première.' And thus the mountain labored, and scarce a mouse.

(Olin Downes, New York *Times,* December 19, 1929)

-:-

Snickers became guffaws when Anton von Webern's Symphony for Chamber Orchestra was played. The program note spoke of 'tonal pointilism,' 'tonal fractions' and 'differentials.' What the audience heard suggested odd sounds in an old house when the wind moans, the floors creak, the shades rustle, and the doors and windows alternately croak and croon. The work had von Webern's cardinal merit of brevity.

(Oscar Thompson, New York *Evening Post,* December 19, 1929)

-:-

The fragmentary Mr. Anton von Webern was represented by a Symphony for Chamber Orchestra written at the request of the League of Composers. This piece, the League scribe contended, was 'a sort of tonal pointilism . . .' composed of 'differentials. . . .' These commentaries proved to be all true—too true. . . . Mr. von Webern's Symphony was a sort of tonal pointilism and was composed of differentials, or, in other words, the fractional sounds uttered at night by the sleeping inhabitants of a zoo.

(Samuel Chotzinoff, New York *World,* December 19, 1929)

Webern is the one outstanding disciple of the Schoenberg idiom who clings to his master's methods even after his master has moved on a bit. The audience laughed him and his whines out of court. Quite right! If modernism depended for progress upon the Weberns, it would get nowhere.

(*Musical Courier*, New York, December 28, 1929)

-:-

A stir was created at a concert by the Philharmonic Trio in Wigmore Hall when James Whitehead, cellist, walked off the stage after playing only a few bars of Webern's String Trio, op. 20. Exclaiming 'I can't play this thing,' Mr. Whitehead quitted the stage . . . He said that it was 'a nightmare—not music at all, but mathematics.' The majority of musicians will doubtless agree with him.

(London dispatch in the *Musical Courier*, New York, May 1, 1938)

-:-

[This quartet of Anton von Webern] . . . is Dead Sea fruit, and Dead End music. . . The windows were closed, because, as it was remarked, the delicate music of Webern could not be heard if they remained open. Not for this music the fresh air or the crude turbulences of the world. For it is the ultimate of orderly and deliberate disintegration. . . Is it any wonder that the culture from which it emanates is even now going up in flames? To which is here added the plaint of the mosquito. . . By the time the Webern quartet ended, the room was as mephitic as the composition; the windows, following the intermission, were hermetically closed, so to remain until the end of the concert; and at this point nature rebelled. Your correspondent left. He needed fresh air as much as the music.

(Olin Downes, New York Times, May 22, 1941)

INVECTICON

INDEX OF VITUPERATIVE, PEJORATIVE AND DEPRECATORY WORDS AND PHRASES

INDEX OF NAMES AND TITLES

SUPPLEMENT

Viel Schimpf, viel Ehre . . .

BEETHOVEN Beethoven's one hundred and thirty-fifth work was one of his latest, and gives painful evidence of an unbalanced mind, or at least of a morbid sentiment which has grown into a disease. It may, however, be maintained by those who admit of no faults in Beethoven's works, who worship him in all his moods, that its abstruse sublimity places it above the rules of criticism and beyond the comprehension of critics. We agree to both propositions, confessing that we can see no reason for its construction, and declaring that we could understand no part of it, save the few magnificent phrases at the beginning of the *Lento assai*, which are sublime in their beauty. The rest is a chaos of unfinished forms, dreary, dreamy, lugubrious—a succession of painful imitations, with discords carried to the point of agony, without any tangible result. It was curious to watch the faces of the audience as movement after movement of this dreary, unintelligible composition came on and passed away with but one spark of Beethoven's grand inspiration. It seems to us that Wagner commenced where Beethoven left off; that he has inherited to a certain degree the morbid and confused mind which afflicted the great composer in his last days. Wagner has certainly flashes of clear and brilliant thoughts, but Beethoven's one hundred and thirty-fifth work seems to have been his starting-point. This work must have been well played to have rescued any clear points out of the tangled chaos. We trust, however, for the sake of these very pleasant soirees that no more of such works, which are at all events *caviare* to the multitude, among which we are included, will be placed upon the programmes. As curiosities it is well enough to attempt to master their obscureness in private, but it is poor policy to make the public swallow so distasteful a dose.

(*American Art Journal*, April 25, 1866)

DEBUSSY La musique traverse en ce moment une crise de tous points analogue à celle de la peinture. Après le réalisme, l'impressionisme, jusque dans les formes les plus morbides et qui confinent à l'égarement. Nous avons eu, et nous avons, des peintres qui voient violet, ou par taches, ou à travers une brume, une fumée, qui ignorent lignes et couleurs précises. Nous avons maintenant une musique sans formes, sans dessin mélodique ou harmonique, sans motifs, ondoyante et trouble comme les reflets sur l'eau d'images agitées par le vent. Quand cette musique se borne à caresser un rêve que nous écoutons les yeux fermés, en songeant, en tâchant de nous griser un peu de cette impression même qui n'est pas sans charmes, passe encore. Mais quand elle prétend revêtir un drame si symbolique qu'il soit, c'est de la simple aberration, c'est de l'égarement. Certes, on peut discuter et réprouver le réalisme brutal d'un Charpentier, mais c'est une musique robuste et saine, sans aucun doute. Celle de *Pelléas et Mélisande* est décevante, maladive, presque sans vie même. . . . De phrases mélodiques, dans le dialogue ou la symphonie, pas une; d'élan et de vraie et saine poésie, pas davantage; pas même cette saveur pittoresque que les instruments donnent à l'orchestre. . . . On attendait plus, même de l'impressionisme raffiné et énigmatique qui avait charmé dans quelques-unes des œuvres purement symphoniques de M. Debussy.

(Henri de Curzon, *La Gazette de France*, Paris, May 3, 1902)

[Music traverses at this moment a crisis analogous in every respect to that of painting. After realism came impressionism, reaching the most morbid forms that border on aberration. We have had, and we have, painters who see violet or see spots, or through a mist, or through smoke, who ignore lines and precise colors. Now we have music without form, without melodic or harmonic design, without motifs, wavy and troubled like reflections of images in water agitated by the wind. When this type of music limits itself to caressing a dream and we listen to it with the eyes closed, meditating, and trying to absorb a little of the same impression, which is not without charm, this we can accept. But when such music pretends to characterize a drama, no matter how symbolic, this is plain aberration. True, one can discuss and disapprove the brutal realism of Charpentier, but his music is robust and unquestionably healthy. The music of *Pelléas et Mélisande* is deceptive, sickly, almost lifeless . . . . There is not a single melodic phrase in the dialogue or in the instrumental interludes; no flight of true and healthy poetry; even the picturesque color which instruments impart to an orchestra is absent here. . . . We expected more, even from this refined and enigmatic impressionism, which has charmed us in some purely symphonic works of Debussy.]

-:-

La Mer, de M. Debussy, formait l'inédit de la séance. M. Debussy s'est, en musique, voué à la notation de l'impalpable. Il fait de l'impalpable une sonorité. C'est un art très curieux, parce que la recherche de l'impalpable est chez lui un but, alors que l'impalpable est chez d'autres une résultante et même plutôt un moyen. Pour réaliser ce qu'il rêve, ce musicien renverse d'abord toutes les règles de l'harmonie, tout le formalisme existant, et il bâtit son harmonie à lui. Cette harmonie arrive à force d'art à des effets qui paraissent d'une simplicité mediévale. Elle est, en verité, très compliquée. La simplicité de M. Debussy récèle un sous-sol d'harmonies étagées, une pluralité tonale que tient du prodige. Par là, M. Debussy arrive à donner des sensations d'une infime tenuité, quelque chose comme du frôlement orchestral. Il semble ne pas écrire. Il est Éole, qui souffle à travers une immense harpe qui serait l'orchestre. Et c'est par là que vaut sa nouvelle œuvre, *La Mer*, travail de micrographie musicale. Dans *La Mer*, il semble, du reste, que M. Debussy se soit assagi et qu'il ait fait quelque concession au développement symphonique; ou trouve ça et là quelques phrases qui se perdent dans l'écume orchestrale.

(Louis Schneider, *Gil Blas*, Paris, October 16, 1905)

[*La Mer* by Debussy was the novelty of the program. Debussy devotes himself in music to the transcription of the impalpable. He produces a sonority out of the impalpable. This is a very curious art because the search of the impalpable is for him the goal, whereas the impalpable to others is a product, or a means. To realize his dream he turns upside down all the rules of harmony, the entire set of formulas, and builds his own harmony. This harmony creates effects that seem to be of medieval simplicity. In reality, it is very complex. The simplicity of Debussy conceals a basement of terraced harmonies, a tonal plurality which is prodigious. In this manner Debussy succeeds in giving a sensation of infinitesimal tenuousness, something like orchestral friction. He does not seem to be writing at all; he is Eolus blowing across an immense harp which is his orchestra. And so *La Mer* becomes a labor of musical micrography. It seems also that in *La Mer* Debussy has become more prudent and that he makes some concessions to symphonic development; one encounters here and there some phrases lost in orchestral foam.]

-:-

À force de regarder la mer par le petit bout de la lorgnette, comme le fait M. Debussy, il vous donne plutôt l'impression du bassin des Tuileries. Il n'y a pas d'idée qui vienne planer sur ces harmonies juxtaposées comme pour faire un costume d'Arlequin; l'art qui en résulte est pour ainsi dire invertebré; c'est de la marqueterie, ce n'est plus un tableau. Le public a paru assez désappointé: on lui avait annoncé la mer, quelque chose de grand, de colossal, et on lui a servi de l'eau troublé dans une cuvette.

(Louis Schneider, *Gil Blas,* Paris, October 23, 1905)

[By dint of looking through the small end of his lorgnette, Debussy gives us the impression not of the ocean but of the basin at the Tuileries Gardens. Ideas that float over these juxtaposed harmonies seem like a costume made for Harlequin, and the music that results from this is, so to speak, invertebrate. It is inlaid-work; it is not a painting. The audience seemed rather disappointed; they expected the ocean, something big, something colossal, but they were served instead some agitated water in a saucer.]

-:-

Some of the music performed by the Boston Symphony Orchestra in Carnegie Hall last night seemed to have been chosen by Dr. Muck to make his threatened parting easy. The Boston Symphony's patrons are a loyal and affectionate folk, but their loyalty and affection were put to a severe strain by last night's program, which began with a lot of impressionistic daubs of color, smeared higgledy-piggledy on a tonal palette, with never a thought of form or outline or purpose or logical procedure, but dignified with no less vast a title than *The Sea*. There were three of these groups of daubs and splotches, which the composer Debussy designated respectively as *From Dawn Till Noon on the Ocean, Frolics of Waves,* and *Dialogue of the Wind and the Sea,* but so far as a merely musical mind could determine, the order of the pieces might have been reversed and the music itself played backward without disturbing or changing in any way their significance, their effectiveness or the intellectual quality of the pretty rhapsodies of unmeaning words which the expositors of the French composer have superimposed upon all of his music. One thing only was obvious, and that was that Debussy's ocean was a frog pond, and that some of its denizens had got into the throat of every one of the brass instruments and stayed there from beginning to end, with woeful results.

(H. E. Krehbiel, New York *Daily Tribune,* March 22, 1907)

-:-

Some encouragement of the hope, long entertained, of the founding of a really representative American national music school may have been afforded to musicians and lovers of music on this side of the Atlantic by the decided success that was achieved by Frederick Converse's orchestral fantasy *The Mystic Trumpeter*. Coming as it did, the second of the evening's offering by the Boston Symphony Orchestra conducted by Dr. Karl Muck, the Converse fantasy proved a delightful and exhilarating relief from the bewildering chaos and dissonant jumble of the imported novelty that preceded it—Debussy's suite of orchestral sketches entitled *La Mer*. Dawn, wave frolics and moaning sea—these have inspired the Gallic composer with little of harmonic and nothing of melodic invention that the illimitable vastness of the Sahara desert, the lofty heights of the Andes, or the fastnesses of the African forests might not have suggested in precisely the same manner and with resort to the same mechanical tricks that have produced the sea sketches. The composer of *The Mystic Trumpeter,* on the contrary, at no time denies his hearers the benefit and pleasure of logically, attractively formed musical expression. His work abounds in dainty bright effects that were well brought out by the Boston symphonists.

(*The Evening Telegram,* New York, March 22, 1907)

The concert of the Boston Symphony Orchestra began with three orchestral sketches called *The Sea* by Claude Debussy, given for the first time in New York. M. Debussy, in this group of descriptive tone poems, has contrived to break down every one of the old rules of harmony. In the order of progression of incomprehensibility first comes Wagner; second, Strauss, and third, Debussy. He does not write for the person of ordinary, healthy mind, but for the ultra psychic creature, and even the most highly cultured of Boston music lovers found Debussy almost unintelligible. The best description of this mysteriously involved music is to be found in his commentator's words: 'There are times when his melody verges upon obviousness.' Few of the auditors found even the verging places.

(New York *American*, March 22, 1907)

-:-

The Debussyites regard *Pelléas et Mélisande* as a work marking a new stage in the evolution of opera. They are mistaken. Debussy is unique; he is as individual as an orchid. He does not stand in the direct line of operatic evolution, but on a sideline, which points backward rather than forward. What struck last night's audience most in listening to this music was its utter lack of melody. It will not do to say that this remark is as foolish as the accusations of a lack of melody once made against such operas as *Lohengrin, Faust* and *Carmen*. Debussy abjures melody deliberately . . . He eliminates the melodic element, and this marks a step backward. The French opera of the future will be much more like *Carmen* than like *Pelléas et Mélisande*. Is not Debussy's contempt for operatic melody a case of sour grapes? A step backward also is Debussy's treatment of harmony—or rather discord, for he abjures harmony of the euphonious sort almost as completely as he does flowing melody à la Bizet. He seldom writes a chord as other composers write it; by altering a semitone he gives it a changed aspect which is new, but not always valuable. Caviar, camembert and cayenne pepper are good relishes, but a whole meal of them is not desirable.

(*Evening Post*, New York, February 20, 1908)

-:-

He who would enjoy Debussy's musical integument of *Pelléas et Mélisande* must have cultivated a craving for dissonance in harmony and find relish in combinations of tones that sting and blister and pain and outrage the ear. He must have learned to contemn euphony and symmetry, with its benison of restfulness, and to delight in monotony of orchestral color and monotony of dynamics and monotony of harmonic device.

(H. E. Krehbiel, *Daily Tribune*, New York, February 20, 1908)

-:-

M. Debussy a peut-être tort de se confiner dans l'étroitesse d'un système. Il est probable que ses imitateurs navrants, les Ravel, les Caplet, ont contribué pour beaucoup a détourner de lui les foules dont la faveur est si fugace. Son *Ibéria* ne diffère cependant en rien, hormis le titre, de ses précédentes productions. L'auteur a désiré, nous assure le programme, peindre des *Images* dont l'Espagne aurait fourni le cadre. Avouons-le humblement: le fourmillement orchestral délicieux, entendu hier, nous parut bien peu espagnol. . . . Absence de couleur, monotonie, voilà les deux principaux défaits de cet art trop subtil, qui veut exprimer l'inexprimable, décrire l'indescriptible.

(Louis Schneider, *Gil Blas*, Paris, February 21, 1910)

[Debussy perhaps makes a mistake in confining himself to the narrow limits of a system. It is probable that his pathetic imitators—the Ravels, the Caplets—have been instrumental in turning away from him the crowds whose favor is so fickle. His *Ibéria* does not differ in anything, except the title, from his previous productions. The composer has intended, so we are assured by the program, to paint the images of which Spain is the framework. We must humbly submit that this delicious orchestral anthill appears to us not very Spanish. The absence of color, monotony—these are the two principal defects of this subtle art which endeavors to express the inexpressible and to describe the indescribable.]

-:-

Vint l'*Ibérie* de M. Debussy. Ah! ce n'est plus l'Espagne de Bizet ou de Chabrier! Quelles brumes, quelles visions nostalgiques! Peut-être y a-t-il une erreur d'impression sur le programme? J'y suis! La première lettre du titre est tombée, et il faut lire *Sibérie*. Tout s'explique.

(René Brancour, *Le Ménestrel*, Paris, June 28, 1913)

[Then came *Iberia* by Debussy. Ah! This is no longer the Spain of Bizet or of Chabrier! What fog, what nostalgic vision! But perhaps there is a typographical error in the program. I have it! The first letter of the title fell off, and one must read *Siberia*. Then everything becomes clear.]

PUCCINI The first principle of music, which is melody, is sacrified, for what Puccini puts in the orchestra can scarcely be called melody under the most liberal interpretation of the term. Quite as significant as the degradation of music thus illustrated is the degradation of the drama which has brought it about. There has always been a restrictive and purifying quality in melody. It is that which has turned our souls to sympathy with the apotheosis of vice and pulmonary tuberculosis in Verdi's *Traviata*. Without such palliation, the vileness, the horror, the hideousness of a play like *La Tosca* is more unpardonable in an operatic form than in the original. Its lust and cruelty are presented in their nakedness. There is little or no time to reflect upon the workings of perverted minds, except in the moments, so plentiful in Puccini's opera, in which music becomes a hindrance and an impertinence, and phrases of real pith are mixed with indescribable balderdash.

(*Daily Tribune*, New York, February 5, 1901)

-:-

It has been supposed by many that music is an art which should be devoted largely to the exploitation of rare, subtle, higher emotions. The Italian composers today, however, believe differently. Their idea is that the promised land into which music should take us is the land of savagery, where lust, attempted violence, stabbing, shooting and suicide rule the day. These are the leading motives, the only motives of Puccini's opera *Tosca*, and they seem even more gross and barbarous than they do in Sardou's play, because the action is more concentrated and the horrors follow one another more promptly. Were this opera Puccini's first attempt, one might pardon it as the sin of a passionate musician sowing his wild oats. But Puccini is forty-three years old and this is his fifth opera. That he should under the circumstances choose so vulgar a subject, one so ill-suited for alliance with the divine art, is discouraging—no less discouraging, however, than his music itself. He teaches composition and harmony at the Milan Conservatory, and if his title does not read Professor of Harmony and Discord, it ought to be. For the old-fashioned *bel canto* Puccini seems to have tried to substitute the *bell canto*. Such incessant clangor of bells has never been heard in any opera or operetta. Act one, act two, act three, all are full of the din of chimes. How chaste and moderate is Wagner in comparison, and how much more effective are the bells in *Parsifal* than in *Tosca*. The time has come when Wagner may he held up as a model of conservatism and classical restraint!

(*Evening Post*, New York, February 5, 1901)

-:-

Fiasco! Ma buon Dio, como si possono musicare episodi, scene inconcludenti, che non hanno nessuna finalità lirica? La personalità di Puccini pecca di uniformitá. Gli eroi e le eroine dei suoi drammi non presentano varietà di tipi e di sentimento. Quasi tutti si rassomigliano. Ma *Butterfly* parve un *bis in idem* di *Bohème*, con minor freschezza. Abbonda invece l'enfasi e la musica frammentata, senza un carattere precisato che esprima un sentimento, che identifichi tipi.

(Gian Battista Nappi, *Perseveranza*, Milan, February 1904)

[Fiasco! But good Lord, how can anyone expect to set to music episodes, incomplete scenes lacking lyric substance? The personality of Puccini sins on the side of uniformity. The heroes and heroines of his musical dramas do not present variety of type or sentiment. Almost all resemble each other. *Butterfly* is a replica of *La Bohème*, but with less freshness. Instead, there is exaggerated emphasis and musical fragmentation, without precise character which would express sentiment, and identify types.]

RAVEL Maurice Ravel's *Rapsodie espagnole* was a toothsome morsel for those musical gourmets who look with lackluster eye upon the diatonic scale, the old (but still fairly healthy) harmonic system and the natural voices of orchestral instruments. . . . Dr. Norman Macleod in his notebook characterized Spanish music as 'a hot night disturbed by a guitar.' M. Ravel has conceived it to be a hot night disturbed by two piccolos, two flutes, two oboes, one English horn, two clarinets, one bass clarinet, three bassoons, one sarrussophone, four chromatic horns, three trumpets, three trombones, one tuba, four kettledrums (tuned chromatically), one big drum, a pair of cymbals, one triangle, one Basque drum, one tam-tam, one xylophone, one celesta, two harps and the usual complement of strings variously subdivided. And yet with all this apparatus he does not create a violent disturbance of the atmosphere, because he keeps his hands on the throat of every instrument and seldom permits it to utter its native and normal sound. One device which provoked the risibles of yesterday's hearers was a glissando in open fifths on the strings, which involuntarily and irresistibly invited a prescription of paregoric or a soothing syrup.

(New York *Tribune*, November 22, 1909)

SCHOENBERG La soirée d'hier mérite de retenir notre attention à un titre historique. C'est, en effet, le 28 mai 1913, vers dix heures du soir que le cubisme musical a fait son apparition dans la bonne ville de Paris. Par une ironie du sort assez singulière, c'est dans la vénérable salle du Conservatoire, temple de toutes les traditions, que cette révélation a eu lieu. La Société Musicale Indépendante y donnait un concert et offrait à ses habitués la primeur de trois pièces de piano d'Arnold Schoenberg. Cet auteur nous arrive de Vienne, précédé d'une réputation alléchante. Chaque audition d'une de ses œuvres en Autriche et en Allemagne a provoqué des émeutes, des charges policières, des transports de blessés à l'hôpital et de cadavres à la morgue. Au dernier accord les auditeurs en venaient aux mains, on voyait les chaises sillonner le ciel, et on ramassait par grappes les mélomanes jonchant le sol. On attendait donc avec impatience le premier contact de cet art explosif et de la sensibilité française, et les organisateurs avaient fait préparer des civières et mobiliser des ambulanciers pour déblayer la salle après la déflagration. Mais toutes les prévisions ont été trompées. Le pianiste E.-R. Schmitz, qui était chargé de mettre le feu à la mèche, put accomplir son dangereux exercise dans un silence parfait. Il y eut bien quelques sourires inquiets, quelques soupirs angoissés, quelques plaintes étouffées mais aucun scandale n'éclata. Arnold Schoenberg ne voudra pas le croire! Le public français s'est resigné à voir la musique lui échapper et a renoncé à s'en plaindre publiquement. . . . Et l'on demeure épouvanté de la rapidité avec laquelle les conceptions musicales se remplacent l'une et l'autre, se chassent et se détruisent; les auteurs comme Debussy et Ravel n'ont pu conserver, plus d'un an ou deux l'étiquette révolutionnaire, les voici maintenant rangés dans le parti retrograde avant même d'avoir pu se faire comprendre de la foule. C'est, hélas! en musique, que les astres nouveaux deviennent le plus vite de vieilles lunes!

(*Paris-Midi*, May 29, 1913)

[Yesterday's concert merits our attention for historic reasons. It was indeed on May 28, 1913, at about ten o'clock in the evening that musical cubism made its appearance in the fair city of Paris. By singular irony of fate, it was in the venerable hall of the Conservatoire, the temple of all tradition, that this revelation took place. The Société Musicale Indépendante presented a concert there offering to its habitués the first performance of three piano pieces by Arnold Schoenberg. This composer hails from Vienna, preceded by an intriguing reputation. Every performance of one of his works in Austria and Germany has provoked disorders, police intervention, transportation of the wounded to the hospital and of dead bodies to the morgue. At the sound of the last chord the listeners would come to blows, and music lovers strewn on the floor would be picked up in bunches. So we awaited with impatience the first contact of this explosive art with French sensibilities, and the organizers had provided stretchers and mobilized ambulance drivers to clear the hall after the deflagration. But all expectations were deceived. The pianist E. R. Schmitz, who was assigned the task of igniting the fuse, could accomplish his dangerous exercise in perfect silence. True, there were some uncomfortable smiles, some anguished sighs, some stifled groans, but no scandal erupted. Arnold Schoenberg would not believe it! The French public has resigned itself to the fact that music eludes it and has renounced public protests. . . . And we are appalled by the speed with which musical conceptions replace each other, overtake each other and destroy each other. Composers like Debussy and Ravel could not preserve for more than a year or two their revolutionary label and they are already relegated to the retrograde group even before they have succeeded in making themselves comprehensible to the crowd! It is, alas, in music that new stars rapidly become old moons!]

-:-

Arnold Schoenberg's famous, or notorious, *Five pieces for Orchestra* are worse than the reputation that preceded them. . . . There were doubtless few, if any, in last night's audience to whom the pieces bore any relation to music at all. They would agree with the critic who called them 'the freakish product of an overcultivated musical brain.' There is not the slightest reason to believe that their squeaks, groans and caterwaulings represent in any way the musical idiom of today or tomorrow or of any other future time. Hard words have been said about the most recent output of Messrs. Casella, Stravinsky, Prokofiev and others of the same kind, but most of what they have done is innocent, lucid and reasonable compared to Schoenberg's achievements. Possibly some sort of apology is due them.

(Richard Aldrich, New York *Times*, November 30, 1921)

The *Five Orchestra Pieces* by Schoenberg had already been hissed in Vienna and Philadelphia, and their reception last night was of mingled enthusiasm, amusement and disgust. The opening number, *Premonitions*, hinted at none of the madness to come. There was a blast of sound, but it was still sound and not yet noise. The audience, prepared by the program notes for the worst, seemed pleasantly surprised. But pleasure soon gave way to bewilderment. *The Past, The Changing Chord, Peripeteia, The Obbligato Recitative,* such titles convey little of the consistent clangor, the shifting pallors and suffusions, the vortex of whirling shrieks and whines that proceeded from the Philadelphia Orchestra. Whether in pain or at play, the instrumentalists seemed to know what was expected of them; their leader implied by his directions that he expected definite things. No one else could foretell or understand or appreciate. And the finale of the third act of *Die Walküre* was received with a burst of applause, as if in protest at the preceding atrocities accomplished in the name of music.

(*The Sun,* New York, November 30, 1921)

-:-

Cette séance était en majeure partie consacrée à la musique—le reste du programme était dévolu à des produits de M. Arnold Schoenberg. . . . C'est le plus incohérent et le plus vulgaire des charivaris. Que l'on se figure la représentation 'musicale' d'un bal dans une maison d'aliénés ou d'une crise de delirium tremens en un poulailler! Mis à part une cinquantaine (peut-être moins) d'auditeurs aux masques exotiques et aux applaudissements savamment disciplinés, les autres temoignèrent par les rires, des sifflets et des huées de leur mépris pour cette méchante cacophonie—d'ailleurs encore plus bête que méchante.

(René Brancour, *Le Ménestrel,* Paris, April 28, 1922)

[The concert was dedicated in the major part to music—and the rest of the program was assigned to the products of M. Arnold Schoenberg. This is the most incoherent and the most vulgar of charivaris. Let one imagine a 'musical' representation of a ball in an insane asylum, or an attack of delirium tremens in a chicken coop! Discounting some fifty (perhaps less) of listeners of exotic countenances whose applause was carefully disciplined, the rest of the audience manifested their contempt for this evil cacophony—or rather more stupid than evil—by laughter, hissing and booing.]

From the standpoint of music as developed by Bach, Haydn, Mozart and Beethoven, Schoenberg's *Pierrot Lunaire* is mere trash. Judged as music, it is hideous. It is not the sort of thing that an American audience can enjoy.

(*Evening Telegram*, New York, February 5, 1923)

-:-

Abseits von der Strasse geht er seinen verlorenen Weg; ein Einsamer, ein Fanatiker, ein Märtyrer seiner intellektuellen Eigenbrötelei; ein Verlorener in sich selbst, meinetwegen ein Verrückter, aber doch ein Charakter. Ich vermag daher nicht zu lachen, wenn ich diese unnatürlichen Klanggebilde höre; mich packt vielmehr die Tragik eines Menschen, der bewusst seinen Weg in eine Vergessenheit nimmt, die ihn voraussichtlich noch bei Lebzeiten ereilen wird. . . . Diese Musik insofern man die nach eigenen Gesetzen ausgeklügelten Tonkombinationen überhaupt als solche bezeichnen kann, stellt eine Klangwelt in sich dar, die unseren Ohren und Gehirnen nicht zugänglich ist. . . . Es kam in der Hauptprobe der Variationen für Orchester und auch im Hauptkonzert zu einem gewaltigen Skandal. Das Publikum beginnt sich gegen Vergewaltigungen seines besseren Selbst zu wehren. Solche Vorgänge mögen an sich zu beklagen sein, aber sie werden angesichts der hier vor sich gehenden Nerven-Tortur begreiflich. . . . Schönberg hat mich gedauert. Trotzdem muss ich die ernste Frage stellen: Wie lange noch soll der unhaltbare Zustand weitergehen, dass ein der Welt und Kunst Verlorener wie Arnold Schönberg, in Berlin als Vorsteher einer staatlichen akademischen Meisterklasse für Komposition wirkt und unabsehbares Unheil unter der vertrauensseligen Jugend anrichten darf? Wann endlich erfolgt der energische Eingriff ins preussische Kultusministerium, der solche Kulturschädigung für die Zukunft unterbindet? Man gebe Schönberg in Gottes Namen eine anständige Abfindung oder Staatspension, aber man enthebe ihn sehr bald seines Lehramtes.

(Paul Schwers, *Allgemeine Musikzeitung*, Berlin, December 7, 1928)

[Far from the main road, Schoenberg goes his own way—a loner, a fanatic, a martyr of his intellectual snobbism; lost in himself, a madman as I see him, and yet a man of character. I therefore cannot laugh when I hear his unnatural tone poems; I am much more concerned at the tragedy of a man who deliberately takes the road leading him to oblivion that will overtake him predictably still during his lifetime. . . . His music, insofar as these tonal combinations, derived from self-made rules, can be described as music, presents a world of sound which is inaccessible to our ears and brains. . . . During the final rehearsal of Schoenberg's *Variations for Orchestra*, a strong demonstration took place. Audiences begin to protect themselves against such violations of their better nature. Such occurrences are to be regretted, but they are understandable considering the torture inflicted on the nervous system. . . . I feel sympathy for Schoenberg. Nevertheless, I must pose a serious question: how long will the untenable situation continue whereby a man, lost to the world and to art as completely as Arnold Schoenberg, is allowed to be in charge of a master class for composition in a State Academy, causing unforeseeable harm to innocent and trusting youth? When will an energetic protest be made to the Prussian Ministry of Culture to stop such cultural damage in the future? In God's name, let them give Schoenberg a decent severance pay, or a state pension, but let him be removed, and very soon, from his position as a teacher.]

-:-

Schönbergs *Begleitmusik zu einer Lichtspielszene* ist in die drei ineinander übergehenden Teile, *Drohende Gefahr, Angst, Katastrophe* gegliedert, jedoch soll die Musik nach Schönbergs Absichten keine detaillierte Illustrierung dieses psychologischen Vorganges geben, der nur eine Art Gerüst für den streng formalen, mehr dem dramatischen als dem rein konzertmässigen Typus zuneigenden musikalischen Verlauf bildet. . . . Ob man sie sich als Begleitmusik zu einer ideell vorgestellten Lichtspielszene oder als 'absolute Musik' denkt, ist für das Verständnis völlig belanglos. Sie ist absolute Unmusik.

(*Signale für die Musikalische Welt,* Berlin, November 12, 1930)

[Schoenberg's *Accompaniment to a Cinema Scene* is divided into three overlapping parts: *Menacing Danger, Fear, Catastrophe.* However, the music is not supposed, according to Schoenberg's intentions, to give any detailed illustration of these psychological events, which serve only as a framework for a strictly formal, more concert-like than dramatic, composition creating a congenial musical picture. But whether one regards it as musical accompaniment to an ideally imagined motion picture scene or as absolute music, is entirely immaterial. For it is absolute unmusic.]

-:-

The Prelude to *Genesis* was by Arnold Schoenberg, the text for which was 'The Earth was without form, and void.' This reviewer has never heard music that had less form or was more nearly void than Mr. Schoenberg's contribution. It was simply a succession of ugly sounds bearing no relation whatsoever to the thing generally known as music.

(*Pacific Coast Musician,* Los Angeles, December 15, 1945)

-:-

For nearly forty years the corruption of atonality has exercised its pernicious influence on contemporary bourgeois music. The founder and leader of this thoroughly formalistic and consistently cosmopolitan method is the Austrian composer and theoretician Arnold Schoenberg, the creator of a system of musical composition that leads to the liquidation of music as an art, to the substitution of nonsensical cacophonic combinations of sounds for musical works. At present the atonal school has become some sort of sect with representatives in all European countries except Russia, and in America. This proliferation of Schoenberg's anti-people heresy is a symptom of the most profound decline and disintegration of the spiritual culture of capitalist society. . . . For several millennia, in the process of social experience, humanity has selected and elaborated diverse melodic patterns. These intonations have become emotionally logical formulas of musical art, intimately accessible to millions of people. The words of V. I. Lenin in regard to the nature of logical patterns may be applied here: 'The practical experience of man must have led billions of times to the reiteration of various logical figures so that these figures have become axioms.' In his remarkable characterization of decadent modernistic music Comrade A. A. Zhdanov spoke of the coarse, inelegant, vulgar type of music based on 'atonalities, unrelieved discords, so that consonances become exceptions and wrong notes and their combinations become laws.' Schoenberg's aim is to express pathological conditions on the base of abnormal world outlook. This is confirmed not only by Schoenberg's music but by his paintings, for Schoenberg has frequently exhibited in galleries specializing in decadent art. . . . The well-known anti-Fascist composer Hanns Eisler sees in Schoenberg's music the expression of the 'mad despair of the little man.' Indeed, Schoenberg has attempted to portray the mad despair of a petty bourgeois of Western Europe, mainly Austrian and German peoples thrown out of their customary routine by socio-historical conflicts of tremendous dimensions. From this despair and anger on the part of petty-bourgeois artists arose individualistic contempt for listeners. As Schoenberg states it, he and his adherents are compelled to address themselves to audiences only for acoustical reasons, for 'music in an empty hall sounds even worse than in a hall filled by empty people.' Atonal composers reject the depiction of any concrete subjects in their music. The content of their works is expressed in complete spiritual desolation. In his piano piece, op. 33a, Schoenberg sets down the expression mark *cantabile.* It is hard to find a more insulting use of the term than the first two bars of this piece: here the *cantabile* quality is applied to six cacophonic chords that come down crashing on us like six huge rocks! Arnold Schoenberg, who settled in California, became in fact the tutor and guide of many American composers. He seeks contacts with wider circles of bourgeois society. The desolate psyche of atonal composers is now permeated by the spirit of obeisance to the 'iron heel,' as Jack London characterized the dictatorship of the financial oligarchy. The reactionary circles of the United States support the cult of Caesarism and Bonapartism. Accordingly, Schoenberg composes an *Ode to Napoleon.* The same circles are strengthening their bonds with the Vatican. Thus Ernst Krenek writes choral pieces in the Roman Catholic style emphasizing the kinship of Gregorian chant with atonal music. The decisive reason for the support of atonal composers by the reactionary bourgeoisie is that the hermetic sect of atonality has proved to be a suitable tool for the reckless propaganda of repugnant cosmopolitanism leading to the separation of the intelligentsia from the people. The center of this sect is situated in the United States, but its branches are dispersed all over the world.

(I. Ryzhkin, *Arnold Schoenberg, Liquidator of Music,* in *Sovietskaya Musica,* August 1949)

-:-

I read with great interest the Editor's lecture on serial music, and when therefore on November 30th 1960 there was a programme of this sort of music broadcast in the Third Programme I was careful to tune in. It was Peter Maxwell Davies playing five of his own pieces Opus 2, followed by three pieces by Schoenberg, Opus 11. Against the player's technique I have nothing to say. The piano was a very fine one, rich and sonorous. But the 'music'! HORRIBLE! How anyone has the nerve to call that kind of stuff music I just do not know. None of it had any tune and most of it could equally well have been our fat old tabby cat jumping on and off the piano chasing after a marmalade jar cover. The better parts reminded me of my seven-year-old daughter letting off steam by banging up and down the keyboard. I was obliged to turn off the Schoenberg after five minutes of exquisite agony and consider I displayed a fortitude of the front rank by enduring it at all. It was a great relief to turn the nasty sounds off. I await a torrent of abuse from all quarters, but I shall stand fast in my opinion, that only a moron with a warped mind could find real enjoyment in this kind of music. You know—the kind of fellow who sits in a padded cell thinking he's the G string of a double-bass.

(Letter to the Editor of *Musical Opinion,* London, January 1961, signed Michael Jack at Hythe)

STRAVINSKY Si M. Igor Stravinsky ne nous avait pas donné un chef-d'œuvre, l'*Oiseau de Feu*, et cette œuvre pittoresque et charmante, *Petrouchka*, je me resignerais à être déconcerté par ce que je viens d'entendre. Je me bornerais à constater un orchestre où tout est singulier, étrange, multiplié pour confondre l'ouïe et la raison Que cet orchestre soit extraordinaire, rien n'est plus certain; je crains même qu'il ne soit que cela. Pas une fois, le quatuor ne s'y laisse entendre; seuls y dominent les instruments aux sons violents ou bizarres. Et encore M. Stravinsky a-t-il pris soin, le plus souvent, de les dénaturer dans la sonorité qui leur est propre. Aussi nulle trêve, qui ne serait que simplicité, n'est-elle accordée à la stupeur de l'auditeur. Écoutez le prélude: un instrument à vent y prédomine; on s'interroge: 'Lequel produit de tels sons?' Je réponds: 'C'est un hautbois.' Mais mon voisin de droite, qui est un grand compositeur, m'assure que 'C'est une trompette bouchée.' Mon voisin de gauche, qui n'est pas un moins savant musicien, opine 'Je croirais plutôt que c'est une clarinette.' A l'entr'acte, on s'informe auprès du chef d'orchestre lui-même; et l'on apprend que c'est un basson qui nous a mis en si grande incertitude. J'entends bien que tout cela, où certains ne discerneront que des signes de démence, est froidement et méticuleusement volontaire. Il n'est peut-être qu'ordre, harmonie et clarté, ce *Sacre de Printemps* où je n'ai guère discerné que de l'incohérence des dissonances, de la lourdeur et de l'obscurité. J'ai pensé dès l'abord, que ce n'était là qu'une exception dans la manière de M. Stravinsky et que cette musique qui m'ahurit était exclusivement limitée à l'évocation des quelques aspects de la préhistoire russe. J'eusse admiré, une fois de plus, la singulière logique qui veut que les instincts, les sentiments et les gestes les plus primaires nous soient évoqués par les musiques les plus savantes et les plus compliquées. Mais il n'en faut pas douter: ce n'est point là une exception; l'art de M. Stravinsky, m'affirme-t-on, commence seulement de nous étonner.

(Georges Pioch, *Gil Blas*, Paris, May 28, 1913)

[If Igor Stravinsky had not given us a masterpiece, *The Firebird*, and that colorful and charming piece *Petrouchka*, I would be bewildered by what I have just heard. I would confine myself to comment on the orchestration, in which everything is odd and strange, multiplied to confound the ear and reason. That this orchestration is extraordinary is quite certain; I fear only that it may be nothing but that. Not once are the strings allowed to be heard; only instruments producing violent or bizarre sounds predominate. And even then Stravinsky takes care as often as not to denature their sonority. No reprieve, in the form of simplicity, is accorded to the stupefaction of the listener. You hear the prelude, where a wind instrument is dominant. We ask each other, which instrument can produce such sounds. I reply: 'This is an oboe.' But my neighbor to the right, who is a great composer, assures me that it is a muted trumpet. My neighbor to the left, no less learned in music, opines: 'I would rather think that it is a clarinet.' During the intermission we ask the conductor himself, and we learn that it was the bassoon that put us in such great doubt. I understand that all this, which some would recognize as signs of dementia, is coldly and meticulously intentional. Perhaps not everything is order, harmony and clarity in this *Sacre du Printemps*, where I found only incoherence of dissonance, heaviness and obscurity. I thought at first that this was an exception in Stravinsky's style and that this music which baffles me is limited exclusively to the evocation of certain aspects of Russian pre-history. I would have admired once more the singular logic which demands that instincts, sentiments and gestures of the most primitive sort should be evoked by the most scientific and intricate type of music. But there is no doubt: this is not an exception. Stravinsky's art, so I am told, is only beginning to astonish us.]

-:-

La musique du *Sacre du Printemps* de M. Stravinsky est déconcertante et désagréable. Sans doute s'est-elle proposé de ressembler à la chorégraphie barbarescente. On peut regretter que le compositeur de l'*Oiseau de Feu* se soit laissé aller à de telles erreurs. Mais dans le désir, semble-t-il, de faire primitif, préhistorique, il a travaillé à rapprocher sa musique du bruit. Pour cela il s'est appliqué à détruire toute impression de tonalité. On aimerait à suivre sur la partition ce travail éminemment amusical. Vous pourrez en prendre une idée qui corresponde à mon impression: jouez à deux pianos, ou à quatre mains, en transposant d'un ton une partie mais non l'autre: ainsi, par exemple, quand vous aurez *do-mi-sol* d'un côté, vous aurez ré-fa-la de l'autre côté, et en même temps. D'ailleurs, si vous préférez désaccordez d'un demi-ton, ne vous gênez pas. Il s'agit seulement de n'obtenir presque jamais un de ces ignobles accords, qui passaient jadis pour être consonants.

(Adolphe Boschot, *L'Echo de Paris*, May 30, 1913)

[The music of *Le Sacre du Printemps* by Stravinsky is disconcerting and disagreeable. Perhaps he had intended to assimilate it to barbarescent choreography. One can regret that the composer of *The Fire-Bird* has let himself fall into such errors. But in his desire, so it seems, to go primitive and prehistoric, he labored to approximate his music to noise. For this purpose he made an effort to destroy every vestige of tonality. One would like to follow this eminently amusical work from the score. You can get an idea corresponding to my impression: play on two pianos, or four-hands, transposing by a whole tone one part but not the other; thus, for example, when you have C-E-G in one part, you will have D-F-A in the other, both at the same time. However, if you prefer to play out of tune by a semitone, do not feel embarrassed. Just make sure that you never, or almost never, use these ignoble chords which once upon a time passed for consonances.]

-:-

Pour suggérer l'inharmonie d'un monde à demi humain seulement, plongé encore dans la barbarie et presque dans l'animalité, M. Stravinsky dans son *Sacre du Printemps* écrit une partition qui, presque d'un bout à l'autre, est délibérement discordante et ostensiblement cacophonique. Ce ne sont que frottements rugueux, rendus plus âpres par les sonorités dénaturées auxquelles M. Stravinsky demande ses effets de rudesse préhistorique. Je regrette qu'un artiste aussi ingénieux que M. Stravinsky ait cru devoir adopter un parti aussi désagréable.

(Jean Chantavoine, *Excelsior*, Paris, May 30, 1913)

[To suggest the disharmony of a world only half-human, still dwelling in barbarism and near-animalism, Stravinsky writes in his *Sacre du Printemps* a score which, almost from the beginning to the end, is deliberately discordant and ostentatiously cacophonic. It is a series of rough frictions rendered more acrid by the denatured sonorities from which Stravinsky demands the effects of prehistoric rudeness. I regret that an artist as ingenious as Stravinsky has chosen to adopt such a disagreeable method.]

-:-

À un signal donné par le kapellmeister tous les musiciens improvisèrent sans le moindre souci de tonalité, de nuance ou de mesure. Au bout de dix minutes, estimant la plaisanterie suffisamment longue, ils se turent, fiers d'avoir ainsi mis au jour l'Introduction au second tableau de *Sacre du Printemps* de M. Igor Stravinsky.

(René Brancour, *Le Ménestrel*, Paris, June 28, 1913)

[At a sign given by the conductor, the players began to improvise with no concern about tonality, dynamics or measure. At the end of ten minutes, having decided that the amusement had gone far enough, they became silent, proud for having thus performed the introduction to the second scene of *Le Sacre du Printemps* by Igor Stravinsky.]

-:-

Grande journée! Branle-bas général! Monteux va jouer *Le Sacre du Printemps.* Cette nouvelle met les musiciens dans un état d'exaltation voisin de délire. Tous n'éprouvent pas une satisfaction sans mélange; certains en lisant ce titre redoutable, serrent les poings et froncent les sourcils. Cette partition tombe en effet dans nos discussions esthétiques comme un obus à la mélinite au milieu d'une assemblée d'entomologistes. Nos subtilités alexandrines, nos fines recherches, nos scruples et nos cas de conscience ont été balayés et dispersés aux quatre vents du ciel par l'explosion de ces harmonies fracassantes. Une stupeur indignée nous rendit d'abord muets, puis, peu à peu, on s'explique. Et tandis que les uns criaient à la violation du droit des gens, les autres avouaient timidement que le viol a quelquefois du bon.

(*Paris-Midi,* April 5, 1914)

[A great day! General commotion! Monteux will play *Le Sacre du Printemps!* This announcement has put our musicians in a state of exaltation bordering on delirium. Not all of them have experienced unmixed satisfaction; some, reading this formidable title, clenched their fists and raised their eyebrows. This composition drops into our esthetic discussions like a shell of melinite in an assembly of entomologists. Our Alexandrine subtleties, our fine studies, our scruples and our consciences are swept to the four winds by the explosion of these shattering harmonies. An indignant stupefaction renders us mute, then, little by little, everything is explained. Some cry that the rights of men are violated, while others admit timidly that there is something good in this violation.]

TCHAIKOVSKY Tschaikowskys Violin Konzert klingt in seiner brutalen Genialität, in seiner Vernichtung aller Formschranken, wie eine Rhapsodie des Nihilismus.

(Dr. Königstern, *Illustriertes Wiener Extrablatt*, Vienna, December 6, 1881)

[Tchaikovsky's violin concerto sounds, in its brutal genius, in its abolition of all formal limits, like a rhapsody of nihilism.]

Über Tschaikowskys Violinkonzert in D von Brodsky vorgetragen hat sich bereits das Auditorium mit voller Deutlichkeit ausgesprochen. Ein solcher aus buntscheckigen Phrasenlappen zusammengesticktes Tonstück mag neudeutsch sein, es ist unter allen Umständen abscheulich und barbarisch, und wir wissen es uns nicht zu erklären, wie die Philharmoniker, die sich sonst gerne als die Hüter der Classik loben lassen, plötzlich diesem abgeschmackten Charivari in ihren Konzerten Raum geben konnten. Schade um die Virtuosität, welche Brodsky auf dieses Attentat wider den Kunstgeschmack der Wiener verschwendet hat. Dem Namen Tschaikowskys gereicht es aber nicht zur Ehre, die hehre Muse der Tonkunst zur Culturstufe einer Zigeunerbande erniedrigt zu haben.

(Florestan [pseudonym of Dr. Wörz] in *Wiener Sonn- und Montagszeitung*, Vienna, December 8, 1881)

[The audience had already spoken out with full clarity about Tchaikovsky's Violin Concerto. Such a piece of music, made up of motley bits of phrases stitched together, might be neo-German, but it is under any circumstances repulsive and barbaric, and we cannot understand how the Vienna Philharmonic which accepts praise as defender of classicism suddenly gives place in its concerts to such tasteless charivari. It is a pity that Brodsky had to waste his virtuosity on this affront against the artistic tastes of the Viennese public. And it does not do honor to Tchaikovsky's name to have debased the lofty muse of tonal art to the cultural level of a gypsy band.]

WEBERN Anton von Webern appears. I never saw an angrier man; he is about 35, dry and thin, as though pickled in perennial fury, and erect as a ramrod. It was amusing to see him face up to each of the four executants of his five pieces for string quartet, as if he were going to kill them, then relent, wring his hands bitterly, glare defiance at the audience, and rush off stiffly into the artists' room. Thereupon, one suddenly became aware of the sixth furious man (who, I subsequently learned, was an architect and stone-deaf), passionately reproaching the audience, and more especially a certain Kapellmeister there present, for laughing and spoiling everything. Most ungrateful, since but for those ever-recurring scenes, the school, whom no one takes seriously except Schoenberg, would have fizzled out long ago. Webern's five pieces follow his very subjective formula. One long-drawn note upon the bridge of the first violin (pause); a tiny scramble for viola solo (pause); a pizzicato note on the cello. Then another pause, after which the four players get up very quietly, steal away and the thing is over. And now, snorts and laughter are heard in the audience, while four furious admirers clap and yell amid not ill-natured giggles.

(*Daily Telegraph*, London, September 9, 1922)

-:-

Man fragt sich, beinahe erschreckt, danach, wie ein Gehirn organisiert sein muss, das solcher Eingebungen fähig ist. Man scheut sich, das Wort 'abnorm' auszusprechen, aber man kann anderseits auch nicht behaupten, dass in diesem Trio Anton Weberns irgendwelche Beziehungen zu unseren gewöhnten Vorstellungen von Musik zu finden sind.

(*Deutsche Allgemeine Zeitung*, Berlin, May 24, 1928)

[One wonders, almost in horror, what kind of organization a brain must have to be capable of such productions. One is reluctant to utter the word 'abnormal,' but on the other hand one cannot assert that there is any connection in this Trio by Anton von Webern with our accustomed ideas about music.]

Wir lächelten über Weberns *Streichtrio*. Vielleicht wird man dafür einst über uns lächeln. Wir denken mit Bedenken an den Opelschen Raketenwagen, der eines Tages Kunde von einem musikalischen Aschenbruchdrama der Stratosphärenmusik zu uns verkalkten Trommelfellbanausen herniedertragen könnte. Aber trotzdem: ein entschiedenes Nein.

(*Hamburger Courier*, May 29, 1928)

[We laughed over Webern's *String Trio*. Perhaps we will be laughed at for this. We think wonderingly about Opel's rocket ship which might one day bring down to us, calcified drumheaded Philistines, the news of a Doomsday drama of stratospheric music. And yet: a decided No!]

-:-

Weberns Streichtrio ist eine völlig lebensunfähige Arbeit, eine Mikrothematik von winzigen, beschämend primitiven Motivabfällen. . . . Substanzlos in ihrem gesamten Verlauf, unverbunden lose, ein Spiel mit Septimen und Nonen nach oben und nach unten, mit Seufzen und Zirpen, Flageolett-Klängen; spukhaft traurig, trostlos in der Armut und Unfähigkeit Sprache und Form zu bilden.

(*Neue Freie Presse*, Vienna, June 19, 1928)

[Webern's String Trio is a completely lifeless work, a piece of microthematics of tiny, pitifully primitive motivic shreds. . . . Without substance in its entire course, disconnectedly loose, it is a play of sevenths and ninths above and below, with sighs and chirps, high harmonics, ghostly and mournful, distressing in its poverty and incapacity to build language and form.]